Coaching Science

Active Learning in Sport – titles in the series

Coaching Science	ISBN 978 1 84445 165 4
Personal Training	ISBN 978 1 84445 163 0
Sport Sociology	ISBN 978 1 84445 166 1
Sport and Exercise Science	ISBN 978 1 84445 187 6
Sport Management	ISBN 978 1 84445 263 7
Sport Studies	ISBN 978 1 84445 186 9

To order, please contact our distributor: BEBC Distribution, Albion Close, Parkstone, Poole, BH12 3LL. Telephone: 0845 230 9000, email: **learningmatters@bebc.co.uk**. You can also find more information on each of these titles and our other learning resources at **www.learningmatters.co.uk**

Coaching Science

Dan Gordon

LearningMatters

First published in 2009 by Learning Matters Ltd

British Library Cataloguing in Publication Data
A CIP record for this book is available from the British Library

ISBN: 978 1 84445 165 4

Cover and text design by Toucan Design
Project Management by Swales & Willis Ltd, Exeter, Devon
Typeset by Kelly Gray
Printed and bound in Great Britain by TJ International Ltd, Padstow, Cornwall

Learning Matters Ltd
33 Southernhay East
Exeter EX1 1NX
Tel: 01392 215560
E-mail: info@learningmatters.co.uk
www.learningmatters.co.uk

FSC
Mixed Sources
Product group from well-managed
forests and other controlled sources
Cert no. SGS-COC-2482
www.fsc.org
© 1996 Forest Stewardship Council

Dedication

This book is dedicated to the memory of Paul Pearce, a friend and inspirational athlete with whom it was a pleasure to have worked and also to Sheila Carey for without your guidance, patience and extraordinary passion for sport I would not have succeeded as an athlete or coach.

Contents

Foreword

Coaching is an art form, a special mix of sociology, psychology and the understanding of an athlete both from a physical and personal perspective. Great coaches are the ones who have the ability to generate performances from their athletes without getting heavy handed or shouting the odds!

I have worked with many coaches, but the best coaches are the ones you spend time with and work with over many years. A coach like this has the ability to adapt to the changing needs of the athlete, is gracious in accepting new ideas and is willing to work through rough times as well as the times when you can't stop winning!

The true colours of a great coach can only be seen in times of hardship and it is during these times an athlete will know whether their coach can take the giant leap from being a successful coach to being an outstanding coach. If a coach can see you through a bad patch and help you come back out on top again, then they are worth their weight in gold medals and deserve the highest accolade!

Sarah Storey OBE
World and Paralympic Champion and World Record Holder
3,000m Individual Pursuit

Acknowledgements

I would like to take this opportunity to acknowledge those individuals who helped both in the production of this book but also in my development within sport and coaching. To my family (Lynne and Daniel) for their unstinting support and help, both when I was an athlete and also in the construction of this book. To those contributors who have provided case studies and notes to expand the learning experience within this book (Ken Kelly, Caroline Heaney, Barney Storey, Phil Hayes and Wayne Buxton), and to Sarah Storey for her Foreword, many thanks – your experience and guidance has been invaluable. To all those coaches and athletes with whom I have worked as both an athlete and a scientist, I thank you for your inspiration and drive in the world of sport. Finally to my parents without whom I would not have had a passion for sport and education.

PART 1

Understanding the coach

Chapter 1

The coaching process

This chapter introduces the concept of coaching. It provides a framework for modelling the role of the sports coach. It also discusses the more general roles of the coach and the coaching philosophy. By the end of this chapter you will have:

- explored and evaluated coaching roles and responsibilities;
- considered the nature of the coaching process;
- discussed the association between knowledge and coaching competence;
- considered the philosophy of coaching philosophy and its impact on the athlete and coach/athlete relationship;
- critically considered the real world application of an understanding of the subject.

Introduction

The lay view of coaching shows that it is seen as a domain of sport constructed by the coach, constituting a series of episodic activities conducted on a week by week basis, with the aim of improving, and thereby enhancing, performance.

Coaches, however, tend to see the process quite differently. Coaching may be seen, not simply as a series of discrete actions, but rather as a complex model of overlapping scenarios, ranging from training supervision to liaison with fellow coaches and peers. As Figure 1.1 illustrates, the coach acts not only as a traditional sports-based supervisor but also as a mentor and pillar of support.

It can be seen that modern advanced coaches have to take responsibility for their athletes, both inside and outside of competition. This is where our understanding of what makes a coach becomes more complex: no longer can we view a coach simply as the individual with a stopwatch barking out lap times, or just as the mentor who offers training advice to groups of athletes. The role of the coach has become still more complicated and diverse.

Let us consider each of the roles that make up 'coaching'. The most obvious ones are those of teacher and trainer. Clearly the role of trainer – the person who facilitates the training sessions and the physical development of the athlete – is the one that most people equate with coaching. The role of teacher is also apparent in that the coach instructs the athlete in the ways of the sport, whether through teaching new skills or

Figure 1.1: The roles of the coach. Adapted from: The Australian Institute of Sport

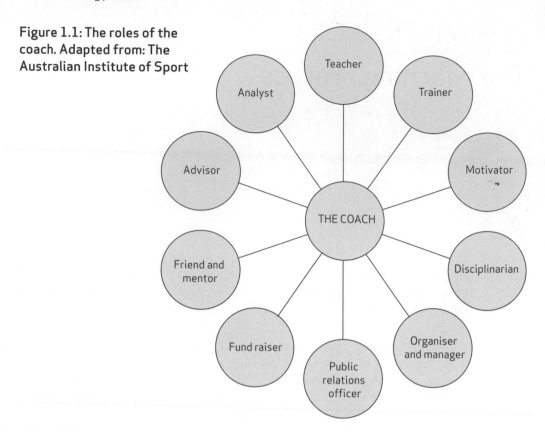

tactics or imparting knowledge on specific aspects of the sport. Many top coaches are not only trainers but real aficionados of the sport.

Associated with the teaching and training components of the role is that of analysis. A good coach will study the performance of an athlete during both competition and training, generating information from which comments can be made, focusing on both the positive and negative aspects of the performance. The coach's analytical role is crucial to the development of the athlete, as it provides feedback on performance and can be used to frame training and competition goals.

Two roles, apparently opposed to each other, are those of disciplinarian and friend/mentor. The disciplinarian role could be viewed as negative and stereotyped as the overpowering coach who controls the athlete at all times. However, it is the responsibility of the coach to ensure that the athletes reach their full athletic potential. To do this, the coach has to instill discipline. The coach/athlete relationship can be extraordinarily close. It is, therefore, important also for the coach to be able to act as friend and mentor – someone to whom the athlete can turn in order to discuss problems or concerns.

A further role is that of motivator. One could argue that athletes should be self-motivated, however, the coach has to be able to pick the athlete up when suffering a 'low', either due to poor performance or from monotony of training. For example, swimmers generally have early morning training sessions for which they have to be motivated enough to attend, but who will often go through the 'motions' of training, rather than actually training hard. At this point the coach (as motivator) needs to step in to drive the athletes on.

The final three categories are perhaps the least recognised, but are just as important to the athlete. Many coaches, especially at amateur level, act as fundraisers for their athletes, generating funding for equipment or competition entry fees. In the early stages of the athlete's development they also act as organisers, arranging everything from training schedules to punctual attendance at a competition. The final role is that of public relations officer. The coach becomes the voice of the athlete, communicating with the press and sponsors rather than putting the athlete under undue pressure. Some of these roles will remain with the coach and some will become less important as the athlete matures and develops.

Recipe for success

When considering the nature of coaching, we need to be aware of the layers of skills and competencies required and how these interact with each other and consequently impact on the athlete as a performer. To do this we need a model of coaching, one that includes both the artistic and scientific aspects of the profession. One model that effectively describes the intricate nature of coaching was developed by Côté et al (1995), as illustrated in Figure 1.2. Think of a model as a construction where we attempt to fit all the key elements into a structured format that best describe the nature of the discipline; in this instance, coaching.

According to this model, the primary aim of both the coach and athlete is the production of a developed athlete: the model shows this as the goal of the whole process. The model seeks to indicate the factors that contribute to the coaching process and shows how each factor can have either a positive or negative influence on the attainment of the athletic goal. The central theme of the model is the coaching process. This theme encompasses the components of training, organisation and competition, which would generally be viewed as the primary responsibilities of the coach.

Central to the coaching process is the coach's mental model of athletic potential. According to the model, the coaching process can be affected by the coach's personal characteristics, the athlete's personal characteristics, and the level of athletic development. It also encompasses an extra category, perceived as being integral to the overall coaching approach: that of contextual factors. We can refer to these variables as peripheral components to the coaching model. The final component is the goal of the athlete and coach. We will now consider each of these separately.

The coaching process

This is the relationship between training, organisation and competition, thereby including the 'nuts and bolts' of coaching. Within this process there is one overarching factor, namely knowledge. Often it is the coach's knowledge that marks the difference between the novice and experienced coaches. For more details on the spectrum of coaching, refer to the *Concept box*.

Figure 1.2: The coaching model. This schematic shows the factors that contribute to the process of coaching and how they interlink with each other, with the overall aim or goal being the development of the athlete. Adapted, with permission, from: J. Côté et al. (1995) The coaching model: A grounded assessment of expert gymnastic coaches' knowledge. *Journal of Sport and Exercise Psychology*, 17: 1–17

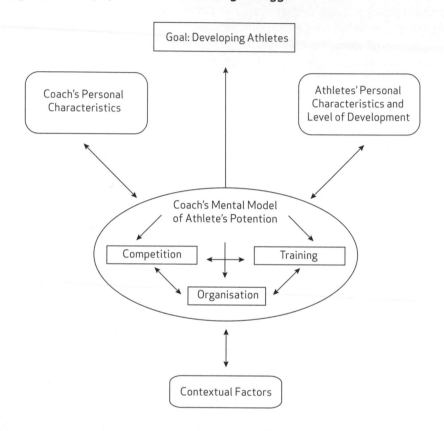

Concept 1.1: Categorising novice and advanced coaches

We can classify levels of coaching according to such criteria as years of experience, qualifications, quality of athlete worked with, overall knowledge base of the coach and whether they used to be an elite athlete themselves.

A high level of knowledge, although crucial, may not directly relate to the quality and ability of an individual to coach. Can we classify a coach as being advanced just because they have the requisite qualifications associated with that sport? The answer has to be a cautious 'no'. Just because someone has the qualifications does not mean that they can convey knowledge and expertise to the athlete. Similarly we may ask, can a coach be described as advanced just because they have worked with high calibre athletes in the past? Generally, the more advanced and developed coaches are able to work with the best athletes. However, caution should be employed here in that some coaches work with the best athletes by chance or through their association with others.

Concept 1.1: Continued

If we apply Côté's model of the coaching process, we can begin to understand the spectrum of coaching expertise. An advanced coach will have a well-developed mental model of athletic potential through both education and application. Furthermore, they will be comfortable in their personal development of coaching characteristics. Conversely, the novice coach will not have a well developed mental model of athletic potential, either because of lack of experience or lack of knowledge, and may not have developed to be comfortable with their own characteristics.

As the coach develops, knowledge base will increase in relation both to the process and the needs of the particular athlete. It is the coach's responsibility to impart to the athletes the knowledge that they have obtained from either experience or through practice. This is why it has sometimes been suggested that coaching is in fact a form of teaching (Drewe, 2000).

The transference of that knowledge is a rather complex process that depends on a number of key factors. To understand more about the levels of knowledge, refer to the *Concept box* below.

Concept 1.2: Knowledge

There are many models and theories which have been proposed as descriptors of knowledge (Schön, 1987; Shulman, 1986; Carr, 1989) However, if we wade through these theories we begin to recognise that there are some broad themes which we can apply to our understanding of what is knowledge.

There are two broad forms of knowledge which we can relate to the 'coaching process': these are first, theoretical knowledge – that which is learnt or acquired perhaps through education, such as coaching qualifications and courses. The second form is that which is developed in response to actually coaching, we could view this as 'on the job' experience or knowledge. The literature refers to theoretical knowledge as professional knowledge (Martens, 1987) but although important to the overall development of the coach, it is perhaps too rigid in its structure and does not allow for the acquisition of knowledge through experience.

On the job or experience-acquired knowledge has been termed in the literature as 'knowledge-in-action' (Schön, 1987). This model suggests that knowledge is composed of many inter-related factors such as ethical, personal, aesthetic and empirical knowledge. These four classes of knowledge are underpinned by social norms, prejudices, values and other sources of knowledge (Anderson et al, 2004). What makes the knowledge-in-action approach is that it recognises the requirement for both theoretical and that which could be classified as 'artistic development', i.e. knowledge which can be quantified and non-quantified. As a coach though, something that is crucial to the development of this knowledge base is the ability to continue the learning process and a

Concept 1.2: Continued

powerful tool that is at the disposal of all coaches is the use of 'reflective practice'. Reflective practice is the process whereby the coach examines issues that have occurred during the process of actually coaching and conceptualises them and so helps to bridge the gap between theoretical and on the job experience. This is very much a self-driven process of reviewing both the positive and negative aspects of the coaching process and addressing those through the development of an action plan. An approach that is often adopted in reflection is that of Gibbs' (1988). This approach has six stages which begin with describing what happened during the coaching session. The second stage involves the coach listing their own thoughts and feelings that occurred during the session, i.e. listing both the positive and negative responses. This is followed by the third step which requires the coach to evaluate the coaching session and examine what were the strengths and weaknesses there. Upon completion of the evaluative process, the coach is asked to analyse the session, which constitutes stage four. Within this stage, the coach must draw upon the information gathered from stages two and three and attempt to make sense of it all. Once the coach has made sense of the issues through analysis, a conclusion to the process is then encouraged. This is stage five and encourages the coach to consider what could have been done to facilitate a stronger coaching session. The final stage is the development of the action plan which, as stage six, asks the coach a single question: 'if you were to conduct that or a similar coaching session again what would you now do?'

Thus, through reflection, the ability of a coach can be developed and knowledge-in-action widened.

The model in Figure 1.2 showed us that the ability to train an athlete is a fundamental component of coaching: this will be dealt with in greater detail in Chapter 8. However, we should consider training in terms of the process rather than simply outcome. In this respect, the coach applies knowledge to the need of the athlete to acquire the essential elements of fitness, skill and tactics in relation to their sport. The coach also trains the athlete's mental capacity for performance.

The ability of the coach to implement training methodologies is dependent on organisational skills.

A coach might have a wonderful scientific understanding of training principles and responses, yet be unable to organise sessions efficiently within a coherent training plan. As a result, the athletes would almost certainly fail to reach their true athletic potential, despite the knowledge base that the coach possesses. Therefore the coach must have the ability to implement and establish optimal conditions for training and competition. The coach's ability to organise also relates to the ability to work with other coaches and in some cases, even parents.

The final piece of the coaching process is the competition component. This strand of the model allows us to differentiate coaching from teaching: teaching is not considered to be truly competitive, certainly within the classroom environment, whereas the coach has to apply knowledge in order to allow the athletes to compete at their optimal level.

An understanding of competition rules and the responsibilities of the coach under competition conditions can be of utmost importance to the success of the athlete. When considering the rules of the game we tend to focus on those rules established by National/International Governing Bodies of Sport and which should be considered as doctrine by the coach. An advanced coach is expected to know these rules and how to apply them in order to get the best out of the athlete, especially in competition.

Coaching processes are best seen as fluid. The coach will need to constantly monitor each of the components and when required, make appropriate adjustments. How the monitoring and adjustments are determined depends upon the interaction between the three process variables, the coach's acquired knowledge and resultant mental model of athletic potential.

All these 'processes' are aimed at producing or attaining an end-product – *the goal*.

The goal

This is the fundamental aspect of the coach's role: the ability to develop an athlete in order to reach and maintain a pre-determined level. All athletes wish to 'develop', no matter what their current performance level, be that elite, club or novice athlete – the end-point is the same: 'I want to improve'. Let's consider how this goal can be attained.

First, note that the term 'develop' is fluid: it may be adapted to meet the needs of the athlete to whom it is being applied (Côté et al, 1995). Second, the goal within each of these groups may differ. Two Olympic 800m runners under the guidance of the same coach may have different goals, despite the event being identical. Third, we need to consider what we actually mean by the 'goal' and how this is derived by the coach.

The coach's mental model of athletic potential (MMAP)

This represents the coach's mental interpretation of what needs to be completed in order for the athlete to reach the desired goal (Côté et al, 1995). What becomes apparent from discussions with coaches is that their MMAP is determined primarily by their evaluation of the peripheral components of the coaching model. It is also determined in part by the coaching philosophy that has been adopted, as this will help to drive the direction and style of the coach.

Peripheral components

The model proposes that there are three peripheral components that can interact with the coach's MMAP. Each of these peripheral components may have either a positive or negative effect, depending on the specific circumstances.

Coach's personal characteristics

Here we have to consider any of the coach's personal characteristics that could have a positive or negative influence on the coaching process. These could include the coach's philosophy, style, beliefs, perceptions and even personal life. Each of these can impact on the coaching process and therefore directly affect the attainment of the goal.

Athlete's personal characteristics and level of development

The athlete's character and level of development can have a direct effect on the attainment of the goal; indeed the nature of the athlete will have a direct bearing on the coaching process adopted by the coach. Within this component, we need to consider such issues as the athlete's learning style, stage of learning, motivation, personal abilities, identity and acquisition of skills.

Contextual factors

A saying often applied to sport is 'control the controllables'. Many aspects of the coaching process may be controlled. Some, such as illness and environmental conditions, may not be fully controllable but can still be addressed by both the coach and the athlete. Those factors that neither the coach nor athlete can control are termed contextual factors. An example of a contextual factor would be losing a competition as a result of a poor ruling from an official or referee. The athletic component may have been controlled, but the decision of the *official* is not controllable, and may be something that has to be accepted without necessarily agreeing with it.

Contextual factors can have a profound positive or negative effect on the coaching process and the attainment of the goal. (Goals will be discussed in more detail in Chapter 4.)

Activity 1.1: Controlling the controllables

A key facet of the coaching process is the ability of the coach to deal with all eventualities and to attempt to control as much of the competition environment as possible. Either in the classroom or in the field, consider how you would do this.

Start by stating the goal of the session or competition for the athlete or team.

Now make a list of all the variables that contribute to the session. For each variable decide if you can control it and if so how this will be achieved. For those variables that you feel are not controllable, decide why this is the case and more crucially how you can minimise their impact.

This should be an approach taken to all training and competition sessions.

Coaching philosophies

A variable that always arises in the coaching process is the philosophy and beliefs of the coach.

We can view a coaching philosophy as a set of principles, beliefs and personal practices that help to guide the coach and are used to construct their MMAP. The philosophy developed by the coach will form the framework by which the athlete will be coached and guided.

At this stage, we should not judge a coach's philosophy, but rather consider the reasons behind the philosophy. A coach's philosophy provides a series of boundaries to which both the coach and athlete can agree and participate within; it also helps the athlete to appraise the coach – something which is important when trying to develop a successful coach/athlete relationship and working partnership.

The primary source forming these beliefs and driving the philosophy is the coach's education and prior experience as either coach or athlete. Although the coach's philosophy is rooted in prior experience, it is a dynamic construction and hence one that can be influenced by new experiences and pressures.

The pressures that affect a coach are complex. Typically, they comprise peripheral components of the coaching model: an athlete's personal characteristics and development and the contextual factors. Although the beliefs of the coach may not change due to these pressures, they may change the boundaries within which they operate. This is an important consideration that will help us to discriminate between advanced and novice coaches.

The seasoned coach who has formed a well-honed philosophy should recognise that in order to best serve the needs of their athlete, they need to be flexible in their coaching style and philosophy. In so doing they may well continue to work within their constructed belief system, but will 'bend the rules' in order to accommodate the influencing contextual and athlete-based factors.

A novice coach, on the other hand, is generally less sure of their knowledge base and has less coaching experience from which to frame this philosophy. So although their belief system (morals, ethics, etc.) may be identical to the advanced coach, their ability to *interpret* these beliefs in relation to pressures and expectations will be less developed. Their approach is therefore likely to be more formulaic (Côté et al, 1995).

Coaches should be encouraged to articulate their attributes and values. As with goal setting, writing down the philosophy helps to formalise the whole process.

Defining a coaching philosophy

The literature base (Lyle, 2002) suggests that by using reflective practice in relation to the coach's present MMAP and their own characteristics, a coach's current philosophy can be honed further to become deeper and more fluent. In order to develop effectively and maintain a balanced athlete/coach relationship, the coach needs to establish a philosophy reflecting their ethos and values.

What makes a good coach?

Thoughts and reflections of elite athletes
This opening chapter has helped us define what constitutes a coach, in terms of roles and responsibilities and also the factors which contribute to the overall coaching process. However, it is also interesting to know what athletes feel constitutes a good coach and how important they are to their ability and pursuit of success. To do this, we will reflect on a document produced by the United States Olympic Committee (Gibbons et al, 2003).

The information provided is based on the responses of 2,100 US Olympians who competed for their country between 1984 and 1998. When asked what they perceived to be the top ten most important factors that contribute to success, athletes indicated that the most important factors were dedication and persistence, followed by support of family and friends, with excellent coaches considered to be the third most important factor. Interestingly, when asked what were the ten most crucial obstacles to success, lacking coaching expertise or support was the third most critical factor behind conflict of roles in their lives and lack of financial support.

When the same athletes were asked what factors contribute to the value of a coach, they identified the ability to teach, motivate and to be able to demonstrate training knowledge, skill development and strategic knowledge (Gibbons et al, 2003).

The data from the report of Gibbons et al (2003) becomes more pertinent when viewed in conjunction with that of Greenleaf et al (2001) which examined the factors perceived to contribute to successful coaching. These athletes reported that an effective coach was someone who did not over coach, who had a clear performance plan, who kept things simple, who were fully committed to their profession, who had realistic expectations but at the same time showed belief in their athletes and who athletes felt they could trust.

Given these indications, it is perhaps not surprising that the report of Gibbons et al (2003) highlights that the second largest component of the budget spent on PODIUM (elite) athletes was for coaching and support (23 per cent), just behind athlete stipends (25 per cent), which are the funds used to support the athletes' day-to-day expenses.

Take home message

Understanding the coaching process against the backdrop of a theoretical framework allows us to appreciate both the roles of the coach and the way in which coaching is a complex series of factors. If we consider the factors that contribute to the overall process, we begin to appreciate how to construct individual sessions and also the whole training plan.

The process is governed by the knowledge of the coach and the way in which they convey this knowledge to the athlete. Remember that the ability of the coach to impart this knowledge is governed by their own philosophy and belief systems. Coaching involves both scientific and artistic attributes which, when controlled and focused, can lead to the development and attainment of the athlete's goal.

Further study

In order to assist your learning and understanding for the coaching process, the following literature base has been compiled. It contains resources related to coaching styles, athlete preferences, coaching models and the roles of the coach in the coach athlete relationship.

Australian Sports Commission (2006) *Beginning Coaching General Principles*, pp3–54

Cote, J and Salmela, J H (1996) The organisational tasks of high performance gymnastics coaches. *The Sports Psychologist*, 10: 247–60

Drewe, S B (2000) An examination of the relationship between coaching and teaching. *Quest*, 52: 79–88

Knowles, Z, Borrie, A and Telfer, H (2005) Towards the reflective sports coach: Issues of context, education and application. *Ergonomics*, 48: 11–14

Lyle, J W B (1993) Towards a comparative study of the coaching process. *Journal of Comparative Physical Education and Sport*, 15: 14–23

Price, M S and Weiss, M R (2000) Relationships among coach burnout, coach behaviours and athletes' psychological responses. *The Sport Psychologist*, 44: 393–409

Samela, J H (1994) Learning from the development of expert coaches. *Journal of Coaching and Sport Science*, 1: 1–11

Shulman, L (1986) Those who understand: Knowledge growth in teaching. *Educational Researcher*. 15: 4-14

Terry, P C and Howe B L (1984) Coaching preference of athletes. *Canadian Journal of Applied Sports Sciences*, 9: 188–93

Timming, R (1982) Improving coaches' instructional effectiveness. *Sports Coach*, 4: 37–41

Turman, P D (2003) Coaches and cohesion: The impact of coaching techniques on team cohesion in the small group sport setting. *Journal of Sport Behaviour*, 26: 86–104

Woodman, L (1993) Coaching: A science, and art and emerging profession. *Sports Science Review*, 2: 1–13

www.ausport.gov.au/coach/tools.asp – Australian Institute of Sport: Massive website devoted to the promotion of elite performance and sport within Australia. This specific link takes you to articles related to coach education and knowledge.

www.ausport.gov.au/ethics/coachofficial.asp – Australian Institute of Sport: Massive website devoted to the promotion of elite performance and sport within Australia. This specific link takes you to articles related to ethics in coaching.

www.athleticscoaching.ca/default.aspx?pid=7&spid=80 – Canadian Athletics Coaching Centre: Site containing information relating to coaching and sports science. This link relates to coach education and development.

www.mysport.net – My Sport: An online community for coach education and discussion.

www.sportscoachuk.org – Sports Coach UK. National body responsible for regulating and overseeing coach education within the UK. Site contains information relating to coaching courses and contacts through to coaching resources and support.

www.uksport.gov.uk – UK Sport. National body supporting elite world class performers. Useful resources related to coach education and drug free sport.

Chapter 2

Leadership and the coach/athlete relationship

A question asked by coaches, athletes and the media is what makes a good coach? We recognise that there are some extremely successful coaches and others who, despite their best efforts, are not productive. Why should this be the case? And how crucial is a positive coach/athlete relationship to the success of the athlete? This chapter will address these questions, therefore upon its completion you will have:

- explored the difference between traits and behaviours;
- addressed the main theories relating to leadership and their application to the sporting environment;
- considered the coach/athlete relationship and its implications to the success of the athlete and the partnership;
- applied the knowledge gained to the role of the coach.

Introduction

There is little doubt that a significant portion of the England rugby team's success in winning the World Cup in 2003 can be attributed to Sir Clive Woodward, the then head coach of the team. Woodward was described in the press as a coaching genius and an individual who appreciated how to get the absolute best from every player in the team and squad. When we sit and reflect on that World Cup, the role of Woodward will come to the fore. We can recognise that Woodward was a great leader and an individual who pushed the boundaries of professional rugby in England and who led from the front. Some may disagree with the manner in which Woodward approached his tasks, but few could argue that he was not effective.

In order to recognise a successful leader, we need to address what makes a leader and how to distinguish good leaders from poor leaders. This is where our understanding becomes clouded, because although we recognise the greatness of a coach like Woodward, it is hard to define and quantify their contribution. We have a clear understanding of the coach's interface with the athlete and role, but what makes an effective coach is a much more complicated question. There is also the question of what may be learnt from good coaches such as Woodward.

The purpose of this chapter, therefore, is to examine coaching in terms of leadership and examine the coach/athlete relationship.

Constructing a leader

Understanding the coaching process (Chapter 1) has helped us to define the role of the coach and, perhaps more significantly, the way the coach reacts to the needs of the athlete and the environment in which they are working. Given that the coaching process is a framework from which all coaching strategies should begin, we will use this as our starting point for examining leadership.

The coaching process model of Côté et al (1995) recognises that the coach requires specific knowledge and skills in relation to both the athlete and sport, but also needs to be an effective practitioner in implementing those skills. These tenets of the coaching process have been defined as traits and behaviours. We will consider each in turn, before examining some of the theories that surround leadership.

If we consider great leaders from sport (or business) we can, no doubt, compile a list of characteristics that help to define these individuals, e.g. intelligence, persistence, assertiveness and independence. These characteristics are termed 'traits', i.e. qualities common to all leaders (coaches) under all conditions. When we think about the people we went to school or university with, we can often recount individuals who were described as having leadership potential because they possess these underlying traits. This informs us of an important consideration relating to traits: that they remain stable over time and within situations. Reflect on this for a moment, for it would be unusual for an individual to lose those traits that we have highlighted.

There is however a recognised difference between what we classify as a *trait* and what we term as a *behaviour*. Indeed we generally accept that there are a set of traits which all coach's need and these are defined as being *universal*. However, we also appreciate that coaches display differing behaviours when faced with changing scenarios and as a result, we can describe these as being *situational* or *environmental*.

This distinction is important: it suggests that a behaviour or trait used in one condition may not apply to another, therefore implying that coaches need to be flexible in their leadership style.

Activity 2.1: Great leaders

Construct a list of the traits and skills that you consider are required of a great coach within your chosen sport.

Universal traits

There is a set criteria of traits that can be used to identify and thereby distinguish 'great' leaders from their less successful counterparts (i.e. universal traits for all occasions).

The universal trait theories suggest that we take our 'great' leader or coach and because they possess all the required traits, they could lead/coach in any situation or sport. This is the ideal; we can understand what makes a great coach simply by studying their traits, which must be universal to all 'great' coaches.

This conception is highly attractive in that it attempts to explain what makes a great coach. When studying the literature base however, the support for such a universal theory is less compelling. Indeed most academics and coaches would agree that there is no universal set of traits that can be used to define 'greatness'.

Does this mean we discount universal trait theories altogether when discussing leadership? It would be unfortunate if we did, for there must be combinations of traits that when combined together help to define leadership.

Universal behaviours

Another leadership option prescribes the notion of a set of behaviours which allow the coach or leader to be effective in any situation or environment. As with trait theories, these are a generic set of values universal to all 'great' coaches and leaders.

Note the difference between trait and behaviour theories: universal behaviour theory predicts that, once generic behaviours are identified, they can be learnt and mastered by any individual – hence any individual can become a 'great' coach or leader.

What are these behaviours that best describe a leader or coach? Not surprisingly, given that we have already identified that behaviours are the characteristics of the coach that define style and approach to coaching, these behaviours are reflections of the basic underlying traits and also the environment in which the coach or leader is currently working. Behaviours mentioned in the literature include: trust, respect, communication and organisation. Again, think back to Chapter 1 and you will recall that the 'coaching process' is made up of many factors, one of which is the coach's personal characteristics, a component being the behaviour of that coach.

As an athlete myself, I used to encounter many different coaches, some with whom I worked well and some with whom I worked less well. A primary reason for this was the behaviour (approach) of the coach in the session and their interaction with me. Some of my past coaches were very good at interacting with me as an athlete, whereas others were more interested in my performances and less interested in me and my personal development. Indeed a coach once told me that we did not have to get on with each other to be successful; he was very much driven by performance outcomes rather than what is often defined a being athlete-orientated.

When we consider coach behaviours then, it could be suggested that there are a series of almost opposing behaviours which we have all seen in coaches and leaders. The task below is designed to help you to consider these more carefully and appreciate the 'behaviour game'.

Activity 2.2: Universal behaviours

This task is designed to address the various forms of behaviours that exist within the realm of coaching and leadership. Using the list of terms below, you need to provide the opposite term and also the relevant meaning. For example:

Activity 2.2: Continued

'Athlete centred' would have an opposing behaviour to 'performance centred' (meaning that the coach is more interested in the performance than the athlete and their own personal development).

Selected terms:
- 'Laissez faire';
- Authoritarian;
- Democratic;
- Hierarchical.

The above list of behaviours prompts a number of questions. For example, which of these behaviours are best for coaching? and can we learn or adopt these behaviours? Let us consider the first question. The ideal scenario would be to have a coach who possesses all of these behaviours and can initiate a particular behaviour pattern when either engaging a particular type of athlete or when exposed to a particular environmental condition such as their own response to their athlete winning or losing. This poses a problem for, if the ideal solution is to have a coach/leader possessing all the behaviours highlighted in the task, they may find themselves suffering from internal conflicts due to their being comfortable with one set of the behaviours and not another. The literature base suggests that a more profitable and effective solution would be to have two coaches each providing opposing sets of behaviours (Smoll and Smith, 1989). Remember that the process of coaching aims to extract the best performance from an athlete and therefore the coach requires the ability to be both outcome and athlete orientated, which is not always the case. There are many great examples within sport, e.g. Clive Woodward and Andy Robinson when they guided England Rugby to World Cup success in 2003 of having two coach's with different styles who together made an ideal coaching philosophy. This approach of combining different styles to generate the most profitable outcome for the athlete has been termed the 'functional model of leadership'.

We should now be able to appreciate that there are different behaviour traits that contribute to the make-up of the coach and that although they appear independent of each other, some convergence may be acceptable and indeed encouraged.

The second question posed above was whether these behaviours can be learnt. To a certain degree we have addressed this previously in recognising that, although the ideal would be to have a coach possessing all the recognised leadership behaviours, this could prove problematic for the coach as it may not feel comfortable to apply them. The behaviours may, for example, conflict with a coach's personal ethos and coaching characteristics. Thus, the answer is, 'Yes, these behaviours can be learnt'. This is something which is evident in the business world (Lei et al, 1999) where management courses are held to develop and foster more effective and productive managers/leaders.

We can now conclude that there are no *universal* traits and behaviours, applicable to *all* situations and environments. In contrast, therefore, let's now examine theories of situation-specific leadership styles and conditions. Before we do so, however, we should acknowledge that many of the models that follow have developed from the earlier work of Fiedler (1967), which provided the initial insight into leadership behaviour and the association between the situation and the personality trait.

Path Goal theory

A key component of the coaching process is the coach/athlete relationship and principally the goal of the athlete. Path Goal theory defines how the coach facilitates the athlete in attaining this goal. In order to achieve the goal, the coach must accomplish two principle tasks: first, they must emphasise realistic and achievable goals and second, they must facilitate the path that the athlete will take in reaching these goals. Some research in relation to Path Goal theory (Terry and Howe, 1984; Chelladurai and Saleh, 1978) suggests that there is some evidence to support the use of a Path Goal orientated approach as a preferred leadership style by athletes.

Lifecycle theory

One component that should be considered in any of these theories is that of the developmental stage of the athlete (see Chapter 14). We all recognise that there has to be a different approach taken by coaches, teachers and leaders when working with athletes at different developmental stages; in other words the behavioural approach taken by the coach has to be adapted to meet the demands of the athlete/population group. This is the premise that forms the basis of the Lifecycle theory. This theory recognises that, as athletes develop, they mature and therefore start to become more capable of setting their own goals; they become more responsible as both the learner and the practitioner and will have developed a greater experience base on which these processes can be established.

What we see is that the task-orientated behaviour of coaches is lower with less mature athletes, while at the same developmental stage, the relationship behaviour of the coach is high. As the athlete starts to mature as a performer, however, the need for a more task-orientated approach from the coach is required, with less desire for a relationship-orientated approach. There is however, an interesting twist to this theory, in that as athletes mature (in relation to their sport) they desire a decrease in the task-orientated approach of the coach but an increase in behaviour orientation.

Multidimensional model of leadership

Two key components of the athlete's progression in their sport are their performance outcome and level of satisfaction. This model defines an association between these athlete outcomes and the behavioural approach adopted by the coach. The behaviours exhibited by the coach are highlighted in Table 2.1.

We should think of this as a mixing pot, whereby the athlete's desired outcomes for the session (performance/satisfaction) are directly affected by the leadership behaviour that is adopted by the coach. Imagine a spectrum of response from the athlete (performance/satisfaction) in relation to the behaviour displayed by the coach. At the opposing ends of the spectrum would be either high performance outcomes and high satisfaction or poor performance and poor satisfaction. According to the model, the former would be associated with a behavioural pattern from the coach where they

Table 2.1: Leadership components associated with the multidimensional model of leadership

Component	Description
Prescribed leader behaviours	A team or organisation has an ethos which is taken as being the template on which all coaching approaches and thereby behaviours are based.
Preferred leader behaviours	From the behavioural package that the coach possesses, the athletes in the team or individuals will have preferred approaches and styles.
Actual leader behaviours	These can be defined as the difference between what is actually expected by the team/organisation/athlete and what behaviour/approach the coach actually exhibits.

exhibit a positive overlap between the leadership components displayed in Table 2.1. Of course the opposite extreme of poor performance and satisfaction would be associated with almost no positive overlap between the leadership components.

Where this model becomes more interesting is when it predicts what happens with overlap between two of the components. An athlete would display a high level of performance but poor satisfaction if the coach were to exhibit positive prescribed and actual behaviours but these were opposed to the preferred behaviour.

Activity 2.3: Multidimensional model of leadership

The purpose of this task is to develop your understanding of how the Multidimensional model of Leadership predicts athlete outcomes in relation to the displayed behaviour of the coach. Using the analogy of the spectrum discussed previously, you should consider the following two scenarios and state what the athlete outcomes (performance/satisfaction) would be in relation to those displayed behaviours.

- *Scenario 1:* The coach displays a positive overlap between the preferred and actual behaviours but they are directly opposed to the prescribed behaviour.
- *Scenario 2:* The displayed actual behaviour of the coach is directly opposed to both the prescribed and preferred behaviours.

Once you have considered the spectrum of responses and also worked through the tasks, you will begin to appreciate why the Multidimensional model of leadership has been suggested to be a solid descriptor of coaching behaviours (Bean et al, 2004; Shields et al, 1997).

Leadership behaviour model

In Chapter 1, we discussed the nature of the coaching process and how the coach's philosophy is affected by personal beliefs, those of the athlete, personal knowledge and the goals of the athlete/group. The leadership behaviour model (LBM) (Smoll and Smith, 1989) is the closest example that fits with the coaching process model proposed by Côté et al (1995).

The LBM attempts to knit together the coach's behaviour to the athlete's perception of the coach's behaviour, resulting in the athlete's responses to these perceptions. This approach is very similar to that proposed in the multidimensional model of leadership. There are, however, some striking differences. The LBM suggests ways in which the 'central process' can be affected by various factors, all playing a role in the coach/athlete relationship and thereby athlete performance. The contributing factors include: coach and athlete individual differences; the coach's perception of the athlete's ability; and specific situational factors.

Activity 2.4: Leadership behaviour model

From your understanding of leadership qualities and the coaching process, discuss the factors which could contribute to the aspects of the LBM affecting the central process. In particular, consider what factors would fall into the following categories:

- Athlete individual differences;
- Coach's perception of the athlete;
- Situation-specific variables.

Having viewed a number of models of leadership and coaching behaviour, we have identified several key principles, the most fundamental of which is the importance of the coach/athlete relationship.

Quite often in the media we hear of athletes splitting from their coaches on mutual terms because they did not get along. The coach/athlete relationship has been described by one leading coach in the UK as being akin to marriage, in that there are a number of possible outcomes. The coach and athlete can generate a highly compatible relationship that is a 'match made in heaven', or they initially fall for each other but soon realise that they are not suited but do not know where else to turn, so the relationship becomes one built on mutual gain. Another is where the coach and athlete initially fall for each other but then drift apart, ending in 'divorce'. There is of course another group that we should mention: those coaches and athletes who just never fall for each other; there just isn't that spark!

The coach/athlete relationship

A strong coach/athlete relationship is associated with high levels of athlete performance and satisfaction. If we look at a poor relationship or incompatibility between the coach and athlete, we will begin to appreciate the characteristics associated with strong relationships.

The two primary variables associated with poor relationships are lack of communication and lack of rewarding behaviour from the coach. Poor coach/athlete relationships are associated with lack of mutual respect, no real appreciation for either person's role and perhaps the most serious of all, lack of honesty between both parties when communication does occur. Think again of the marriage analogy and you will see why the two kinds of relationship are similar.

An interesting point here is that there is no mention of the coach and athlete actually liking each other. As mentioned above, when I was an athlete I was once told by a National coach that we did not have to like each other – we did however have to respect each other. I had to respect his abilities and credentials as a coach and he had to respect my abilities and credentials as a performer. This is a working relationship and as such both coaches and athletes need to ask themselves the question, 'what is this relationship for – to get results or get another friend?'

Given that it is clear what makes a poor relationship, it should be clear what makes a strong relationship: good communication, mutual respect, rewarding behaviour from the coach and a strong appreciation for each other's role. This is easier said than done, but they are fundamental to the coach/athlete relationship.

Communication – the key to success

Open dialogue between the coach and athlete is associated with greater degrees of athlete satisfaction and better performances. Good performances should be praised, with the coach providing insightful information on that performance. A poor performance should not be openly criticized; instead, the coach should highlight any good aspect of the performance, no matter how minor and praise that. They should then use communication skills to apply constructive criticism to the performance, allowing the athlete to learn and theoretically correct mistakes that were made. This praise and criticism approach to coaching can only come about through a solid coach/athlete relationship built on mutual respect.

Activity 2.5: Constructive criticism

Coaches need to be strong and assertive communicators. Constructive criticism is founded on the knowledge of the appropriate language to use to convey mistakes but at the same time not alienating the athlete. In this task you should discuss and list terms and phrases that could be used under the challenging conditions listed below. Try this as a role-playing exercise. Remember that you need to be highlighting weaknesses but not criticising without support. The suggested scenarios are:

- An athlete who no-jumps three times at their opening height in a high jump competition and is therefore eliminated;
- An athlete who drops the ball/misses all the passes during a field game and is substituted;
- An athlete who despite all their efforts cannot master a specific skill in a training session.

CASE STUDY: COACHING LEADERSHIP   Ken Kelly

. . . it's a people thing . . . !

Getting someone to go where they may never have been before is never easy. Some exceptional individuals achieve this through sheer force of personality. For other, mere mortal individuals, the task can be somewhat more challenging. In disability sport, the challenge facing both athlete and coach in their pursuit of excellence is in many ways the same as for any other aspiring high achievers, while at the same time presenting its own unique set of challenges.

The quality of the athlete/coach relationship is crucial in determining the extent to which the athlete's identified, latent or even dormant potential is ultimately realised. Without an open and honest relationship between athlete and coach, lasting success at the elite end of sport is rarely achieved. Coaches who are leading exponents of their craft will, over time, carefully and sensitively nurture what they see and know to exist within a performer. Sadly, those less enlightened often try to 'shoehorn' skill and capacities into performers ill equipped to accept due to their innate abilities.

All top quality coaches who are masters of their craft have one eye on the future. They continually seek to clear a path along which the athlete can travel and for some the road is in better shape than for others. The result is that potential trainwrecks spotted by coaches in their forward planning are no longer there once they and the athlete arrive at that point along their performance pathway. Good coaches always plan for what comes next and seek to minimise being caught by surprise, but as coaching is a far from exact science, being caught by surprise can happen from time to time. The quality and strength of the athlete/coach relationship will determine ultimately, how rough the waters are that they will be required to negotiate.

Coaches must always be flexible in their approach to their work and by being so are able to ensure that the athlete/coach relationship – itself a continually evolving association – remains a healthy one. Within teams, both inside and outside sport, the extent to which leaders are able to empower other individuals and make them feel a genuine part of the decision-making process is a key component of high levels of achievement. In sport, this happens when coaches, without consideration or thought, place those who have entrusted them with their sporting futures at the centre of each and every activity.

In disability sport this is an evolving process, for some athletes have rarely been encouraged to offer their view or opinion about anything, including their own involvement in sport. Coaches who aspire to achieve such degrees of trust and understanding must be patient and support the development of confidence and self-esteem, both in themselves and the performers they work with. In the arena of elite sport, most performers have to operate on their own, with no time to seek counsel over the split-second decisions they are so often required to make.

CASE STUDY: Continued

There is a saying that:

Success has a thousand fathers – but that failure is an orphan.

Over time and either through observed or actual experience, most coaches will have contemplated the situation implicitly described in the saying above. It should be the aspiration of all good coaches to ensure that they do what they can to minimise the occurrence of the message it seeks to convey. Here again, we return to the nature and strength of the relationship between athletes and those people who advise and guide them.

High performance is about living on the edge, it is the world of no compromise. Coaches and athletes are able to create this environment together by expertly cultivating an ethos of *collective responsibility*, implying choice and encouraging freedom rather than *selective accountability*, implying judgement and apportioning blame.

Throughout the continually changing life-cycle of an athlete/coach relationship that leads to high performance and may well extend over a number of years, successful coaches initially lead but later support their charges through a range of experiences that are appropriate at certain points along the performance pathway. They repeatedly prepare the way and continually equip the performer and themselves with the necessary range of skills required to operate effectively in an extremely complex and stressful environment.

Many performers succeed at the highest level because, to begin with, someone believed in them, and made them believe in themselves – often a coach, perhaps more than one – who was then able to go on and bring out the best in them.

Good coaching?
It's not difficult. If it is – you're not doing it right!

Ken Kelly
Coaching Officer
British Paralympic Association
UKA Level 4 Performance Coach
UKA Technical Director Disability Athletics – 1999 to 2005
Athletics Team Leader Sydney 2000 and Athens 2004 Paralympic Games

Take home message

Are leaders born or made? It is for you to decide. However, what we do know is that good coaches need to be effective leaders. There are many theories of leadership, some of which we have studied in this chapter, none of which gives us the definitive answer as to what makes a great leader, although all lend aspects that should be adopted and respected when coaching. Remember that coaches and athletes both have a set of universal traits and behaviours and it is the behaviours that can be manipulated and moulded to generate the coach/athlete behaviour. The coach should always be aware of the needs of their athletes; of their goals and desires.

Question the perceptions of the athlete of the relationship and the process of coaching and how these marry up with the philosophy adopted by the coach. Is the relationship built on mutual respect and open to communication in both directions? There is little doubt that the role of the coach as a leader is fundamental to the success of the athlete as a performer.

Further study

The material listed below has been selected to assist you in developing a wider understanding of the role of a coach as a leader and the coach/athlete relationship. As such, there are publications related to leadership models, the role of the coach in the coach/athlete relationship and the preference of athletes in terms of coach behaviour.

Allen, J B and Howe, B L (1998) Player ability, coach feedback and female adolescent athletes' perceived competence and satisfaction. *Journal of Sport and Exercise Psychology*, 28: 280–99

Barrow, J (1977) The variables of leadership. A review and conceptual framework. *Academy of Management Review*, 2: 231–51

Bloom, G A, Crumpton, R and Anderson, J E (1999) A systematic observation study of the teaching behaviours of an expert basketball coach. *The Sport Psychologist*, 13: 157–70

Chelladurai, P (1990) Leadership in sports: A review. *International Journal of Sport Psychology*, 21: 328–54

Coleman, D (2000) Leadership that gets results. *Harvard Business Review*, 4: 78–90

Jowett, S (2003) When the honeymoon is over: A case study of a coach/athlete dyad in crisis. *The Sport Psychologist*, 17: 444–60.

Riemer, H and Chelladurai, P (1995) Leadership and satisfaction in athletics. *Journal of Sport and Exercise Psychology*, 17: 276–93.

Smith, M and Cushion, C J (2006) An investigation of the in-game behaviours of professional top-level youth soccer coaches. *Journal of Sports Sciences*, 24: 355–66

Terry, P (1984) The coaching preferences of elite athletes competing at Universiade '83. *Canadian Journal of Applied Sport Sciences*, 9: 201–08

Terry, P and Howe, B (1984) Coaching preferences of athletes. *Canadian Journal of Applied Sport Sciences*, 9: 188–93

www.ausport.gov.au/coach/tools.asp – Australian Institute of Sport: Massive website devoted to the promotion of elite performance and sport within Australia. This specific link takes you to articles related to coach education and knowledge.

www.ausport.gov.au/ethics/coachofficial.asp – Australian Institute of Sport: Massive website devoted to the promotion of elite performance and sport within Australia. This specific link takes you to articles related to ethics in coaching.

www.athleticscoaching.ca/default.aspx?pid=7&spid=80 – Canadian Athletics Coaching Centre: Site containing information relating to coaching and sports science. This link relates to coach education and development.

www.eis2win.co.uk/gen/news_copingpressure230603.aspx – English Institute of Sport: National organisation who support and work with elite athletes in England. This link is directly related to coping with pressure.

www.sportscoachuk.org/ – Sports Coach UK. National body responsible for regulating and overseeing coach education within the UK. Site contains information relating to coaching courses and contacts through to coaching resources and support.

www.uksport.gov.uk/ – UK Sport. National body supporting elite world class performers. Useful resources related to coach education and drug free sport.

Chapter 3

Skill acquisition and learning

The ability to learn a skill or technique is integral to athlete development and is therefore a component which needs to be addressed by the coach and athlete throughout all stages of the development process. This chapter will introduce the process of skill acquisition and motor learning. Therefore upon completion of this chapter you will have:

- understood the term 'skill' and how this differs from 'ability';
- addressed the different types of skill and how these can be associated with different sports;
- explored models of skill acquisition and learning;
- examined the role of memory and memory processing in the acquisition and learning of skill;
- addressed the models related to motor learning;
- applied the models and theories to the role of the coach.

Introduction

Anyone who competes in sport at any level will be aware that an integral part of success in sport is derived from the level of possessed skill or proficiency. Athletes and coaches often describe the development of skill within the training process and overall growth of the athlete, implying that skill can be both innate and learnt. Furthermore, it is clear that different sports require different sets of skills, e.g. a sport such as rifle shooting requires proficiency in 'fine' motor skills, whereas cycling requires 'gross' motor skill proficiency.

What we need to consider is how athletes learn skills and why some naturally acquire skills more effectively than others. By understanding the nature of skill acquisition within sport we begin to address two major coaching concepts: (1) How to structure training sessions in order to optimise the development of the athlete; (2) The best way to teach the skill to an athlete.

I have pondered these tenets for sometime. As an athlete, I have been lucky enough to be good at any sport I tried (400m running, swimming, track cycling), yet when I decided to take up golf, I hit a hurdle – it did not come easy. I have consistently struggled to develop as a golfer despite practicing and playing on a regular basis, so why should this be? Why can I acquire the skills of some sports and not others? Through this chapter, we will explore the nature of skill and how we learn and develop as a performer.

From this starting point we will begin to better understand what differentiates elite and novice athletes.

What is skill?

When we start to consider skill as a concept and try to develop a consensus statement which caters for all sports and abilities, we are faced with a massive task.

Activity 3.1: What is skill?

Consider your own sport and create a list of the skills that contribute it. Then make a second list for a sport which is *completely* different, e.g. if your sport is soccer then perhaps a different sport would be synchronised swimming. For both sports, list skills that you consider pre-requisites to success in that sport. Once you have the two lists, consider the differences and similarities of both.

It is known that there are a set of physical traits which contribute to athletic performance, the so-called Ss of training (see Chapter 7): Speed, Strength, Stamina and Suppleness, and that each sport requires each of these fitness components in varying degrees. It is these basic fitness components that underscore our skill levels.

What distinguishes these Ss of training which we class as being skills from such traits as academic achievement and the ability or skill of learning? The answer lies in the prefix term that we apply in relation to sport, that of motor (skill). The term motor is used to categorise the movement of the body and limbs and so for the purposes of this chapter and your understanding, we will define motor skills as 'skills in which both the movement and the outcome of action are emphasised' (Newell 1991).

As all sporting events require the co-ordination of motor skills, it is perhaps not surprising that there are many classifications of skill which contribute to athletic performance. An overview of these skill classifications is presented in Table 3.1.

Table 3.1: Classification of skills

Skill type	Classification
Fine and gross skills	Motor skills can be subdivided into those skills which require co-ordinated sequencing of large muscle groups, e.g. for shot putting or triple jumping (gross skills) and those requiring more precise, controlled muscular movements and sequencing, such as archery and gymnastic events.
Open and closed skills	Skill can be classified by the degree to which the external environment affects the performance of the skill. In sports such as rifle shooting, archery and diving, the environment is highly predictable, therefore they are classified as closed skills in that they are discrete and have minimal external influences. Conversely, there are those skills which can be influenced quite considerably by external factors such as in team sports, racquet sports and the combat sports. These sports are classified as

Table 3.1: Continued

Skill type	Classification
	having an open skills base, as they are open to influences which are external to the athlete.
Skill cycles	Some skills have a very clear start and end point to their execution, such as in the golf swing or penalty stroke in hockey. Once they have been executed, the skill is complete and there is a clear end point, therefore we classify these as being discrete in nature. At the other end of the skill spectrum are those which have no clear start or end point, such as in running and swimming, where there is a cyclical nature to the skill, the distinction being that once the action is stopped, the movement is not rendered incomplete. Therefore these skills are classified as being continuous in nature. Many sports require a combination of both discrete and continuous skills, such as in sprinting where we can view the drive phase out of the blocks as a discrete skill and the acceleration and speed maintenance parts of the dash as continuous in nature.
Serial skills	Some skills do not conform to being either discrete or continuous, such as when a sequential series of different skills are performed to produce the overall action, such as in gymnastic events.
Skill pace	An action or skill that is under the control of the athlete is deemed to be internally controlled, such as pitching in baseball or a free throw in basketball. Those skills whose timings are affected by external conditions are referred to as being external skills, such as saving a penalty in soccer or returning a serve in tennis.

Activity 3.2: Classification of skill

Table 3.2 lists a series of sports or sporting actions. For each, identify the level of motor control and whether the skill is open or closed, the skill cycle and the pacing of the skill. Just tick the box(s) which best classify each action.

Table 3.2: Sports or sporting actions

Action	Skill classification								
	Fine	Gross	Open	Closed	Discrete	Continuous	Serial	Internal	External
Pitching									
Sprint start									
High dive									
Archery									
Canoe slalom									
Snooker									
Darts									

Models of skill acquisition

When we study the literature relating to skills acquisition, it is possible to identify an evolution in the development of both understanding and construction of the proposed models and concepts. The model that has perhaps had the greatest influence on the study of skill acquisition is the Closed Loop theory of Adams (1971), which proposed that in order to learn a skill, two memory domains must exist.

The memory domains were separated by the distinction that one was associated with the initiation and implementation of the skill, while the other acted as the template or benchmark against which the actioned skill is compared. The former memory domain was termed the 'memory trace' and the size of this trace or file grew in proportion to the amount of time spent practicing the skill. The later memory domain was according to the model termed the 'perceptual trace' and its size was based on prior experiences in the form of both proprioceptive and exteroceptive actions. If you would like to gain a greater understanding of proprioception refer to the *Concept box* below.

Concept 3.1: Understanding proprioception

What is meant by the term proprioception?

This is a term used to describe a form of sensory information which relates to the position of the limbs and the body within time and space. In other words, proprioception information informs us through the central nervous system (CNS) what our muscles are doing during any action and how much tension is being applied through a muscle and our bodily orientation. Quite commonly, proprioception is referred to as kinesthetics, which is a term used to imply the same form of information.

How is this information derived?

Within the body there are many forms of receptors which provide the information regarding a specific limb or position. For example, within the muscle we have two forms of receptors: the Golgi tendon apparatus which senses the amount of force being applied through a muscle and the muscle spindles which inform us (through the CNS) about the changes in muscle length.

What is proprioceptive feedback?

Given that we now recognise what is meant by the term 'proprioception' the concept of proprioceptive feedback should be the next logical step. Imagine performing a somersault on a trampoline. You would initiate the movement generating tension in the muscles to swing the arms, creating a rotation in the body and attempting to land back on your feet. Throughout the whole movement you would be aware of your position within time and space. These processes and actions are centred on feedback loops: the action is performed; the position/ tension, etc. are indicated; the information is interpreted in the brain and the information is then relayed back through the CNS to the requisite structures, whereupon the appropriate action is implemented. Therefore, there is generation of feedback to the information generated from the receptors.

How does this work in a sporting context? When the individual practices a skill, a series of sensory files are produced, very much like the way in which files are produced on a computer. This perceptual memory file is amended each time the skill is performed, but all actions are compared with the most up-to-date file. This is a fascinating model and one which received some attention in the mid- to late-1970s, but which finally became subsumed by a larger more robust theory of skill acquisition, namely Schema theory (Schmidt, 1975).

Schema theory extends the framework of Adams by still retaining the concepts of motor recall and recognition (Newell, 1991) but provided a link (schema) between these two areas. Consider the schema as being a master file which contains all of the necessary information required for completion of a movement as highlighted in Table 3.3. So as with Adam's theory when an action is performed, the movement is compared with the schema. Thus, the more a skill is practiced and feedback provided, the more both the recall and recognition schemas will develop.

So far, there would appear to be very little difference between Schema theory and the Closed Loop theory of Adams. However, on closer inspection, we note that there are two clear distinctions. The first is crucial in that unlike Closed Loop theory the model of Schmidt does not propose a feedback loop and is explicit in suggesting that feedback does not necessarily directly transfer from one schema to another, in other words recognition does not always provide feedback to recall. The second distinction is something that, as coaches, we witness in sport, the issue of transference. Schema theory suggests that skill is developed in relation to a movement rather than that movement in relation to one specific scenario. As such, Schema theory allows for the idea of transference of skill from one situation to another.

So why did Schema theory come about? According to Newell (1991) there were two reasons which prompted this change in thinking. First was the issue of novelty. How could a new skill be framed when in theory there would be no perceptual trace from which to draw comparisons? Second, and perhaps less of an issue, was that of storage. How many motor programs could be stored before the file became overloaded?

Table 3.3: Classification of information types according to the scheme theory

Information type	Clarification of the information
Environmental	The place and conditions in which the actions were performed, such as indoors or outdoors or in competition or training.
Body form	The position and shape of the body required for the action, encompassing the mechanical components of the movement, such as speed, direction and force.
Results	For any action to be performed there has to be an initiation followed by a response, the response is therefore the result of the action, so we need to recognise the results or response to various actions.
Sensory	The sensations associated with movement need to be recognized; we need to get a feel for the movement pattern.

Activity 3.3: Reflecting on skill

Think about a particular skill either from your own sport or from a skill-based sport, such as diving or cricket.

Why do athletes report that they are aware almost immediately during the performing of an action that it has not been executed correctly? HINT: think about the Closed Loop theory.

Some sports require extremely rapid motor skill and movement patterns. Consider if the Closed Loop theory would apply to these rapid-based programmes. HINT: think about the timeframes involved for both the skill and also the interpretation of the information.

Activity 3.4: Schema theory applied to sport

One of the main advantages of Schema theory is the universal application of a learnt skill. There are two tasks related to this topic:

1. Reflect on why this should be an advantage to the acquisition of skill when compared with the Closed Loop theory; think about issues of processing capacity and storage of information.
2. Think of a skill that can be learnt in one sport that can be applied to another and whether the athlete would need to re-learn the skill, or simply adapt the skill for the new circumstances.

Practice and mastery

It is the coach's responsibility to coach and develop the athlete ensuring that they acquire the skills and skill mastery as they progress. There are a myriad of methods that can be adopted as part of the coaching manual, which will help us in this process, as presented in Table 3.4.

For the coach, the key facet to this process is the degree of guidance and support that is provided to the athlete. There is little doubt that athletes who are supported and guided through their training prosper when compared with the non-guided athlete. The question however is, 'In what guise should the support come?

The guidance given can be in the form of hands-on support: physically manipulating the athlete's body parts into the correct position during an action. We see this often used by tennis coaches where they stand behind the player and move the player's arm through the trajectory required for the swing.

A very common form of guidance is through the use of verbal support and instructions, where the coach explains what is required and the athlete follows these instructions when performing the skill. The final form of guidance is that of demonstration, which could simply be the coach demonstrating the skill through the use of video support and diagrams. This approach is used a lot in sports such as American Football when players needing to learn new skills can view video analysis from multiple

Table 3.4: Methods of practicing and developing a skill

Practice type	Method of practice
Mental rehearsal	In Chapter 6 we refer to the concept of mental rehearsal through imagery. This is a powerful tool but should not be used as the only means of developing a skill but rather in conjunction with the physical practice.
Whole practice	This is where the entirety of the skill is practiced. It is ideal for skills which are continuous in nature such as running and cycling.
Combined practice	A single skill is selected for the session but rather than being practiced for the entirety of the session it is combined with bouts of different activities. This is very useful with younger athletes and also where the skill, if repeated too often, could be associated with an overuse injury.
Mass practice	Under conditions of massed practice, the skill is rehearsed or practiced over a prolonged period of time (up to 3 hours) on a single skill, such as free kicks in soccer. Athletes tend to remember the skill through massed practice mainly because the process has been ground into them. This approach may prove to be problematic for younger athletes.
Part practice	Many of the serial skills benefit from being broken down into their constituent parts in order to master each sequence of the action. Part practice on its own, though, should be avoided as this may lead to disjointed and ill fitting skill patterns.
Physical practice	Practicing the skill through the recognised movement patterns is integral to the development of that skill as a whole.

angles. What is clear however, is that athletes benefit from a mix of all forms of guidance and that the coach should not rely solely on one approach; also we need to recognise what kind of learner the athlete is and take this into account when structuring the session (see Chapter 1).

Coupled with the ability to impart the requisite knowledge and instructions to the athlete, there is the need for appropriate feedback, which is discussed below.

At this point, we have managed to address what is meant by the term 'skill' and the variety of forms of skill that can be expressed by the athlete. We have also briefly examined different means of practicing and rehearsing these skills. However, in order to appreciate how skill is actually developed and improved upon, we need to address how skill is acquired, enhanced and expressed and this will become the focus of the following sections of this chapter.

Sporting ability

Skill proficiency is dependent on the ability of the individual. Ability therefore implies a restriction on the degree to which skill can be acquired within a sport, so highly able athletes are likely to acquire skill more effectively than those with lesser athletic abilities.

The nature of ability is important to our understanding of the processes of both long-term athlete development (Chapter 15) and talent identification (Chapter 14), because, e.g. an athlete with high cardiovascular fitness and speed but poor hand–eye coordination will probably not excel in rugby, but could be directed to endurance-based sports.

A word of caution however, for the implication here is that ability is in fact an innate factor dictating the degree of both achievement and development within a sporting pursuit. This is not entirely the case however, because the development of core athletic abilities of a given sport will, over time, allow for an enhanced capacity to acquire specific skill traits, thereby implying that abilities are trainable and not fixed.

Feedback and athlete support

All skill development requires feedback in order to allow for development of that skill. When we refer to the literature base it becomes apparent that there are many issues which relate to feedback, such as the timing, the form, the nature and its relationship to different skill sets and programmes (Schmidt and Wrisberg, 2000). From this information, we can observe that there are two very basic forms of feedback: that which comes from the athletes themselves and that which is derived from the coach and/or other observers. It is of course the latter that is affected by the coach.

Within coaching, we have to be effective at providing feedback to the athlete and in doing so recognise that there are two types of feedback: that which is performance-orientated and that which is outcome-directed. These forms of feedback are very much associated with the structures identified in Chapter 4 on goal setting.

Coaches need to make use of both forms of feedback to ensure that they communicate their message in a manner that is not perceived to be overly critical by the athlete, but at the same time not so diluted that the athlete fails to recognise which part of the skill was performed incorrectly.

Take home message

The learning and acquiring of skill is a process which needs to be nurtured by the coach allowing the athlete to develop at an optimal rate. We need to recognise however, that there are many forms of skill and that the ability of the athlete to acquire that skill is dependent not only on the stage of learning development, but also on the level of guidance and support provided by the coach.

Furthermore, although there are competing models of skill learning and acquisition, we should be aware of the common themes, such as the role of memory and information processing. Whichever school of thought you subscribe to, there is little doubt that motor learning and development is an integral part of the development of an athlete and of the process of coaching and coach support.

Further study

The list below highlights a series of selected articles and books that will support your learning and understanding in relation to motor learning and development. As such, the list contains publications related to forms of feedback given to the athlete, the concept of innate talent and the principles of motor learning.

Ericsson, K A, Krampre, R T and Tesch-Römer, C (1993) The role of deliberate practice in the acquisition of expert performance. *Psychological Review*, 100: 363–406

Handford, C, Davids, K, Bennett, S and Burton, C (1997) Skill acquisition in sport. Some applications of an evolving practice. *Journal of Sports Sciences*, 15: 621–40

Hodges, N J and Franks, I M (2002) Modelling coaching practice. The role of instruction and demonstration. *Journal of Sports Sciences*, 20: 1–19

Howe, M J A, Davidson, J W and Sloboda, J A (1998) Innate talents: Reality or myth. *Behavioural and Brain Sciences*, 21: 399–422

Magill, R A and Wood, C A (1986) Knowledge of results precision as a learning variable in motor skill acquisition. *Research Quarterly for Exercise and Sport*, 57: 170–73

Newell, K, M. (1991) Motor skill acquisition. *Annual Review of Psychology*. 42: 213–237

Salmomi, A W, Schmidt, R A and Walter, C B (1984) Knowledge of results and motor learning: A review and critical reappraisal. *Psychological Bulletin*, 95: 355–86

Schmidt, R A and Wrisberg, C A (2000) *Motor learning and performance: A problem based learning approach*. 2nd edition. Champaign, IL: Human Kinetics

Weeks, D L and Anderson, L P (2000) The interaction of observational learning with overt practice. Effects on motor skill learning. *Acta Psychologica Scandinavia*, 104: 259–70

Walf, G and Prinz, W (2001) Directing attention to movement enhances learning: A review. *Psychonomic Bulletin and Review*, 8: 648–60

Walf, G, Shea, C H and Matschiner, S (1998) Frequent feedback enhances complex motor skill learning. *Journal of Motor Behaviour*, 30: 180–92

www.bases.org.uk/newsite/home.asp – British Association of Sport and Exercise Sciences: National body for sport and exercise science within the UK. Useful contacts and documents related to physiology, psychology, biomechanics, health and coaching.

www.elitetrack.com/ – Elitetrack: A website which houses both peer reviewed and lay articles. All papers are referenced and are either written by coaches or sports scientists. A very good resource for all disciplines within coaching.

www.eis2win.co.uk/gen/ – English Institute of Sport: National organisation whom support and work with elite athletes in England.

www.everythingtrackandfield.com/catalog/matriarch/OnePiecePage.asp_Q_PageID_E_350_A_PageName_E_ArticlesGeneralCoaching – Everything Track and Field: Articles related to coaching and training.

www.sirc.ca/ – SIRC: Sport, Research, Intelligence, Sportive: An international database which lists articles and publications related to coaching. Also has links to International Governing Bodies of Sport and Sport Institutes.

PART 2

Psychology of sports performance

Chapter 4

Goals and goal-setting

Athletes and coaches often refer to their 'goals' or objectives for the forthcoming season or tournament. The use of goals and goal-setting is a recognised practice among athletes from many sports. It is now widely recognised that there are different forms and approaches that can be adopted. It is these aspects, along with relevant theories that will be discussed in this chapter, upon completion of which I hope you will have:

- established how the setting of goals can impact on the athlete's development;
- addressed the questions of goal level and how each level produces different responses in the athlete;
- considered how coaches can use goal-setting in an effective way;
- determined how we can establish goals in an effective and applied manner.

Introduction

We often hear athletes stating their goals for the season or a match/competition and that these goals come in many shapes and sizes; some referring to winning, others relating to perhaps just completing a match or game. As discussed in Chapter 1 (The coaching process) the whole aim of coaching is to develop the athlete to achieve the goal that has been agreed.

So how can we set achievable and realistic goals that are challenging enough to the athlete? In order to establish a physiologically structured training plan (containing the components of sporting fitness: strength, endurance, speed, flexibility) which contributes to overall sporting performance, we need to know what the desired end-product of the season or period of training is going to be. If goals are set at an inappropriate level, the structured training plan can result in athletes either not being pushed hard enough or failing to cope with the training – or, at worst, becoming burnt out, possibly resulting in under-performance syndrome (UPS).

This chapter will explore the concepts of goals and goal-setting as part of the development of peak athletic performance.

Goals and goal-setting

Achievement of peak athletic performance is dependent on steely resolve, motivation and the stringent setting of goals (see Chapter 1). The goals that an athlete works towards may be set on a daily, weekly or long-term basis (such as for Olympic Games or National Championships). Goal-setting is a motivational tool used by athletes and coaches to produce more effective and perfective performances.

Loche and Latham (1985) support the use of goal-setting in sport, describing three types of goal as demonstrated in Table 4.1.

Table 4.1: Classification of goals used by coaches and athletes

Process goals	Designed to focus on a specific facet of the athlete's behaviour during the performance or action. They allow the athlete to register and address key issues relating to technique and skill attributes during the actual performance. Examples of this are trying to avoid over-rotation in the triple jump or ensuring a correct catch phase is conducted during a rowing cycle.
Performance goals	Rather than focusing on the outcome, these goals are directed towards the specifics of a performance such as a personal best for the 1500m or more than 30 conversions in a rugby season. These goals are independent of the outcome goal (see below) but are also athlete specific, meaning that within a team, each player can have their own performance-orientated goal.
Outcome goals	The simplest form of goal focussing is on the absolute outcome of the sporting situation and considers placing in a competition or training session. This does not have to be a podium position; it could instead be a pre-determined placing established by the coach and athlete.

Activity 4.1: Establishing a set of goals

Apply goal-setting to your sport or to the scenarios set out below. In either case you should come up with a series of outcome, performance and process goals which meet the needs of the athlete.

For each goal show some justification as to why you have chosen it (as a fundamental key in coaching is writing down and contextualising the goal).

Consider the following scenarios:

- An 800m runner (junior) who wishes to race at the National Championships. She has a current PB of 2min: 14s, with an entry time of 2min: 10s being required.
- A developing striker in a soccer team who consistently under performs.
- A gymnast who has been selected for the Olympic Games in three months time, but who is struggling with her beam work.

We should now consider which types of goals are the most effective and which are the least effective.

Weinberg et al (1993) suggest that using outcome goals on their own is not a productive way of motivating and enthusing an athlete. There is of course a simple reason for this, in that the goal may consist purely of a placing (1st, 2nd, 3rd, etc.), therefore if the athlete does not achieve this goal they could perceive this as failure, as could the coach. Thus, outcome goals should not be set on their own.

We do know however, that the effectiveness of outcome goals is increased when used in conjunction with both performance and process goals. A successful coaching strategy then would employ all three goals to best aid the development of the athlete. When we consider the use of performance goals, it is important to recognise that generally if an athlete manages to attain their prescribed performance they are quite likely to have also attained their outcome goal. Also, the balance between outcome- and performance-orientated goal-setting is important, for although an athlete may not attain their outcome goal, they may indeed realise their performance goal and, as a result, derive some satisfaction from the performance. This derived satisfaction is important as we will discuss in Chapter 5.

Note that the coach will also have a series of goals which can be considered under these headings. In order for the athlete to develop they must be able to access their coach's knowledge. This knowledge can be acquired only by the coach through 'education' and so the coach should also have a series of personal goals in relation to their own coaching development.

Using goal-setting effectively

The key for goal-setting is to know your athlete. Without an understanding of what makes them tick, the establishment of goals may be fruitless. By knowing your athlete you can devise specific goals. Think back to the coaching model (Chapter 1) and the athlete's personal characteristics and level of development, in particular the factors of the athlete's learning style, ability, motivation and stage of learning. We can add to these anxiety, self-confidence and attitude.

For novice athletes, we would prescribe a short-term goal of mastering a skill, achievable within an allotted timeframe ensuring that the athlete will benefit not only from acquiring the skill but also from the confidence that such an achievement generates. An advanced athlete would follow the same structure, the difference being that the goals set will be particular to their needs and level of development. It is evident that the use of goal-setting has received considerable attention within the literature (Hall et al, 1987; Mento et al, 1987; Weinberg et al, 2000; Tenenbaum et al, 1999). From this research base we are able to derive the 'tools of the trade', as highlighted in Table 4.2.

Table 4.2: The tools of the trade for goal-setting as used by the coach

Timeframe for goal-setting	The goals need to be constructed in accordance with appropriate timings. This is a process and skill that comes from understanding the development of the athlete. The goal attainment should be constrained by a timeframe, however this needs to be considered carefully. A window of opportunity exists for achievable goals, which avoids those which take too long to achieve and so promote disinterest and those which are too short and promote little sense of accomplishment.
Range of goals	The coach should make use of both long- and short-term goals. The long-term goal for a marathon runner may be to attain a place in the final at the Paralympic Games, while the short-term goals may be to qualify for the Paralympic Games and set a personal best in the 10,000m. The reason for the combination is that long-term goals can appear too distant and hence unachievable, whereas short-term goals can be used as stepping stones to the overall long-term goal.
Difficulty in attaining the goal	The goal that has been set must be realistic. It has to be achievable but not so easily that the athlete loses interest or motivation. If the goal is too difficult, they will not engage in the process. The reverse is also evident: set the goal too low and the athlete will not be challenged and will lose motivation, potentially disengaging from the process.
Control of the goal	The goals that are set should be controllable by the athlete and not depend on the performance of others. Performance goals can be controlled by the athlete as they are not dependent on others, whereas an outcome goal is. For example, team performance can affect the attainment of an individual's outcome goal. The best approach is to use more controllable performance-orientated goals to supplement the less controllable outcome-goals.
Specifics of the goal	Specificity of goal-setting is a fundamental rule that must be adhered to. The athlete needs to appreciate both the nature of the goal and how it relates to their overall performance plan, but the coach must also ensure that the goal set is specific to the needs of the athlete. In essence, the goal has to be personal to the athlete to ensure their needs are met and so that the athlete 'buys into' the overall plan.
Measurable goals	If they cannot measure how well the athlete is doing in relation to the goal how can the coach formulate appropriate strategies? In this instance, it is easy to see why outcome goals become the obvious choice as they can be measured (won/lost, etc.). However in order for a goal to be measurable it has to be specific and essentially observable. Observable goals can be measured because they can be seen.

An issue that should be quite apparent is the nature of the athlete. Generally, there are two types of athletes: those who are performance-orientated and those who are outcome-orientated. By their nature, games players (soccer, rugby, hockey, etc.) tend to be outcome-orientated as they chase nominal or ordinal goals (win/lose, place in the league, etc.). Performance-orientated athletes like to be in control of their environment and hence focus on goals which are measurable (interval and ratio).

Activity 4.2

Using the outcome, performance and process goals that you developed in Activity 4.1, explain how they would be: measurable, controllable, attainable, varied and within a timeframe.

For each component, provide some justification.

Two final points to debate in relation to setting goals for an athlete are to know what goals to set and how to monitor them. Both are related and help to conceptualise the coaching process.

The needs analysis

In order to generate a series of goals, the coach and athlete should engage in the needs analysis process. This is a great way of focusing both athlete and coach on the requirements for the forthcoming season and also on formalising and reviewing the athlete's progress to date.

The process allows both parties to reflect on the previous season/campaign and thereby highlight strengths and weaknesses which can be addressed through goal development. This should be an independent process where the coach and athlete complete the analysis separately and then discuss together their scores and comments. This encourages the athlete to engage in the review process and the establishment of new goals.

The development of a needs analysis ProForma (Table 4.3) must take into account all the components addressed within the coaching model so that both coach and athlete can evaluate the athlete's position within the long-term performance strategy.

This ProForma addresses key components of the coaching model and although the example has been tailored to an endurance athlete, the principle can be adopted for any athlete within any sport. The sport-specific components can be altered to meet the requirements of the event and the comments can be re-worded to be athlete and sport-specific. Both coach and athlete would then rate each profile category out of ten (10 being the highest/best rating).

By using this systematic approach, we are able to cover the second fundamental key of goal-setting: monitoring the progress of the athlete. By having written information agreed by both coach and athlete, both parties can review and reflect on the goals in order to check their progress against what is required and expected.

Table 4.3: Example ProForma for the needs analysis process

Profiling category	Example topics and issues	Self-rating		Coach-rating		Comments
		Current level	Ideal level	Current level	Ideal level	
1 Ambition	Clarity of long- and short-term goals. Are they realistic?					
2 Self-belief	Score your self-confidence. How often do you doubt your ability to achieve your goals?					
3 Lifestyle management	Discipline, organisation, social skills, function in a team, outside interests, financial management, etc.					
4 Endurance 1	Considers aerobic power. How well do you cope with top end speed? Think about lactate tolerance.					
5 Endurance 2	Considers aerobic capacity. How well do you cope with sustained aerobic performance? Think about aerobic base work and economy.					
6 Conditioning	Core stability, flexibility and mobility and general conditioning.					

		Example topics and issues	
7	Nutrition	Considers macro- and micro-nutrient intake. Think about food types consumed for training and competition and also hydration awareness.	
8	Technical skills	Consider the issues related to training and racing with a guide-runner. Pacing strategies and the use of heart rate zones.	
9	Tactical skills	Appreciation of the tactics needed for both track and road races.	
10	Rules and regulations	Appreciation of the rules of track and road running relating to the AAAs, IAAF, IBSA and IPC.	

Guidance notes on completing the assessment: 1. Define or clarify your long-term goals. 2. For each of the ten categories in the profile, consider how important you think these are in order to be a podium athlete. 3. Now consider yourself against the same categories and score yourself out of ten. 4. You should now be able to identify where you feel you have the most ground to make up in order to achieve your goals. ProForma used for the assessment of an athlete, in this case a visually impaired marathon runner. The specifics within the 'Example topics and issues' box can be changed according to the sport. Adapted from a worksheet used by British Cycling.

CASE STUDY: GOAL-SETTING AND PERFORMANCE, A PERSONAL PERSPECTIVE

As an athlete I must confess that I have often struggled to come to terms with the use of personal goals. I often fell into the trap of setting goals that were too long term, forgetting to use short-term stepping stone goals to reach the main one. As a result, I quite often lost enthusiasm and motivation for the training. Interestingly, I started to become more proficient with the use of goal-setting as I matured as a performer; indeed my most productive years as an athlete came when I was older and using a serious of well established goals. The needs analysis was also something that I found extremely useful as an athlete, as it allowed me to both assess where I came from and gauge this against the expectations of my coach and performance director for the journey ahead. Through the use of needs analysis I was able to set a series of goals that were both realistic and ultimately achievable.

CASE STUDY: GOAL-SETTING AND PERFORMANCE   *Caroline Heaney*

I believe that effective goal-setting is a vital part of the coaching process. Without goals, both coach and athlete have no direction. Goals help to focus effort and attention and increase motivation. An athlete who is preparing for a specific competition or performance target will train harder than one who does not know what they are training for.

I hold regular performance meetings with the athletes I coach which involve setting goals for the coming period as well as evaluating goals set in our last performance meeting. The evaluation part is important and something that many coaches often forget. Evaluating goals gives me a chance to see if our training strategies are working and if changes need to be made. If one of my athletes isn't achieving a set goal, we need to understand why and address the issue. In contrast, if an athlete has achieved a goal we set, then the performance meetings provide a forum to 'formally' recognise that and give the athlete a confidence boost.

I think goal-setting is a two-way process; therefore I set goals *with* my athletes and not *for* my athletes. I believe this gives them more ownership of their goals, which in turn increases their commitment to achieving them. This two-way process sometimes involves a bit of negotiation.

For example, one of my athletes always underestimates her abilities and so tends to set herself targets that are too low. At the beginning of last season when we sat down together to identify her goals, she said that she wanted to run 60 seconds for the 400m. I felt she could run faster than this, so we discussed how well her winter training had gone and that because she was quite new to the event she could probably take a significant chunk off her personal best time. After this 'confidence building' chat we eventually negotiated a target time of 59 seconds. Sure enough, she finished the season with a time of 59.3 seconds. This shows that setting realistic, but challenging goals is really important. Perhaps if we had set a goal of 60 seconds, she would have been happy to achieve that and would never have gone on to run below the 60 seconds.

CASE STUDY: *Continued*

The opposite problem can also occur. Sometimes my athletes overestimate their abilities and want to set unrealistic targets. This is a tough one because I want them to be ambitious and set their sights high, but at the same time I am conscious that if they don't achieve those unrealistic goals it will knock their confidence. Again it's a process of negotiation. I might say something like 'Okay that's great that you want to run below 11 seconds [for the 100m], but as your personal best is currently 13 seconds, why don't we break that down into stages and focus on breaking 12 seconds for now and when we achieve that we'll move on to 11 seconds?'. That way you set a realistic target, but you don't make the athlete feel like you don't believe in them.

So far, I have focused on time-based (performance) goals, but my goal-setting with athletes goes far beyond that. Obviously we set outcome goals as well, for example many of my athletes have goals to medal in specific championships. I know some people aren't keen on outcome goals because they are externally referenced, but at the end of the day, that's what competition is about – pitting yourself against other people.

I think that as long as you set other types of goal to support the outcome goals then they are fine. An athlete of mine might have an outcome goal to win the County championships, but if on the day a much faster athlete unexpectedly shows up and wins, but my athlete runs a time that exceeds the target time we set, then we will still be happy and feel satisfied that the performance goal has been achieved. Achievement of the outcome goal would have been a bonus, but turned out to be unrealistic given the unexpected opposition. Our evaluation of the race would reflect that.

Process goals are perhaps the 'secret ingredient' of good goal-setting. We all know athletes who talk a good game but don't deliver and that's where setting process goals makes a difference. I might say to an athlete, 'Okay, so you want to get down to 24 seconds this year [for the 200m]. What do you need to do to be able to achieve that?' Outcome and performance goals are great because they tell us where we want to go, but without the support of process goals that tell us how we are going to get there, they are meaningless.

So in a nutshell, what do I think about goal-setting? I think it's probably one of the most essential tools in a coach's armour. It feeds into everything we do as coaches.

Caroline Heaney
Level 3 UK Athletics coach and BASES accredited Sport Psychologist.
Caroline coaches track and field and works as a psychologist with athletes from a number of sporting backgrounds.

Take home message

The use of goals and goal-setting is integral to both the development of the athlete and the process of coaching as a whole. The setting of goals should be achieved in discussion between the athlete and coach and set against the background of the needs analysis and long-term strategy. The goals need to be achievable and realistic and measurable; remember if we cannot quantify the goal, can we cannot measure or assess improvements.

Further study

The list below highlights some key publications and supporting material that will assist you in your understanding and appreciation for the application of goal-setting to sport. As such, there is literature related to the role of the coach in goal-setting, the use of different goal strategies and the use of long-term goal-setting programmes on athletic performance.

Boyce, B A (1990) The effects of instructor-set goals upon skill acquisition and retention of a selected shooting task. *Journal of Teaching in Physical Education*, 9: 115–22

Hollingsworth, B (1975) Effects of performance goals and anxiety on learning a gross motor task. *Research Quarterly*, 46: 162–8

Kingston, K M and Hardy, L (1997) Effects of different types of goals on processes that support performance. *The Sport Psychologist*, 11: 277–93

Locke, E A and Latham, G P (1990) *A theory of goal-setting and task performance*. Englewood Cliffs, NJ: Prentice Hill

Miller, J T and McAuley, E (1987) Effects of a goal-setting training program on basketball free-throw self-efficacy and performance. *The Sports Psychologist*, 1: 103–13

Poag, K and McAuley, E (1992) Goal-setting, self-efficacy and exercise behaviour. *Journal of Sport and Exercise Psychology*, 14: 352–60

Weinberg, R and Weigand, D (1993) Goal-setting in sport and exercise: A reaction to Locke. *Journal of Sport and Exercise Psychology*, 15: 88–96

www.bases.org.uk/newsite/home.asp – British Association of Sport and Exercise Sciences: National body for sport and exercise science within the UK. Useful contacts and documents related to physiology, psychology, biomechanics, health and coaching.

www.eis2win.co.uk/gen/news_copingpressure230603.aspx – English Institute of Sport: National organisation who support and work with elite athletes in England. This link is directly related to coping with pressure.

www.eis2win.co.uk/gen/psychology_confidencepart1.aspx – English Institute of Sport: National organisation who support and work with elite athletes in England. This link is directly related to confidence (Part I).

www.eis2win.co.uk/gen/psychology_confidencepart2.aspx – English Institute of Sport: National organisation who support and work with elite athletes in England. This link is directly related to confidence (Part II).

www.eis2win.co.uk/gen/psychology_confidencepart3.aspx – English Institute of Sport: National organisation who support and work with elite athletes in England. This link is directly related to Confidence (Part III).

www.mysport.net – My Sport: An online community for coach education and discussion.

www.uksport.gov.uk – UK Sport. National body supporting elite world class performers. Useful resources related to coach education and drug free sport.

Chapter 5

Motivation

It is widely recognised that in order to succeed at the highest level in sport, both athletes and coaches need to be highly motivated to achieve their goals. What do we mean by 'motivation' and why do athletes and coaches exhibit different levels of motivation? These issues and their supporting theories will be discussed in this chapter, therefore upon its completion you will have:

- understood what is meant by motivation in terms of athletic performance;
- examined the theories of motivation and their relevance to the development of an athlete;
- appreciated why coaches need to understand what motivates their athletes and how that motivation can be harnessed;
- addressed the negative consequences of motivation;
- appreciated the role of athlete motivation in the context of the overall coaching process.

Introduction

We have all heard or read pre-match interviews with athletes during which they emphasise their desire and commitment to do well and almost all exhibit high levels of self-confidence, e.g.

> I want to make history and be the heavyweight champion

Asked if he would aim to take the yellow jersey in Paris in a fortnight's time he said:

> The way I'm riding, I would be stupid not to.

The above are examples from elite athletes, but we see 'motivation' and 'drive' at all levels of sport. Think about the channel swimmer; what motivates them to swim in water with an average temperature of 15°C for over 10 hours? What motivates amateur golfers to spend hours on the golf range struggling with their swing? These issues lie at the heart of the athlete's personality and philosophy and as a result, our appreciation of what motivates an athlete or coach is crucial to our understanding in the development of an optimal coaching process.

This chapter will focus on the role and development of motivation in the athlete and how understanding motivation is integral to the coaching process.

Understanding motivation – theories

Self-efficacy

Perhaps the mostly widely accepted theory is the self-efficacy model of Bandura (1982). The model proposes that the individual (athlete) has a belief in his/her own ability to produce actions that will meet the desired goal. The underpinning factor to this approach is that the athlete believes he/she is in control of the situation. If they feel that this control will allow them to produce the desired result, they will be motivated to perform.

Self-competence

An extension of self-efficacy is the model of self-competence (Harter, 1978). This suggests that all individuals strive to attain levels of self-competence. In order to become self-competent the individual has to show a level of mastery for the task. The individual's level of self-competence is determined by their level of self-perception for success in the task. Therefore, someone who perceives that they have shown a high level of competence through mastery will gain a positive feeling which will cultivate self-efficacy and hence personal satisfaction. As a result, they gain what is called competence motivation. Conversely, low competence motivation is generated through a perceived low level of task mastery and competence.

Having reviewed the two theories, both containing the generic thread of motivation, we can see a second link between them: that of need. What do we mean by need? Consider Bandura's self-efficacy model which proposes that athletes strive to attain the goal because they feel that they can, because they are in control. Here, the athlete not only has the desire to achieve the goal but also needs to be in control in order to do so. In Harter's model, this need can be viewed as being the desire to become self-competent and thereby derive satisfaction from the mastery.

Needs of the athlete

The realisation of the 'need' of the athlete is important in motivational understanding, primarily because motivation has been defined as 'the desire to fulfil a need'. Within the literature this has been defined within Maslow's *Hierarchy of Needs* (1954). According to Maslow's approach it is not until our basic needs have been met that we can progress to the more advanced and refined needs, such as self-actualisation. By understanding the hierarchy, we begin to understand an athlete's 'needs' in terms of sport and performance.

Achievement motivation

This approach suggests that individuals derive motivation from the process of striving to succeed. Individuals falling within this group show high levels of persistence even when faced with barriers and internal/external pressures.

Achievement can be viewed in two ways: there is the achievement from succeeding and also the achievement derived from not failing. At this stage you could be forgiven for thinking that these are the same thing, i.e. if I succeed I have not failed. This is partly correct but the difference is exemplified in the scenario below.

Scenario
Penalty shootouts in soccer have become the bane of the England team in the last decade or so, generally ending in failure. Put yourselves in the players' positions; what would you honestly do?

Would you view the situation as positive, your chance to be a hero and maybe win the match and therefore you volunteer to the take the penalty?

or

Would you look negatively on the situation? You might not score. If you miss you will be shamed, with the weight of the nation and the wrath of the press upon you. Both are examples of achievement motivation but with distinctly different approaches.

Considerable debate has surrounded the development of achievement motivation in sport and is partly explained by athlete personality. The literature informs us that there are two broad categories of personality: those who want to achieve success and those who want to avoid failure. An overview of the attributes that contribute to these personality types are presented in Table 5.1.

How can we define or measure achievement motivation? Think of it as a calculation, where the difference between positive and negative attributes is the measure of an individual's achievement motivation. Therefore the greater the difference between the two sets of attributes, the higher the individual's score for achievement motivation.

Achievement goal theory

Recent research advocates that different behavioural variations, evident in athletes, are the result of individuals pursuing different achievement goals, rather than an expression of specific levels of motivation (Nicholls, 1984). This is an extension not only of achievement motivation but more specifically, of the models developed by Bandura (1982) and Harter (1978). The overwhelming common feature is the way individuals come to perceive their own ability.

It has been proposed that an athlete who participates in an achievement activity must do so from an initial phase of conception, implying that athletes have different achievement goals and beginnings of commencement. So what does this really mean?

Table 5.1: Athlete personality classifications and their associated attributes

Achieve success attributes	Avoid failure attributes
Actively seek and pursue challenges	Avoid challenges either competing against overly difficult opposition where failure is guaranteed or against overly easy opposition guaranteeing success.
Concerned with excellence and striving for high levels of performance; not afraid to fail	Overly concerned by failure and the fear of failure
Enjoy and thrive on situations where they can be evaluated and given feedback	Dislike situations where the outcome is 50:50 or where evaluation can be provided; both have the potential of bringing embarrassment
Ascribe their performance to factors such as effort and dedication, putting poor performance down to the lack of concentration or application	Attribute their performances to external factors; success is due to luck and chance and failure is due to overly tough opposition

Quite simply, the theory suggests that an athlete's level of perceived ability and therefore motivation is initially the result of early development, learning and cognitive restructuring. Should you wish to explore the concept of cognitive restructuring, refer to the *Concept box* below.

> ## Concept 5.1: Cognitive restructuring
>
> Cognition can be viewed as the knowledge that we have and that develops regarding ourselves, others and the environment, garnered through such processes as perception and problem solving. Therefore cognitive restructuring is the process where we (athletes/coaches) appraise and evaluate our knowledge base and as a result amend our knowledge and thought processes.

What makes this theory appealing to coaches and sports psychologists is the identification of two goal orientations, each of which could be achieved by the individual (athlete).

The first is that of task orientation, where the primary goal is the mastery of a skill. Recent research (Weigand and Burton, 2002) suggests that ability is developed through improvement and that perceived levels of ability are self-referenced (set by the athlete) and dependent upon improvement in both skill and learning.

The task-orientated individual has a tendency to evaluate and reflect on their performance from which they can ascertain whether effort has been expended and crucially if mastery has been achieved. Therefore if an athlete perceives that a higher level of competence has been attained in a task/skill, this would be an indication of increased skill mastery. Trait theory also suggests that the more effort required in mastering a skill, the greater the level of perceived competence. What makes the task-orientated individual all the more compelling is, what happens when they fail, normally the hallmark of distinction between different qualities of athletes. Under such conditions, the athlete would conclude that the adopted strategy used for skill mastery was not sufficient to meet the demands of the skill and so would revise the approach to skill acquisition and start again.

Conversely, we have the ego-orientated athletes whose perception of ability is somewhat different to the task-orientated athletes, in that they have what Weigand and Burton (2002) describe as a differentiated approach, whereby effort does not equate ability. Our ego-orientated athletes will express self-perceptions of ability when they outperform another athlete. These athletes display an inverse relationship between effort and ability in that they believe that the more ability they have, the less effort is required.

The ego-orientated athletes will also show attributes of avoidance when facing the prospect of failure, particularly when perceiving themselves as having a low level of ability. As suggested in Table 5.1, they usually follow one of two actions. They will either: (1) undertake a task which has a low level of skill mastery, with the result of maintaining a level of competence and success in the skill for minimal effort, or (2) they will assess the situation and their perceived ability for both task mastery and competence, conclude that failure is inevitable and as a result will withdraw all effort. The end-product is maintenance of perceived ability because they have not failed the task.

An understating of an athlete's motivational orientation is crucial as it allows for the development of coaching process strategies which ensure that the athlete achieves task mastery at the correct level, while at the same time setting defined and achievable goals (see Chapter 4).

There is also a further point of consideration when focusing on motivational orientation – that of athlete development and understanding how the child develops as a learner and practitioner. We will explore this in greater depth in Chapter 15 (Long-term athlete development) but an overview of the four stages of goal orientation development in children is presented in Table 5.2 (Nicholls, 1984).

Table 5.2: Stages of goal orientation development

Stage 1 – Effort, ability and outcome

The initial stage of a child's development is characterised by the concept of the individual perceiving no difference between effort, ability and outcome. A second concept is that the child cannot differentiate between luck and ability and how one task can be more difficult than another. The key here is lack of differentiation.

Stage 2 – Expenditure of effort

By Stage 2, the child is capable of distinguishing between ability and effort. The primary factor now is the belief of the child that effort equals outcome. Therefore they will believe that the more effort they apply to a task the greater the success at the task.

Table 5.2: Continued

Stage 3 – Does effort equal ability?

The child now begins to make a distinction between effort and ability; they will appreciate that high levels of effort do not necessarily equate to high ability and task mastery. However, on occasion, the child will not differentiate between the two and so revert back to Stage 1 perspectives.

Stage 4 – Understanding of task mastery

The child is now able to discriminate between the concepts of effort, ability, outcome and luck. By this stage of development, the child appreciates that some tasks will be more difficult to accomplish than others. A key facet of this stage is the development of an understanding of the association between performance outcome and effort, whereby they identify that superior ability is associated with a high performance outcome and lower levels of effort.

Stage 1 ages: -0–6 years; Stage 2 ages: -6–9 years; Stage 3 ages: -9–12 years; Stage 4 ages: -12+. Adapted from: Nicholls, J G (1984) Achievement motivation: Conceptions of ability subjective experience, task choice and performance. *Psychological Review*, 91: 328–46 and cited in Cox, R H (2002) *Sport psychology: Concepts and applications*. 5th edition. New York: McGraw Hill, pp 36–7.

Motivational climate

We have focused a considerable amount of attention on the actual motivation of the athlete, whether a child or adult-based performer. Another consideration requiring emphasis when understanding what drives an athlete to develop their performance, is that of the environment in which they learn and develop, the so-called 'motivational climate'.

This motivational climate (Ames, 1992) can be dictated by the coach's own behaviours and philosophy. Remember that the coach imparts their knowledge and viewpoint onto the athletes, which influences the way in which the athletes develop and adapt to the demands placed upon them.

What makes this both fascinating and critical to the coach/athlete interaction is that we can see that the environment in which the athlete works can be classified as being either ego- or task-orientated. As with the athlete characteristics, we can see that the conditions adopted by the coach can have a profound effect on the athlete. The classification of the two environment climates are summarised in Table 5.3.

These motivational climates help us define two further characteristics of the athlete's motivational drive, which relate to whether they are intrinsically or extrinsically motivated. The mastery-orientated athlete is described as being intrinsically motivated, whereas the performance orientated athlete is seen to be extrinsically driven.

Let us define these terms. Intrinsic motivation is when an athlete feels self-confident and therefore has the ability for self-determination. This form of motivation is driven by the athlete's beliefs and philosophies; they have an internal reward system which they use as a benchmark for achievement and success. So an intrinsically motivated athlete is motivated by internal perceptions such as setting personal bests or mastering a skill.

Conversely, our extrinsically motivated athletes seek gratification from both tangible (trophies) and intangible (praise) sources. These athletes again have belief

Table 5.3: Classification of motivational climates

Ego-orientated (Performance-orientated)	Task-orientated (Mastery-orientated)
Perceived by the athlete when: • The coach encourages and emphasises success in relation to normative values (winning). • The coach encourages interpersonal rivalries within the team dynamic. • The coach interacts and treats each member of the team differently dependent on their ability.	Perceived by the athlete when: • The coach encourages learning from past mistakes. • Co-operation is openly encouraged. • There is the chance for both individual and team skill development.

Adapted from: Miller, B W, Roberts, G C and Ommundsen, Y (2005) Effect of perceived motivational climate on moral functioning, team moral atmosphere perceptions and the legitimacy of intentionally injurious acts amongst competitive youth football players. *Psychology of Sport and Exercise*, 6: 461–77.

systems which are used to formulate this level of motivation. It would appear therefore that the best approach to athlete development would be to encourage intrinsic motivation and thereby task mastery, through something called a 'TARGET approach' climate to sport (Ames, 1992).

Research suggests that through manipulation of the TARGET components (Task, Authority, Recognition, Grouping, Evaluation and Timing) the coach can actively develop and foster a motivational climate which yields a greater perception of task mastery in their athletes (Ames, 1992). A summary of each component is highlighted in Table 5.4.

Activity 5.1: Motivational climates

Using the classification of Motivational climates presented in Table 5.3, consider your own coach or coaching philosophy and determine whether ego- or task-orientated athletic performances are encouraged.

Activity 5.2: Socioeconomic class

A key factor that contributes to an athlete's motivation may be the desire to escape the life in which they have been brought up. Classic examples are seen in boxing and most notably basketball, where the dream of playing in the NBA is fuelled by role models who have escaped the streets to become both talented sports stars and multimillionaires. The desire to escape from places such as Cabrini Green in Chicago, emulating the likes of Michael Jordan is a massive motivation in many young Americans. The discussion topic is this:

What kind of motivation can this be classified as and how can it be harnessed to get the best out of the athlete?

Table 5.4: Mastery-orientated climate – TARGET

Tasks	The tasks set by the coach are perceived to be both challenging and diverse, thereby establishing that a well-structured set of goals have been developed.
Authority	The coach presents the athlete with choices in terms of training routines and approaches and encourages them to become more leadership-orientated in their athletic development.
Recognition	The coach provides rewards and recognition to the athlete in a personal and private manner. The recognition is based on the athlete's individual progress rather than as a group.
Grouping	In order to promote and accelerate skill development, an environment of close co-operation between athletes is encouraged along with greater interaction between both athletes and the coaching staff.
Evaluation	Evaluation provided by the coach is in relation to the level of mastery accomplished in a skill/task. As a result of the recognition climate this evaluation is individual rather than group-based.
Timing	The amount of time allocated to skill and task mastery is individual and is therefore fluid, in that the coach can adjust the time according to the level of progress and development shown by the athlete.

Adapted from: Ames, C (1992) Achievement goals, motivational climate, motivational processes, in Roberts, G C (ed) *Motivation in sport and exercise*. Champaign, IL: Human Kinetics, pp 161–76; Weigand, D A and Burton, S (2002) Manipulating achievement motivation in physical education by manipulating the motivational climate. *European Journal of Sports Science*, 2: 1–14; Ntoumanis, N and Biddle, S J H (1999) A review of motivational climate in physical activity. *Journal of Sports Sciences*, 17: 643–65.

Take home message

There is little doubt that the motivation of an athlete is a complex web of factors which converge to facilitate the attainment of the goal. It should also be clear that rather than being a discrete entity, motivation can be developed and influenced by the athlete and through the environment in which they train. The role of the coach as an influencing factor therefore becomes of utmost importance in the structuring and nurturing of athlete motivation. Coaches and athletes need to be aware that their beliefs and personal development play an integral part in the motivational profile of the athlete and that the coach/athlete interaction promotes and fosters an optimal motivational approach.

Further study

The following is a list of key publications which will help your learning and application of understanding in relation to motivation. There are resources related to motivational climates, the association between goals and motivation, achievement goal theory and the relationship between coach behaviour and athlete motivation.

Black, J S and Weiss, M R (1992) The relationship among perceived coaching behaviours. Perceptions of ability and motivation in competitive age group swimmers. *Journal of Sport and Exercise Psychology*, 14: 309–25

Hodge, K and Petlichkoff, L (2000) Goal profiles in sport motivation: A cluster analysis. *Journal of Sport and Exercise Psychology*, 22: 256–72

Lemyre, P N, Roberts, G C and Ommundsen, Y (2002) Achievement goal orientations, perceived ability and sportsmanship in youth soccer. *Journal of Applied Sport Psychology*, 14: 120–36

Ntoumanis, N (2001) Empirical links between achievement goal theory and self determination theory in sport. *Journal of Sport Sciences*, 19: 397–409

Pensgaard, A M and Roberts, G C (2002) Elite athletes' experiences of the motivational climate. The coach matters. *Scandinavian Journal of Medicine and Science in Sports*, 12: 54–9

Reiss, S, Wiltz, J and Sherman, M (2001) Trait motivational correlates of athleticism. *Personality and Individual Differences*, 30: 1139–45

Roberts, G C, Kleiber, D A and Duda, J L (1981) An analysis of motivation in children's sport: The role of perceived competence in participation. *Journal of Sport Psychology*, 3: 206–16

Sarrazin, P, Vallerand, R, Guillet, E, Pelletier, L and Cury, F (2002) Motivation and dropout in female handballers: A 21-month prospective study. *European Journal of Social Psychology*, 32: 395–418

Spray, C M, Biddle, S J H and Fox, K R (1999) Achievement goals, beliefs about the causes of success and reported emotion in post-16 physical education. *Journal of Sports Sciences*, 17: 213–19

Weigand, D A, Carr S, Paetherick, C and Taylor, A (2001) Motivational climate in sport and physical education: The role of significant others. *European Journal of Sports Science*, 1: 1–13

Williams, L and Gill, D L (1995) The role of perceived competence in the motivation of physical activity. *Journal of Sport and Exercise Psychology*, 17: 363–78

www.bases.org.uk/newsite/home.asp – British Association of Sport and Exercise Sciences: National body for sport and exercise science within the UK. Useful contacts and documents related to physiology, psychology, biomechanics, health and coaching.

www.athleticscoaching.ca/default.aspx?pid=7&spid=80 – Canadian Athletics Coaching Centre: Site containing information relating to coaching and sports science. This link relates to coach education and development.

www.mysport.net – My Sport: An online community for coach education and discussion.

www.sportscoachuk.org – Sports Coach UK. National body responsible for regulating and overseeing coach education within the UK. Site contains information relating to coaching courses and contacts through to coaching resources and support.

www.uksport.gov.uk – UK Sport. National body supporting elite world class performers. Useful resources related to coach education and drug free sport.

Chapter 6

Anxiety stress and performance

Coaches and athletes often refer to the concept of needing to be 'in the zone' when competing; being psyched up and optimally prepared to compete clearly associated with the emotional arousal state of the athlete and performance. Negative consequences to this relationship are that athletes can become overaroused and so experience anxieties and subsequent drop off in performance.

This chapter will focus therefore on theories surrounding these concepts and suggest strategies that the coach and athlete can adopt to combat the symptoms. Therefore upon completion of this chapter you will have:

- examined the theories relating to stress, anxiety, arousal and athletic performance;
- explored the positive and negative consequences of anxiety and arousal on performance;
- considered the application of the theories to athletic performance;
- examined the application of coping strategies in relation to stress and anxiety;
- understood the application of the theories and knowledge to coaching and athletic practices.

Introduction

A key facet of sports performance is the ability to cope with pressure and the consequent levels of imposed anxiety. Although the majority of research in this field is associated with elite performers, we would be remiss to suggest that pressure and anxiety do not affect novice and amateur athletes.

As highlighted in Chapter 1, the coach also faces increasing pressures from external agencies and factors. We have all witnessed athletes choking or succumbing to the moment at all levels of competition. The statements in the box below show different responses to stress under varying conditions.

> *Having to wait 15 minutes on the fairway doesn't help when you are trying to win the British Open.*

> *The pressure on her had been so intense in the lead-up to the Games that she spent the summer months training in England.*

Given that anxiety and stress seem to be related to performance, it is imperative that the coach is aware both of the causes of these anxieties and stresses but also appreciates how they can influence the athlete both positively and negatively. Therefore throughout this chapter we will address how stress and anxiety manifest themselves in both coach and athlete, suggesting strategies that can be employed to combat these anxieties in both training and competition environments.

Stress, anxiety and arousal

All too often we are predisposed to using the terms stress, anxiety and arousal to describe the same condition. To help avoid confusion as we progress, the terms are defined in Table 6.1.

Table 6.1: Definition of terms related to stress, anxiety and arousal

Anxiety	A form of apprehension that manifests itself as a consequence of becoming aware of an increased state of arousal.
Arousal	Both an anticipatory and alertness-based response and one which reflects both physiological and psychological adaptations.
Stress	A manifestation of both increased arousal and anxiety as the result of the individual perceiving that they will not be able to meet the goal/demand placed upon them.

Models of stress, anxiety and arousal

Drive theory

This is the original theory of arousal and performance and is based around the basic tenet that performance (P) is a function of both drive (D) and what is described as habit strength (H), thereby giving the following equation:

$$P = D \times H$$

In this theory, drive is the term used to describe arousal, although previous studies have indicated that this form of arousal is global in nature, thereby taking into account both physiological and psychological response. Habit strength is the term used to characterise the dominance of correct and incorrect behaviours (Raglin, 1992). The relationship between arousal and performance has been shown to be linear with high levels of arousal being associated with high levels of performance and vice versa.

Therefore, an athlete who is a novice and wishes to develop skill mastery would, in the initial stages, have a low habit strength in response to correct actions but a high habit strength in relation to incorrect response. The resultant outcome at this stage of the athlete's development is a predominance of incorrect actions. However, as the athlete starts to develop and the skill is mastered, there is an increase in the amount of high habit strength therefore implying that the athlete can perform the task under conditions of high arousal.

Although this model helps us to understand where learning can be fitted into the arousal/performance relationship, we should view it with some caution. Although studies have demonstrated the relationship between performance and arousal, there have been suggestions of limitations to this linear approach. How, for example, should we define a 'well learnt task'? What should we make of the fact that coaches, athletes and sports psychologists were reporting that there was an inverted U-relationship between performance and arousal and not a linear one? (Martens, 1971).

Inverted U-hypothesis

The basic principle behind this hypothesis is that when arousal increases at very low to moderate levels, there will be a resultant increase in exercise performance, the so-called Yerkes–Dodson law. However, if the level of arousal continues to rise beyond this moderate level the performance of the individual will decline, thereby producing the inverted-U effect displayed in Figure 6.1.

Within the inverted-U literature a line of enquiry has emerged to suggest an association between the characteristics of the task and the amount of associated arousal. The data suggests that there is a spectrum of response ranging from slight, through to extreme excitement (Raglin, 1992). On this scale, it has been proposed that activities such as archery, shooting and golf putting would be associated with the lowest

Figure 6.1: The inverted-U hypothesis showing the proposed relationship between performance and emotional arousal

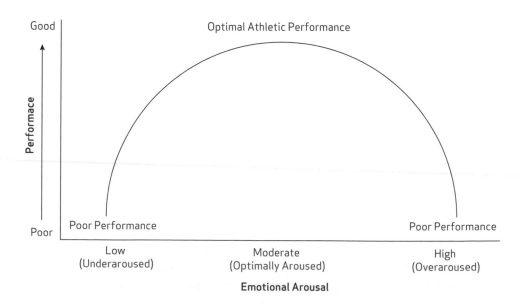

levels of arousal above the normal state, whereas the highest levels of arousal would be associated with such activities as tackling in rugby, 400m running and boxing. So the inverted-U form shifts from actions which require precise fine motor skills to those that require more physical effort and more gross motor activity.

A further concept from the literature that has been associated with the inverted-U hypothesis is that of the experience of the athlete. According to the hypothesis, the more skilled the performer the greater their ability to tolerate a given level of arousal.

However, before we leave the inverted-U principle, we should recognise that there is an increasing amount of evidence suggesting that although the inverted-U hypothesis is very attractive as a concept, it actually fails to address issues such as experience of the athlete, physicality of the exercise and even individual athletic differences (Basler et al, 1976; Raglin, 1992). For a further discussion on the inverted-U nature of anxiety, refer to the *Concept box* below.

Concept 6.1: The inverted-U nature of anxiety: fact or fiction?

Although the inverted-U hypothesis has been shown to provide an attractive theory regarding the nature of the relationship between anxiety and performance, it has been criticised. So does this attractive hypothesis need to be discarded? Support for the theory comes in the shape of another model which has been termed 'cue utilisation theory' (Easterbrook, 1959), which states that as arousal starts to increase, the level of attention applied to the task will start to decrease, or more specifically, narrow. The cues can be both internal and external in relation to the performance and by virtue of this can be described as being both relevant and irrelevant to the performance. When arousal is low the athlete is presented with both relevant and irrelevant cues resulting in a reduced performance response due to the distraction of the irrelevant cues. At the opposite extreme of the arousal spectrum when levels are high, the athlete starts to discard both relevant and irrelevant cues due a severe narrowing of their attentional field, with the rejection of the relevant cues causing a subsequent decline in exercise performance. Within the middle of this spectrum where arousal is at a moderate level, there is a narrowing of the attentional field, but due to the moderate levels of arousal this narrowing only causes a rejection of the irrelevant cues, leaving the relevant cues and thereby optimal performance. So when you consider this arousal/ attention relationship you will appreciate that it generates an inverted-U response.

So where does this leave us with the inverted-U response? This is very much for you as the learner and practitioner to decide and perhaps weigh up the evidence from both sides of the debate.

Zone of optimal functioning (ZOF)

A modification of the inverted-U hypothesis was made based on the Yerkes–Dodson law, especially in relation to athletes who, when exposed to the same stressor, respond quite differently. The ZOF model (Hanin, 1986) was developed to offer some insight to this. According to the theory, each athlete has an optimal level of pre-performance anxiety which results in optimal performance attainment.

Therefore, each athlete has a zone of operation, measurable by the coach or psychologist, which is personal to that athlete and reflects their optimal anxiety zone. Operating within this performance zone is good, however should the athlete stray outside the zone (determined pre-performance) they will struggle to produce optimal athletic results. Interestingly, both coaches and research suggest that this relationship produces an inverted-U, however we need to apply caution at this stage, for although the relationship between performance and anxiety is similar to the inverted-U hypothesis, it does not directly validate that model. If you would like to know more about the ZOF and how it can be used as a coaching tool refer to the *Concept box* below.

Concept 6.2: Using the ZOF as a coaching aid

How do I measure and record anxiety levels?

In order to be able to develop a ZOF we need to be able to quantify what is considered to be normal or base-line pre-competition anxiety. The original research for this model proposed the use of the State Trait Anxiety Inventory (STAI). The other method that is more readily associated with sport is the use of the Competitive State Anxiety Inventory (CSAI). Both provide information on the current anxiety status of the individual, however according to the models a baseline score is needed from which the zone is established.

How is the zone of optimal functioning calculated?

Initially you will need to record the anxiety levels on a regular basis in a pre-competition state while at the same time recording the actual attained performance of the athlete. The baseline value of the ZOF is determined when the athlete attains a personal best in a competition environment, therefore the score from either the STAI or CSAI for that performance becomes the middle of the zone. As this is a zone and not just a fixed value, we need to calculate upper and lower thresholds. These are determined by adding and subtracting 4 points from this mid-value of the anxiety inventory scores. According to Raglin (1992) these scores are approximately equal to 1/2 a standard deviation.

How does the ZOF relate to athletic performance, and perhaps more importantly how can this be of benefit to the coach? There is some compelling evidence that suggests that the ZOF is a better predictor of performance than the inverted U-hypothesis (Turner and Raglin, 1991); however some studies have failed to show an association between the ZOF and performance (Randle and Weinberg, 1997).

Up to this point, we have considered how anxiety and arousal are associated with performance and have addressed a number of the proposed models and theories. Using these theories, the coaches can assess their athletes' states of anxiety, but they could also combine this with an analysis of specific physiological responses to be used as indices of arousal. Such measures could include heart rate responses and the beat/beat variation in heart rate, cortisol levels, blood lactate responses or rating of perceived exertion, all of which will be discussed in subsequent chapters.

There are more theories that have been proposed but they are generally beyond the scope of this book. Should you wish to know more, you are referred to the textbook of Weinberg and Gould (2007). The *Concept box* below presents a theory for those who wish a final challenge in relation to the performance/arousal relationship.

Concept 6.3: Catastrophe theory (Hardy and Fazey, 1987)

To best understand this model we should address the terminology used. A catastrophe has been termed: a great, often sudden calamity, or using a more sports-orientated analogy, 'the wheels coming off'. We often see this in sport where something goes wrong for an athlete and consequently their whole performance collapses. If we consider this as a scenario, we begin to appreciate that the catastrophe theory poses a challenge to the traditional inverted-U hypothesis, where an increase in arousal only results in a small decline in performance. According to this theory, there are three zones or levels of arousal, each of which produces a different performance-based response as outlined in Table 6.2.

Table 6.2: Conditions of negative anxiety as predicted through the Catastrophe model of anxiety and arousal

Category	Classification
Low cognitive anxiety	The model predicts an inverted-U relationship between performance and arousal, in accordance with the traditional inverted-U hypothesis. At this level of anxiety the athlete is not concerned about performance but their anxiety will continually oscillate from low to high without becoming an impeding factor for performance.
Moderate cognitive anxiety	When the athlete is faced with moderate levels of anxiety the model predicts an increase in performance with an associated increase in arousal. However, when arousal becomes too high, rather than following the inverted-U form, there is a sudden and rapid drop off in performance. Furthermore, the model then predicts that the level of arousal will have to fall below that at baseline (performance onset) before the athlete can move back towards a high level of performance.
High cognitive anxiety	When the athlete is confronted with high levels of anxiety, the model follows the same form as seen under moderate conditions, i.e. when arousal levels become too high there is a sudden and catastrophic drop in performance. In order for performance to recommence the arousal needs to fall below baseline, but this time the decrease is far greater than for moderate anxiety. Only then can they commence performance again, i.e. move onto the recovery path.

Concept 6.3: Continued

As well as suggesting this drop off in performance rather than a gradual decline, the theory also tries to amalgamate an understanding of both cognitive (mental) and somatic (physical) anxiety. As such, the model is predicting that physiological arousal can directly affect the performance outcome of the athlete, but crucially this is dependent upon the way in which the athlete interprets the associated physiological symptoms.

As a model we need to address the application and validity of the Catastrophe theory to sport. The literature base suggests that the Catastrophe theory provides an effective model for monitoring and assessing the athlete performance/ arousal relationship and that it is able to distinguish between cognitive and somatic anxiety levels (Edwards and Hardy, 1996; Hardy et al, 1994, Krane et al, 1994). However, the model is not without its limitations, a primary one being its inability to take into account the athlete's initial level of self-confidence, which of course has a significant implication for the anxiety levels of the athlete.

Applying theory to practice

There has been considerable research conducted in the field of athlete arousal and anxiety, resulting in a number of theories surrounding this issue. So how do we use the information and understanding to best meet the needs of the athlete?

Novice and elite athletes

Perhaps a crucial factor for both coaches and athletes alike is the way in which different athletes respond to anxiety and stress. If you were to consider two athletes who were faced with the same series of stressors and one was novice and the other was elite it would be useful to know in general terms, which type of athlete will respond more positively to the scenario. The literature base informs us that anxiety levels are higher in novices than elite athletes when both are exposed to the same stressor. (Covassin and Pero, 2004). As a coach it is also important to recognise that novice athletes who compete in individual sports experience higher anxiety levels than novice athletes competing in a team setting (Simon and Martens, 1977).

Why the difference in response between elite and novice athletes? There are a number of factors which should be taken into consideration, the primary one appearing to be the experience of the athlete. The longer the athlete has been involved in the sport the lower their cognitive anxiety. Coupled with this is the fact that well-trained athletes tend to view anxiety as being facilitative to performance, whereas their less experienced counterparts have been reported to view anxiety as debilitative. In other words, the well trained, experienced athletes – although less anxious – consider what they have to be a positive influence.

To understand this profound difference between novice and elite athletes, we need to appreciate the differences between the two groups in terms of past performance, goal-setting and an athlete's perception of preparedness.

It would appear that athletes exhibiting higher levels of anxiety are not proficient at evaluating their own performances, either because they are not sure how, or because they do not have enough performances from which to compile an evaluative approach. As discussed in Chapter 4, goal-setting has been shown to discriminate between elite and non-elite athletes, with novice athletes tending to use the less effective performance-orientated goals as opposed to the spread of approaches used by elite athletes.

An athlete's preparedness comprises long- and short-term adaptations, related to both physical and psychological adaptations and developments, with the optimum result being that the athlete is fully prepared for athletic competition. Although this can be quantified in terms of training responses, we also need to concern ourselves with the athlete's perception; how prepared do they actually feel? The overriding factor that binds the concepts of goal-setting, perceptions of preparedness and past performance together, is self-confidence.

Self-confidence and performance

There is strong evidence (Bejek and Hagtvet, 1996) suggesting that the level of self-confidence differs between elite and novice athletes. This is not entirely surprising given that the primary predictors of an athlete's self-confidence are their level of perceived preparedness, external conditions and level of previous experience. As we have already seen these same parameters can be used to discriminate between our elite and non-elite athletes.

It would appear that self-confidence can account for a greater variance in performance than either cognitive or somatic anxiety. Elite performers who have high levels of self-confidence may use this as a form of protection from anxiety, in other words the higher the levels of self-confidence the lower the perceived anxiety response. This does not mean that the athletes are no longer anxious but rather that they do not perceive the anxiety that they are experiencing to be a threat to their performance.

Teams and individuals

Previously it was suggested that there were differences in anxiety responses between team and individual-based athletes, but why should this be so? What is believed to occur is a diffusion of the anxiety across the group. On their own, an individual will have to cope with the anxiety and stress associated with the competition or performance, with no way of diffusing that anxiety. As part of a team, any player who is feeling anxious believes that they can spread the anxiety across the rest of the players, thereby lightening the load.

How can you diffuse anxiety?

We have to recognise that anxiety felt by the athlete is a consequence of responsibility. When competing as an individual all the responsibility falls on the shoulders of the athlete. Think about this – when you compete on your own who else can you consider responsible for the performance – your coach, perhaps, but overall you are solely responsible for that performance, good or bad. The result of this responsibility is a state of anxiety which can either be facilitative or debilitative.

In the team scenario however, although the perception of demand will still be high, the individual athlete will perceive that they can 'diffuse' their responsibility among the other team members and in doing so perceive a reduction in anxiety.

It is apparent that anxiety exerts numerous effects on athletic performance and that these effects are associated with factors such as gender, sporting activity and the level of experience. What now requires consideration is how coaches and athletes can use and implement coping strategies to best deal with anxiety and stress.

Coping strategies

Athletes and coaches need to be able to control and regulate their arousal and thereby anxiety. They need to recognise the signs and symptoms of debilitative anxiety and put into place an action plan or coping strategy.

The literature base offers a number of approaches that have been shown to be effective in relation to athletic performance; therefore we will now focus on the use of relaxation techniques, mental rehearsal, goal-setting and cognitive restructuring.

Imagery and mental rehearsal

Mental imagery or practice has been defined as: 'the symbolic rehearsal of a physical activity in the absence of any gross muscular actions' (Corbin, 1967). This technique allows the athlete to rehearse a skill through mental processing and thereby groom the action into an automatic learned response. Through the use of mental imagery and rehearsal, athletes can practice the skill without any form of physical exertion and develop their self-confidence and thus reduce their anxiety. Because they can keep practicing the skill or mentally observe another athlete completing the skill in a faultless manner, they generate a form of positive feedback.

The literature informs us that when imagery is applied correctly, there can be positive performance responses and associated reductions in competition anxiety. However, findings of other research studies suggest that the ability of the athlete to use mental imagery and rehearsal is dependent on the degree to which these techniques are used on a regular basis. In other words these processes are trainable and as with all skills, improve the more they are practiced. If you wish to further your understanding of the use of mental imagery refer to the *Concept box* below.

Concept 6.4: Practical approaches to mental imagery rehearsal

What skill should be rehearsed?
The key to mental imagery practice is that the imaged skill should be as realistic as possible. The athlete should be encouraged to picture the environment in which the skill will be performed (stadium, etc.) and should also attempt to incorporate as many sensory memories as possible. The more information applied to the image, the more reliable and realistic the review will be. Think about using a computer to find out some important information; the responses that the

Concept 6.4: Continued

computer gives can only be as good and realistic as the information supplied to it. The same applies to mental imagery. There is no point imaging the skill being completed in a sterile environment because this is not like the sport. When we compete we are bombarded with sensory inputs, all contributing to the 'experience'. Therefore the more that can be applied to the rehearsal the more reflective the rehearsal will be.

What should be done to prepare for an imagery session?
The process of visualisation is dependent on concentration to formulate the experience and therefore give the most realistic feel. Concentration is best achieved in the relaxed state, therefore a period of mental relaxation (one of the proposed coping strategies) is recommended prior to the rehearsal beginning.

Internal or external imagery?
There would appear to be two main types of imagers. The first are those who view the skill from an internal perspective, i.e. as they would see it during the actual competition or practice session. They see everything from their own point of view or visual perspective. The second are external imagers who view the skill from the perspective of a TV camera, i.e. outside of their body and with an external view of the skill. So which is best?

There is apparently no right or wrong approach, although most sport psychologists argue that the most realistic approach is to use internal visualisation. Coaches however, would argue that an ability to view the skill from a 3D multi-angle perspective gives the athlete a greater awareness of the totality of the movement. What is consistent about both approaches is the ability to apply all the senses and to couple these with something known as 'kinaesthetic feedback'. The role of kinaesthetic feedback is integral to a positive response and its importance has been exemplified in blind and visually impaired athletes who have no formal ability to visualise a skill, yet at the elite level report using a form of the technique.

What appears to happen for this unique group of athletes, which should also apply to able-bodied athletes, is that they image the skill from the muscular level. In other words, they feel the movement and generate a feedback mechanism to the brain which helps them to feel what their limbs should be doing during the action.

At what 'speed' should the skill be visualised and rehearsed?
Coaches often use slow-motion video footage to show the phases of a skill so that specific nuances can be highlighted and worked on. This has been proposed as the best way to mentally rehearse the skill, by 'seeing' all of the skill slowly in order to allow for precise replication.

This however defeats the point. The aim is to practice the skill, therefore the overriding consensus suggests that the skill should be imaged at real-time speed. In doing so, the athlete will 'experience' the entire skill and all associated factors

Concept 6.4: Continued

as they occur, thus meeting the primary goal, i.e. that the visualisation is as realistic as possible.

Is this a solely individual process?
On initial inspection, one would assume that mental rehearsal is an individual process and one which can only be controlled by the athlete. However, the use of this approach should be viewed in the context of the coach/athlete relationship. First, when using these techniques, the coach's support will be important to the athlete's self-esteem and confidence. Second and crucially, the coach can help inform the athlete as to what should be imaged and in particular what they should focus on. This helps foster the coach/athlete interaction and ensures that the athlete is being directed correctly.

The key component to mental imagery is communication. A strong communicative relationship between coach and athlete can help to develop the athlete in the long term.

Relaxation

The literature consistently informs us that relaxation techniques can help to reduce both cognitive and somatic anxiety and thereby help to reduce arousal drive, in turn empowering an improved performance.

Our fundamental understanding of relaxation procedures can be dated back to the 1930s. Although the approaches may have changed over time the primary outcome has not, with the outcome being the desire to produce the relaxation response. The relaxation response can be categorised by decreases in oxygen uptake (VO_2), heart rate, respiration rate and even muscle stimulation as evidenced through decreased electromyographic (EMG) output.

If these physiological responses are considered either individually or as a whole, we see that they represent the exact opposite of the classic 'fight or flight' response, where we experience extremes of arousal and associated physiological responses. Although there are many forms of relaxation we will focus here on just three: bio-feedback, progressive muscle relaxation and autogenic training.

Bio-feedback

Before we examine this concept, attempt the task below and consider carefully what happens.

Activity 6.1: Bio-feedback

You will need to make use of the following equipment: heart rate monitor, sphygmomanometer and stethoscope:

1. Write down in as much detail as possible a past event that caused you a lot of stress and anxiety. The key here is to be as explicit as possible. Make a

Activity 6.1: Continued

    series of statements or phrases that you know generate feelings of stress. Once completed, hand the written information to a partner.

2. Ensure that the heart rate monitor and blood pressure cuff are in place correctly but at this stage, do not use the stethoscope. Ask the person wearing the monitor to sit comfortably and quietly; they should not be able to see any data coming from either the heart rate monitor or the sphygmomanometer. Prior to starting the main task, record the resting heart rate (bpm) and blood pressure (mmHg).

3. Your partner should now re-read your statement of stress, emphasising the key statements or phrases. They should repeat this process a number of times. Upon completion, they should note their heart rate (bpm) and blood pressure (mmHg).

4. Note down the peak heart rate and blood pressure and also the delta (Δ) heart rate and blood pressure. Allow the subject to relax and when the heart rate and blood pressure have fallen back to resting values, move onto task two.

5. This time repeat the process with the script being read out aloud but allow the subject to watch their heart rate on the monitor and also listen to their heart rate through the stethoscope.

6. As the script is being read the subject should to try and prevent their heart rate and blood pressure from rising. Use relaxation techniques to try to control the heart rate response. As with trial one, upon completion calculate the delta values and note down the peak heart rate and blood pressure responses.

What has this task demonstrated? Well first, it shows, using empirical data, that there is a physiological (somatic) response (heart rate, blood pressure) to stress. Second, what you should have seen in trial two is that by focusing on images and relaxation techniques we can control stress-based responses. In other words, we have observed increases in the physiological variables and tried to control them. We have used a form of feedback, observed, interpreted and responded, hence the term Bio(logical) feedback.

    This task was a simple introduction to what is considered to be a powerful relaxation technique. In its truest and more applied form, bio-feedback is the use of physiological assessment tools to help promote the desired state of relaxation.

    The aim of this approach is initially to teach mastering control of the autonomic nervous system (ANS). Within this system are two specific pathways: sympathetic and parasympathetic.

    The sympathetic nervous system (SNS) is associated with increases in heart rate, blood pressure and respiration rate, whereas the parasympathetic system (PNS) is the opposite. So through the use of the instrumentation (heart rate monitors, etc.) the athlete can observe how their body responds to stress and anxiety (heart rate increases); they can then interpret this information and decide what it is they wish to do, finally instigating the appropriate response.

It is the response that is of importance as it needs to be learnt and mastered over time. The athlete has to observe how they respond physiologically to different relaxation approaches. As a result once they have mastered a strategy that induces a decrease in sympathetic tone, they can continue with that approach but without the need for the heart rate monitor or sphygmomanometer.

Before we consider the benefits of this approach, we should first consider the limitations to biofeedback as an applied tool. The primary and most obvious limitation to this technique is the need for specialist equipment; indeed previous studies have demonstrated that bio-feedback can be achieved through the use of electromyography (EMG), electroencephalography (EEG), galvanic skin response, HR, BP and skin temperature. All require specialised equipment which can be costly and may not always be portable or readily available.

These limitations not withstanding, we have to acknowledge that the literature base shows us that bio-feedback is a powerful tool for developing a relaxation response but more crucially has been associated with enhanced athletic performances as a result of the decreased sympathetic tone (Bar-Eli et al, 2001). What appears to happen is that the more often bio-feedback training is used, the more proficient the user becomes.

Progressive muscle relaxation (PMR)

The premise behind this approach is really rather simple: if all the muscles of the body are relaxed, then it is reasonable to assume that there should not be any tension anywhere within the body. So extending this a stage further, we could suggest that a relaxed body should promote a relaxed (less anxious) mind.

The original technique begins with the athlete lying flat and still in a supine position without crossing limbs and in a quiet environment. The principle of PMR is to instruct the mind as to how a state of relaxation should feel, therefore in order for the athlete to appreciate the feeling of relaxation, we need to 'calibrate' the mind. This is achieved by comparing the feeling of a tensed, non-relaxed body. The athlete begins by tensing a specific region/limb of the body and holding that contraction for around 10 seconds.

The original method started the individual on the left arm, although nowadays many versions exist, with the most logical following a pattern from the right toes, then left toes followed by right foot and then left, progressing slowly up the body. For each site, the athlete should initially repeat the contraction three times. Once the athlete has followed this process from toes through to scalp, they should have achieved a state of relaxation.

A further understanding and appreciation for the practical approaches to using PMR can be obtained from the *Concept box* below.

Concept 6.5: Practical approaches to PMR

Training and practice of the technique

Mastering PMR and becoming proficient at achieving a state of relaxation takes a prolonged period of training. This is why at the onset of using PMR, the rather long-winded and time-consuming approach highlighted above is recommended. This approach is encouraged as it teaches the athlete how to recognise the difference between an anxious, overly aroused state and a state of relaxation.

Concept 6.5: Continued

How applicable is the use of PMR to sport?

If we consider the full blown beginner's approach of 3 x 10 seconds for each limb, it could be argued quite rightly that this is not at all practical to the athlete wishing to gain some composure during the heat of competition. Clearly then, time is of the essence and the athlete does not have masses of time to go through this routine prior to undertaking the skill.

However, we should view the role of PMR in a wider context. As we get more proficient at the technique, the time required to achieve relaxation is reduced. The full-blown approach has its place when working with athletes who have the time to achieve the state of relaxation prior to competing. Either way, PMR can help to create a state of relaxation and reduce the arousal response.

How proficient is proficient?

Proficiency is when PMR can be used in the middle of a competition almost instantly. Picture the bi-athlete who has been skiing cross country for around 20km before they stop to un-hitch their rifle, lie in the snow and then hit five targets as soon as they can. They have to go from a state of high athletic arousal (HR >190bpm, VO_2 -90% VO_{2max}), to a state of complete control within a matter of 10–15s. This is achieved through relaxation.

Those who are highly proficient at the technique can relax a specific muscle or muscle group without having to start from the toes and work their way around the body. They can also achieve the state of relaxation without having to induce a pre-muscular contraction for comparison. As a result, they can become relaxed within a matter of seconds.

Autogenic training

Autogenic training is very much a relaxation technique, but rather than being concerned with the direct inducement of the relaxation state, it is more focused on the feelings associated with that state. These feelings are described as being warmth and heaviness within the limbs.

If you consider this, both are states of 'comfort' associated with relaxation and wellbeing. As a result it is these feelings and sensations that autogenic training tries to develop. Quite simply, if we can induce feelings of warmth and heaviness in the limbs we have attained a state of relaxation.

The process is comprised of three stages with the first involving the development of the state of relaxation, with the athlete being encouraged to focus on warmth and heaviness in the limbs. The second involves the athlete using imagery to visualise scenes and feelings that they associate with comfort and relaxation. The third and final stage is to reinforce the sensation of relaxation.

As with PMR, the effectiveness of autogenic training is dependent on the degree to which the athlete uses it as a training aid. It is clear that autogenic training has been shown to induce profound states of relaxation (Stetter and Kupper, 2002), but what is less clear is the association with enhancement of athletic performance.

An issue that has been raised both in relation to PMR and autogenic training is the time frame required in order to induce the relaxed state. Remember that an athlete may have a sudden feeling of anxiety minutes prior to competing; therefore can we use such a technique? The literature base informs us that as the athlete becomes practiced with the skill, the quicker the state of relaxation is reached. So in the beginning, when first undertaking this form of training, the process may take up to 30 minutes but once the skill is mastered the relaxation state could be induced in a matter of minutes.

Take home message

There is little doubt that athletes and indeed coaches experience symptoms and conditions of high arousal and anxiety in response to both training and competition. Strategies are available to help alleviate and reduce these symptoms, which if unchecked can become detrimental to performance.

Although we have discussed a number of methods it should be noted that they are not exclusive and that each has both positive and negative aspects. The more each of these skills are used by both the athlete and the coach the more proficient they become. Furthermore, it is important to consider their use in the context of the coach/athlete relationship.

The athlete and coach both need to recognise and appreciate the role and application of the strategies, indeed for the coach this is another piece of knowledge and understanding that helps form their mental model of athlete potential. Remember that an anxious athlete is a poorly-performing athlete.

Further study

The following is a list of peer reviewed publications and books which will help you develop a wider understanding of the issues relating to anxiety and arousal in sport and the use of coping strategies to combat these symptoms. The list contains literature related to the practical application of coping strategies such as bio-feedback, autogenic training and mental imagery and the relationship to athletic performance.

Caird, S, McKenzie, A and Sleivert, G (1999) Biofeedback and relaxation techniques improve running economy in sub-elite long distance runners. *Medicine and Science in Sports and Exercise*, 31: 717–22

Driskell, J E, Copper, C and Moran, A. (1994) Does mental practice enhance performance. *Journal of Applied Psychology*, 79: 481–92

Epstein, M L (1980) The relationship of mental imagery and mental rehearsal to performance of a motor task. *Journal of Sport Psychology*, 2: 211–20

Fentress, D W, Masek, B J, Mehegan, J E and Benson, H (1986) Biofeedback and relaxation response training in the treatment of paediatric migraine. *Developmental Medicine and Child Neurobiology*, 28: 139–45

Hardy, L, Jones, J G and Gould, D (2002) *Understanding psychological preparation for sport: Theory and practice of elite performers*. Chichester: Wiley

Hecker, J E and Kaczor, L M (1988) Application of imagery theory to sport psychology. Some preliminary findings. *Journal of Sport and Exercise Psychology*, 10: 363–73

Jones, G (1991) Recent developments and current issues in competitive state anxiety research. *The Psychologist. Bulletin of the British Psychological Society*, 4: 152–5

Landers, D M (1980) The arousal performance relationship revisited. *Research Quarterly for Exercise and Sport*, 51: 77–90

Shapiro, S (1980) Psychophysiological effects if autogenic training and progressive relaxation. *Applied Psychophysiology and Biofeedback*, 5: 249–55

Swain, A B J and Jones, G (1996) Explaining performance variance: The relative contribution of intensity and direction dimensions of competitive state anxiety. *Anxiety Stress and Coping*, 9: 1–18

Weinberg, R S and Gould, D (2007) *Foundations of sport and exercise psychology*. 4th edition. Champaign, IL: Human Kinetics

www.bases.org.uk/newsite/home.asp – British Association of Sport and Exercise Sciences: National body for sport and exercise science within the UK. Useful contacts and documents related to physiology, psychology, biomechanics, health and coaching.

www.eis2win.co.uk/gen/news_copingpressure230603.aspx – English Institute of Sport: National organisation who support and work with elite athletes in England. This link is directly related to coping with pressure.

www.mysport.net – My Sport: An online community for coach education and discussion.

www.sirc.ca – SIRC: Sport, Research, Intelligence, Sportive: An international database which lists articles and publications related to coaching. Also has links to International Governing Bodies of sport and Sport Institutes.

www.sportscoachuk.org – Sports Coach UK. National body responsible for regulating and overseeing coach education within the UK. Site contains information relating to coaching courses and contacts through to coaching resources and support.

www.uksport.gov.uk – UK Sport. National body supporting elite world class performers. Useful resources related to coach education and drug free sport.

PART 3

Training the athlete

Chapter 7

Variables and components of training

The aim of this chapter is to introduce you to the intricacies of training and in particular, the factors which contribute to the concept of training. We will address the variables of training, examining the issues of training intensity, frequency and duration and how these relate to both training load and volume. We will also consider the specifics of training which make up the profile of any athletic event. Therefore, upon completion of this chapter you will have:

- examined the factors which contribute to the intensity of training and how these are related to the development of the athlete;
- understood the interplay between training intensity and the duration of training effort;
- explored the issue of training frequency and its relationship to athlete development;
- appreciated the interplay between intensity, frequency and duration of training and how these manifest themselves in the form of training load;
- addressed the so-called Ss of training and how these are related to all athletic disciplines;
- considered the types of athlete and how an understanding of them can benefit the coach and athlete development;
- applied this acquired knowledge to your own sport or coaching background.

Introduction

The primary aim of athletes is to attain their athletic goal, whether that be an Olympic title or setting a personal best in a competition; either way in order to attain these levels of athletic performance the athlete will need to be in a 'trained state'.

Training theory can be viewed in many ways. At a simplistic level we recognise that undertaking any form of physical activity exposes the body to a stimulus which drives development of the individual both athletically and in relation to health and wellbeing. We recognise that through this developed stimulus, occurring as the result of stressing the body, we can develop physiologically, psychologically and biomechanically.

This is a simple view of training: we apply a stressor to the body (training) which initiates a stimulus, the result of which is some form of bodily development. What this example does not show is how an athlete would train to improve.

The purpose of training is to stimulate growth and that growth occurs only during periods of rest and recovery. From this simple statement, we have a starting point for the fundamentals of training and athletic development. We recognise that training provides the stimulus for bodily development but crucially we also need to recognise that this development only occurs when the stress is reduced and the body is allowed to recover. Therefore, we can begin to recognise the relationship between the training session or period and recovery time and the associated development of the athlete.

Once we start to appreciate this chain of events, we can begin to ask ourselves some important questions about the training response, such as how we can increase the size of the developmental response and how we go about generating this response.

In order to answer these questions, we will begin by addressing the fundamentals of training which are quite simply – How hard should we train, how long should we train for and how often should we train? It is the association between these variables that forms the framework for our understanding of the training response and athlete development.

Fundamentals of training

Intensity of training

From this point forward, we will refer to the concept of how hard an athlete should train as the intensity of training. Quite simply, intensity can be viewed as the amount of work done (training) within a period of time. Therefore, the more training completed in a specified unit of time (session) the more intense that session is and vice versa.

The intensity of an exercise or training is both sport- and training session-specific. We should also recognise that we need to have some way of evaluating and measuring the level of intensity at which an athlete is working.

If you consider your own sport, or sports that you are associated with, you probably recognise that not all training sessions are conducted at the same intensity; indeed athletes often discuss completing 'light training' or 'full-on sessions'. So what do these terms mean and how can they be quantified in terms of our overall understanding of training?

In considering systems' physiology, we recognise that there is an energy continuum on which sit the metabolic pathways, with aerobic metabolism of proteins and fats at one end and the use of high energy phosphates, such as ATP and creatine phosphate (ATP-PCr) at the other. By recognising this continuum, we can begin to pin down the philosophy of exercise and training intensities.

Training intensities

Low intensity exercise is characterised by the predominance of fatty acid metabolism and the reliance almost entirely on aerobic metabolic pathways (~5% anaerobic; ~95% aerobic). According to the continuum there are two aerobic domains characterised by different physiological and metabolic responses. Whereas we can maintain low intensity exercise for durations of greater than 3 hours, the second aerobic training zone, classified as medium intensity, can only be maintained for between 1 and 3 hours with the metabolic split between aerobic and anaerobic metabolism being ~40% anaerobic and ~60% aerobic ±15%.

The third level of intensity on the energy continuum introduces the onset of lactate production as a result of an increased reliance on anaerobic metabolism from glycolysis. This level has been defined as sub-maximal and can be tolerated for between 30 and 60 minutes. The increased reliance on anaerobic glycolytic energy associated with this intensity explains why this domain can only be tolerated for such a relatively short period of time and why there is such a profound change in the reliance on the metabolic pathways (~60% anaerobic; ~40% aerobic ±20%).

Beyond this point, reliance on energy substrates and metabolic pathways starts to change, with a much greater demand being placed on both anaerobic glycolysis and the use of the high energy phosphates (ATP-PCr). As a result, the intensity of exercise becomes greater as the athlete is able to train harder but such training can only be tolerated for short periods of 60–360 seconds, with the outcome being a significant change in the demand on aerobic and anaerobic metabolism (~80% anaerobic; ~20% aerobic ±10%).

The final domain of intensity is classified as supra-maximal and is defined by almost entirely relying on ATP-PCr as the energy substrate for exercise. As a result, when we express this domain in terms of aerobic and anaerobic metabolism we see that there is almost no demand on aerobic metabolism (~95% anaerobic; ~5% aerobic ±5%). This domain of intensity can only be tolerated for 10–30 seconds.

The identification of these training intensities enables us to grasp how we programme training sessions through the use of intensity. We might want an athlete to complete a gentle period of training where there is a low metabolic demand and cost so we would set this as low intensity training, perhaps the kind associated with recovery training. Conversely, we may want to set a session wherein we want the athlete to work very hard but for short periods of time. This would be high intensity training and would come under the classification of supra-maximal.

Low intensity training

This zone of training places the greatest demand on aerobic metabolic pathways through the use of proteins, fats and carbohydrates. The physiological strain is generally low with no significant demands being placed on the cardiovascular or respiratory systems, with the athlete experiencing a heart rate (HR) in the order of <140bpm.

Because the intensity is low, the total energy expenditure for the session or event can be high, primarily because low intensity work is associated with increased duration of the activity. Because this form of activity is so low and places very little strain on the metabolic and physiological pathways, it is associated with recovery training where we do not wish to cause undue fatigue and distress to the athlete (see Chapter 10).

Prolonged activity in this domain is associated with increased thermal costs as core body temperature starts to rise. This slow rise in core temperature over time results in 'cardiac drift', where heart rate and cardiac output slowly increase.

The literature base informs us that at some point, fatigue will begin to develop within this intensity zone, either as a result of the slowly increasing core temperature or through a slow decline in the available fuel substrates. Neither of these factors however, can explain why individuals performing prolonged low intensity exercise suffer fatigue of the central nervous system. For a greater understanding of fatigue and its associated physiological and metabolic consequences, refer to the *Concept box* below.

Concept 7.1: *Understanding fatigue*

We often refer to being 'fatigued' either through training or through day-to-day stress from things such as work, education or home life. The term is commonly used to describe a multitude of physiological and psychological responses. A definition of fatigue supplied by Edwards (1981) states that: 'Failure to maintain the required expected force leads to a reduced performance of a given task'.

The task could be any activity we wish to perform; all activities require generation of some level of force, whether when generating the force required to lift a weight, or generating the mechanics of motion in swimming. So if we cannot maintain a given level of force thereby completing the task, we are defined as being fatigued. Where this topic becomes fascinating is in discerning what causes and contributes to this fatigue – not all fatigue is the same.

Consider the 400m runner who completes the distance in around 45 seconds. For this athlete, the relative contribution of the metabolic pathways would be ~73% anaerobic and ~37% aerobic, with post-race blood lactate (BLa) scores likely in the order of $10-15mM \cdot l^{-1}$. There is clearly fatigue in such a race because most athletes start to slow down in the final 100m of the race (inability to maintain the desired intensity).

According to Hirvonen et al (1992) there are profound physiological changes occurring during the 400m run, with reliance on aerobic based muscle fibres (Type I) increasing as the distance increases, with concurrent increase in BLa and decrease in the phosphocreatine (PCr) concentrations. The reliance on the type I fibres ahead of the type II fibres is a result of the increasing BLa and decreasing PCr concentrations which start to render these fast glycolytic fibres less than effective.

Now consider the ultra-marathon runner who will be exercising for longer than 3 hours. Under such conditions it has been reported that the athlete has a much slower running velocity of around $2.0m \cdot s^{-1}$ compared with $8.8m \cdot s^{-1}$ for the 400m runner.

The metabolic demand during such long duration events is relatively low but the total energy expenditure is high. The athlete does not produce excessive BLa scores or show any profound changes in PCr stores, so the fatigue mechanisms are different to those experienced by the 400m runner. The ultra-marathon runner will show signs of mental fatigue and distress and in some cases decreases in cognitive functioning.

These forms of fatigue are defined as peripheral and central fatigue, with the 400m runner experiencing peripheral fatigue and the ultra-marathon runner showing symptoms of central fatigue.

Peripheral fatigue: we can classify this form of fatigue as being a point of failure beyond the neuromuscular junction, associating this form of fatigue with a

Concept 7.1: Contined

failure within the skeletal muscle. Classic symptoms of this form of fatigue are increases in BLa, Hydrogen ion (H^+), ADP concentrations and decreases in PCr, calcium release (Ca^{++}) and energy substrates. Interestingly, ATP is not a limiting factor despite concentrations falling as low as 40 per cent during some forms of dynamic exercise (Cady et al, 1989).

Central fatigue: we can classify central fatigue as a failure within the central nervous system (CNS). It is much harder to classify but has been associated with changes in key neurotransmitters in the brain such as serotonin and dopamine (Blomstrand, 2001), changes in the neural feedback from the muscle to the brain which decrease the muscle's force generation efficiency (Kent-Braun, 1999) and some form of psychological fatigue where the athlete becomes either de-motivated or loses the perception of effort (Nybo and Nielson, 2001).

In most cases, the athlete will conform to the symptoms expressed in our definitions of fatigue and will experience a decrease in performance. A further consideration is that fatigue is the primary response to training and the combination of fatigue and recovery results in physiological adaptation.

Medium intensity training

As with low intensity training, this form of work is still associated with predominantly aerobic metabolism but there are increased metabolic and physiological demands placed on the athlete. It is associated with increased HR in the region of 140–160bpm and a greater reliance on carbohydrate as the predominant aerobic fuel.

Importantly we are still exercising below the lactate turn-point (see Chapter 10) and so lactate and H^+ accumulation do not become limiting factors. This intensity of effort is associated with prolonged steady bursts of activity promoting the development of the cardiovascular system and aerobic metabolic pathways. The key point to this intensity of training is that the supply of energy meets the demand of energy by aerobic means.

Sub-maximal intensity training

Unlike the previous two training zones, sub-maximal intensity of training is associated with an imbalance between the delivery and utilisation of oxygen and as a result anaerobic energy is introduced via glycolysis to supplement the aerobic energy provision.

The further intensity increases the greater the reliance on anaerobic metabolism becomes. Therefore this form of training takes place at an intensity which is in excess of the lactate turn-point and would be associated with an HR of 160–180bpm and the further development of aerobic training responses. The athlete may use this form of training to complete what runners call 'Tempo training' where they are completing faster paced efforts than they would in the previous domains, but without inducing profound metabolic stress.

Maximal intensity training

This form of training is associated with a combination of energy derived from the high energy phosphates and anaerobic glycolysis but very little aerobic metabolism. As a result, the ability to sustain such intensity is compromised by the ensuing development of peripheral fatigue. For this level it is not possible to quantify intensity in the form of HR as there is little if no association at all between anaerobic metabolism and HR responses.

This form of training is generally used in interval sessions where the athlete will complete a number of repetitions of the same intensity but with a specified recovery in between. Such training develops lactate tolerance (longer duration efforts with short recoveries) and specific aerobic responses (VO_{2max}), despite not using aerobic metabolism as a primary metabolic pathway. There is of course the development of anaerobic energy supply through the laying down of key anaerobic enzymes and substrates.

Supra-maximal intensity training

As with maximal intensity, this form of training cannot be quantified through the use of HR or even BLa at the higher end of the domain. Such intense training is limited by the ability to generate energy for muscular work rapidly enough to meet the demands of the muscle. As such, the primary limiting factor is the availability of ATP-PCr. Again this form of training is generally associated with either interval training to promote anaerobic development or all-out efforts such as those used in speed and plyometric training.

Activity 7.1: Training intensities

Using the information gathered from the previous section and your understanding of the energy continuum, attempt to develop sample training sessions for your sport for each of the intensity domains. For each session note down:

- The intensity of the session;
- The purpose of the session (i.e. what are we trying to enhance: cardiovascular, strength, power speed, etc.);
- How much work will be completed?
- How much recovery will there be (if necessary)?

Measuring intensity

Let us initially consider sports where distance and time are factors, such as running, swimming and cycling. For these activities, the primary measure of absolute intensity is speed (kph, $m \cdot s^{-1}$). However, not all activities involve covering a specified distance in a set time, such as weight training and resistance work. In these cases the absolute measure of intensity is mass moved (kg, N, N·m). Some sports clearly fit neither of these profiles such as team and racket-based activities. For these sports, we measure absolute intensity as the frequency or pace of movement within a game.

All of these define the intensity required for a session. We can also define the intensity in relative terms through the use of more specific variables. Coaches can establish training intensities based on the percentage of an athlete's personal best time or pace or through the use of a physiological variable such as $\%HR_{max}$ or $\%VO_{2max}$. A further method for the endurance based sports is to establish a training intensity within a zone using HR or BLa.

Intensity and athletic development

Of the three components of training it would appear that intensity is the primary stimulus for athletic development. Indeed the literature shows a clear association between both physiological adaptations to training and intensity of training (Mikesall and Dudley, 1984) and between training intensity and performance (Martin et al, 1986).

On initial inspection one might logically conclude that if the primary stimulus for both performance and physiological gains is intensity, just bombard the athlete with continuous bouts of high intensity exercise because they are bound to improve. However, the literature and evidence from coaches suggests that a large volume of high intensity training is poorly tolerated by the athlete.

Frequency of training

A component of training is how often the athlete trains; from this point forward this will be referred to as the frequency of training. Quite simply the frequency of training refers to the number of training sessions or units that occur within a specified timeframe.

The timeframe could be a day, week, month or year. The frequency of training sessions is dependent on many factors such as training status of the athlete, stage of athlete development, training phase and sporting discipline. The general approach adopted by most coaches and athletes is to complete between 5 and 14 sessions within a one week block of training.

Therefore when we begin to quantify the training response we must know what constitutes a unit so as to maximise our frequency count. Technically a unit of training is any session or activity that contributes to the overall development of the athlete, so whether supra-maximal high intensity or low intensity sessions, all are crucial to the physiological development of the athlete.

Activity 7.2: Frequency of training in the novice athlete

Elite athletes and their coaches report completion of approximately 5–14 training sessions or units per week. Data from novice or amateur athletes shows a considerable difference in the training frequency, with a range of 2–5 sessions a week being reported. You should discuss why there is such a difference between the two sets of athletes in relation to training frequency.

Duration of training

Previously we have described a component of training which classifies how long an athlete trains for; from now on, we will refer to this as the duration of training. The duration of training is a quantitative variable (i.e. can be measured) that signifies the amount of time of training completed in a session or unit (Smith, 2003).

Intensity and duration of training are inextricably linked; for example you cannot programme a long duration session >2 hours at supra-maximal intensities. Even for an interval session, an athlete would not be able to maintain intensity for the full duration. So although programmed separately when structuring training, they are quite obviously linked.

A misconception in relation to common training terminology is that duration of training is the same as training volume, the two terms being used interchangeably within coaching and scientific communities (Bompa, 1999). Training volume is used to clarify the total amount of training performed within a given timeframe such as a week or month, therefore it is the composite of training duration and frequency. The volume of training implies the total amount of work done by the athlete, so an athlete could have a high or low volume training week, depending on the combination of frequency and duration sessions. Either way our understanding of this interplay between frequency and duration is important when exploring the physiological development of an athlete.

There is a strong association between the increase in total training volume and the physiological development of the athlete, especially in endurance based sports. In sports such as marathon running there is a clear association between training volume and the development of the athlete (Billat et al, 2000).

The same association holds true for skill-based sports where the development of skill is achieved through deliberate practice and the more it is rehearsed the more proficient the athlete becomes at implementing the skill in competition.

However, intensity is not included in the volume calculation and is only implied; this is where our understanding of training load becomes apparent.

Training load

Training load reflects the interaction of intensity, frequency and duration of training conducted by the athlete. If structured and sequenced correctly by the coach, training load will provide the overall stimulus for the development of the athlete either physiologically, psychologically or biomechanically.

Through training programme design and structure (Chapter 9), coaches set plans with both short- and long-term focus, developed primarily on the back of the goals set by the athlete and coach at the start of the new season's training cycle (see Chapter 4).

Despite obvious differences between what would be attempted and achieved through long- and short-term planning, we should also recognise that there is a common feature in how the coach structures training load to recovery.

Recall how recovery is the primary phase of training adaptation and development. In order for any athlete to develop there must be an optimal balance between the amount of work done (training load) and the amount of time allowed to recuperate (recovery) (this will be addressed in greater detail in Chapter 10).

The balance between training load and recovery is dependent on many factors such as the current training phase of the athlete, the aim of the current training cycle and the ability of the athlete. When coaches structure training load it can be mapped in two ways, either by identifying the load of a particular training session/unit or through calculating the total training load for a specified training cycle, usually a week. For a more in depth appreciation of the constituents of training load refer to the Concept Box.

Concept 7.2: Constituents of training load

The primary constituents of the training load are training volume (frequency and duration) and intensity of training. We should recognise however, that although these are the overarching components there are other factors to consider.

Specificity of training

When constructing a training plan, it is important to recognise the difference between sport or event specific training and training which is general but still important. When considering any sport, we can differentiate between training conducted to maintain and develop overall athletic fitness and training conducted to develop specific aspects in relation to the overall performance. Either way, both contribute to the overall training load and need to be sequenced accordingly in the overall plan.

Sequencing of the training elements

The sequencing of the elements will dictate the overall load of a larger training cycle (week or month). The elements of the sport need careful consideration, especially in skill dominated sports where a balance must be struck between base athletic development (fitness) and sport specific skill development. Skill development has to be sequenced so that the athlete is not being overloaded too early with a skill that will impinge on subsequent skill training.

Size of the training stimulus: If we consider that training is the ability to apply a stimulus to an athlete and through a subsequent period of recovery induce athletic development, then the simple way to further development is more training! Too much training however, can be detrimental to the development of the athlete and lead to conditions such as under-performance syndrome (UPS). Therefore the size of the training stimulus has to be judged against the current physical status of the athlete.

Training cycles: The training year is divided up into training cycles (see Chapter 9) and the structuring of these blocks contributes to the overall training load of the athlete. This is partly a sequencing issue but is also based on an understanding of how to structure each of the cycles. Two factors contributing to the structuring of a training cycle are the duration and overall intensity of a cycle. Clearly a longer cycle cannot be as intense as a shorter one, but may be needed in order to further develop the athlete's base fitness. So although the athlete's fitness is developed, the overall training load is lowered.

Rest periods: Again this can be viewed as a sequencing issue but should also be viewed in the context of being a training method in itself. The balance between training within specified sessions and recovery is crucial to the development of the athlete. Too little recovery between training units and we may witness an athlete suffering from fatigue, even leading to burnout and possibly UPS. Too much recovery between training units and the athlete will start to lose the physiological development gained from previous sessions. However, there is a caveat to this relationship. The more stressful a session the greater the recovery needed and the greater the subsequent development. We need to be extremely careful as to how we balance recovery and training.

When we start to develop a plan for any athlete we need to be sure that the session or cycle meets the goals of the athlete. One way to ensure this is to recognise the levels of training load that can be used, as highlighted in Table 7.1.

It is clear that training load is a complex variable and one that must be structured and nurtured effectively to be of benefit to the athlete. At the same time, we should remember that the load is a composite of many interrelated constituents and manipulating any one of these factors will lead to a change in training and thereby alter the level of athletic development.

Up to this point we have addressed the variables but not the components of training; in other words those factors which make up an athlete's ability to influence the type of training conducted for a specific sporting event. In order to do this, we need to address what have been described as the 'Ss of training' (Smith, 2003).

Table 7.1: The five levels of training load

Level	Classification
Disproportionate load	A level of training load exceeding the functional capacity and capability of the body which can lead to athletic burnout, overreaching and even UPS.
Trainable load	The level of load that induces specific physiological and biochemical responses (adaptations) over a period of time leading to athletic development.
Conservation load	The level of training load promoting maintenance of physiological and biochemical adaptations developed through training, but not leading to further adaptations. Crucially, conservation load will prevent a detraining effect (loss of physiological and biochemical adaptations).
Recovery load	The level of training load that promotes the recovery processes of the biological systems which will have been stressed during a previous training session.
Ineffective load	The level of load below the minimum intensity which promotes any physiological or biochemical responses. It is of no benefit to the athlete.

Adapted from: Viru, A (1995) *Adaptation in sports training*. Boca Raton, FL: CRC Press; also cited in Smith, D J (2003) A framework for understanding the training process leading to elite performance. *Sports Medicine*, 33: 1003–26.

The components of training

Ss of training

We need to understand the physical demands of the sport by recognising its make up in relation to the basic components of fitness: Speed, Strength, Stamina (endurance) and Skill.

All athletic sports have a combination of these components but the significance of each of these components varies from sport to sport. This is the first stage of the coaching process in terms of developing the training plan. If the coaches do not appreciate the demands of the sport they cannot begin to programme training to meet those demands.

Activity 7.3: Components of sport

Consider a variety of sports and how they are constructed in relation to Speed, Strength, Stamina and Skill. For each sport listed in Table 7.2 rank the importance of each fitness component with 1 being the most important and 4 being the least important.

Table 7.2: Components of fitness

	Speed	Strength	Stamina	Skill
Marathon				
Golf				
Speed skating				
Fencing				
100m sprint				
Judo				
Archer				
Rowing				
Volleyball				
Windsurfing				

What the above task shows is that despite recognising that sports such as marathon running are endurance based, there is a need for athletes to develop, in some part, all the components of fitness. This is a simple concept to acknowledge and comes back to our understanding of the training load, in that we need to strike a balance between the specifics and generalities of a sport.

Assuming that training is the development of each component to a greater or lesser degree, we come across a problem which is a manifestation of our biological and evolutionary development: one type of training can be detrimental and so have negative effects on another type of training. A classic example of this is seen in endurance-based athletes.

The primary aim of endurance athletes is to produce physiological and biochemical adaptations which promote their aerobic capability. Endurance training has been shown to result in increases in mitochondrial size and density, capillary density within the muscle, aerobic enzymes and in the efficiency of type I muscle fibres. These are not the only adaptations that occur and so for a more in-depth exploration of the adaptations to endurance training, refer to Chapter 10. However, they are important to our understanding of the impact of training modalities on physiological responses.

As well as requiring a solid aerobic base it has become recognised that endurance athletes also need some lower limb strength in order to maintain body form and mechanics during exercise. However, strength training has been shown to result in increases in muscle mass (hypertrophy), decreases in capillary density to the muscle and decreases in muscle mitochondria functioning, all of which are detrimental to endurance performance.

There is clear disparity between what we want to achieve and what physiologically happens. Strength training, although important to the development of the athlete, results in negative aerobic physiological adaptations, which potentially elicit a decrement in endurance performance. So coaches must recognise that although each sport requires a combination of the components of fitness, they need to be critical in the way they structure the training plan so as to minimise the cross-over effect from one component to another.

There are however other components of fitness and athletic capability which come under the heading of the Ss of training and these are P(s)ychology, Stature, Suppleness and Sustenance (Smith, 2003). The psychological factors of athletic performance have been discussed in previous chapters.

Stature refers to the morphological make up of the athlete and encompasses factors such as height, mass, muscle mass and body fat composition. All are of importance to the coach and athlete and can be monitored on a regular basis. Clearly certain body shapes and morphological constructs lend themselves better to certain sports and this recognition has formed the backbone of the Talent Identification process as discussed in Chapter 14.

Consider for a moment – How many short basketball players have you seen in the NBA? How many sumo wrestlers have you seen with low levels of body fat? How many gymnasts have a high body mass? Stature is therefore important in terms of understanding the development of the athlete and should be monitored on a regular basis.

Suppleness is the term used to imply flexibility and is probably one of the least well understood components of fitness, yet is a factor which can have a profound effect on the development of an athlete (Chapter 12). Indeed a lack of flexibility has been associated with reduced ability to learn and execute specific skill-based actions, due to greater physical demand being placed on surrounding muscles that would not normally be involved in that action, but are required to stabilise and complete the movement.

However, we should also recognise that lower levels of flexibility have been associated with enhanced running economy in distance runners by reducing the need to recruit additional muscles when performing an action. For a greater understanding of the role of flexibility in training refer to Chapter 12.

Sustenance is the term used to describe nutrition for the athlete. A coach must recognise that all athletes require a comprehensive nutritional strategy, which encompasses the intake of macronutrients (carbohydrates, fats and proteins) on a daily basis, but also optimises their intake pre- and post-training. There must also be a sound recognition of the fluid intake requirements of the athlete, both on a daily basis but also when training. There is compelling evidence to show an association between the ability to recover from training and an athlete's diet. It is important for the coach to balance the Ss of training in order to meet the needs of the athlete and their developmental plan.

Take home message

The overriding message from this chapter is that training is a complex phenomenon and one which is dependent on an appreciation of the variables of training (intensity, frequency and duration) and how these combine to form the concepts of training volume and load. Our appreciation for the nature of the training load drives the training response (adaptation and development) and through this we factor in the role of recovery.

Coupled with our recognition of the variables of training is the understanding of the components of training and how they relate to both the nature of the sport and each other. We must reflect on the fact that the promotion of the components of fitness is dependent on the correct sequencing and implementation of the training plan. Finally, we should always be aware of the nature of the athlete with whom we are working and how their ability and fitness status will determine both the nature of their development and their rate of development.

Further study

The publications listed below are provided to allow you to delve into the issues surrounding the variables of training in more depth. There is literature related to the association between intensity, duration and frequency of training and performance. There are also selected publications which are related to the Ss of training.

Costill, D L, Thomas, R, Robergs, R A, Pascoe, D, Lambert, C, Barr, S and Fink, W J (1991) Adaptations to swimming training: Influence of training volume. *Medicine and Science in Sports and Exercise*, 23: 371–7

Foster, C, Daines, E, Hector, L, Snyder, A C and Welsh, R (1996) Athletic performance in relation to training load. *Wisconsin Medical Journal*, 95: 370–4

Fox, E L, Bartels, R L, Billings, C E, O'Brien, R, Bason, R and Mathews, D K (1975) Frequency and duration of interval training programs and changes in aerobic power. *Journal of Applied Physiology*, 38: 481–4

Gastin, P B (2001) Energy system interaction and relative contribution during maximal exercise. *Sports Medicine*, 31: 725–41

Gleim, G W and McHugh, M P. (1997) Flexibility and its effects on sports injury and performance. *Sports Medicine*, 24: 289–99

Hickson, R C, Kanakis, C, Davis, J R, Moore, A M and Rich, S (1982) Reduced training duration effects on power, endurance and cardiac growth. *Journal of Applied Physiology*, 53: 225–9

Jones, A M and Carter, H (2000) The effect of endurance training on parameters of aerobic fitness. *Sports Medicine*, 29: 373–86

Pate, R and Branch, D J (1992) Training for endurance sport. *Medicine and Science in Sports and Exercise*, 24: 340–3

Paulsen, G, Myklestad, D and Raastad, T (2003) The influence of volume of exercise on early adaptations to strength training. *Journal of Strength and Conditioning Research*, 17: 115–20

Philips, S M, Green, H J, Tarnopolsky, M A, Heigenhauser, G J F, Hill, R E and Grant, S M (1996) Effects of training duration on substrate turnover and oxidation during exercise. *Journal of Applied Physiology*, 81: 2182–91

Shephard, R J (1968) Intensity, duration and frequency of exercise as determinants of the response to a training regime. *European Journal of Applied Physiology*, 28: 272–8

Siorotic, A C and Coutts, A J (2007) Physiological and performance test correlates of prolonged high-intensity intermittent running performance in moderately trained women team sport players. *Journal of Strength and Conditioning Research*, 21: 138–44

Trappe, T A, Gastaldelli, A, Jozsi, A C, Troup, J P and Wolfe, R R (1997) Energy expenditure of swimmers during high volume training. *Medicine and Science in Sports and Exercise*, 29: 950–4

Vermulst, L J, Vervoorn, C, Boelens-quist, A M, Koppeschaar, H P, Erich, W B, Thijssen, J H and de Vries, W R (1991) Analysis of seasonal training volume and working capacity in elite female rowers. *International Journal of Sports Medicine*, 12: 567–72

Wenger, H A and Bell, G J (1986) The interaction of intensity, frequency and duration of exercise training in altering cardio-respiratory fitness. *Sports Medicine*, 3: 346–56

Wilson, G J, Newton, R U, Murphy, A J and Humphries, B J (1993) The optimal training load for the development of dynamic athletic performance. *Medicine and Science in Sports and Exercise*, 25: 1279–86

Zatsiorsky, V M (1995) *Science and practice of strength training*. Champaign, IL: Human Kinetics

www.bases.org.uk/newsite/home.asp – British Association of Sport and Exercise Sciences: National body for sport and exercise science within the UK. Useful contacts and documents related to physiology, psychology, biomechanics, health and coaching.

www.athleticscoaching.ca/default.aspx?pid=7&spid=35 – Canadian Athletics Coaching Centre: Site containing information relating to coaching and sports science. This link relates to training loads and structuring.

www.elitetrack.com/ – Elitetrack: A website which houses both peer reviewed and lay articles. All papers are referenced and are either written by coaches or sports scientists. A very good resource for all disciplines within coaching.

www.everythingtrackandfield.com/catalog/matriarch/OnePiecePage.asp_Q_PageID_E_350_A_PageName_E_ArticlesGeneralCoaching – Everything Track and Field: Articles related to coaching and training.

www.sirc.ca – SIRC: Sport, Research, Intelligence, Sportive: An international database which lists articles and publications related to coaching. Also has links to International Governing Bodies of sport and Sport Institutes.

www.verkhoshansky.com – Verkhoshansky: Site of Professor Verkhoshansky, which contains articles and data relating to training methods and responses.

Chapter 8

Theories and models of training

This chapter will provide an insight into the nature of training responses and adaptations and how the athlete will respond to a period of training. On completion of the chapter you will have:

- examined the laws of training and how an appreciation of these laws contributes to a successful training strategy;
- formulated a physiological and metabolic understanding of how the athlete responds and adapts to training through the study of the concept of supercompensation;
- critically evaluated the negative consequences of training such as fatigue and under-performance syndrome (UPS);
- developed an applied understanding of how to control the load and volume of training completed by an athlete.

Introduction

The aim of training is to allow the athlete the best chance of achieving their performance goal or target. For this to become a reality, the athlete must develop on all levels, but principally there needs to be a profound physiological and physical development in order for this to occur.

It is this recognition of athletic development and enhancement that we shall explore in this chapter. The ability to develop depends on the relationship between the training load (intensity, frequency and duration) and recovery components of the training plan. The ability to develop is a manifestation of the relationship between the amount of fatigue induced during a training period and the timeframe allowed for athlete recovery. By manipulating this relationship, we can control the degree to which the athlete will develop.

This association between the training load and recovery period is paramount to the overall success of the training plan. Too much recovery and an athlete will not show signs of progression; too little rest and athletes may burnout, become stale or show symptoms of UPS.

These concepts provide the framework for this chapter and will be explored in order to better understand how an athlete develops and how this knowledge can be used by the coach when designing and planning a fully structured and sequenced training programme.

The laws of training

In previous chapters we alluded to the development of the athlete and the concept of adaptation. What precisely do we mean by this? If an athlete follows a structured and well-developed training routine, over time they will experience a gain in their overall physical fitness (general fitness) and in the components of fitness relative to the training undertaken (specific fitness). These athletic developments can be seen at all levels of the athlete's make up, from morphological through to physiological, bio-chemical and cellular responses.

Training can be viewed as a very powerful stimulus which evokes a response in the body, the result of which is adaptation. In order to best understand how the athlete will respond to training and thereby show adaptations, we need to grasp a number of key concepts which are highlighted in Table 8.1.

Overload

In order for athletes to improve they must experience an overload. Overload is the term used to describe the magnitude of the training stimulus which must be greater than the existing homeostatic level of the athlete. For any physiological or metabolic system to adapt, the stress placed on it (training) must be greater than the current level of that system. If the stressor is less than the current capacity of that system, an overload will not occur and therefore will not induce an adaptation. There are two primary ways of manipulating and thereby increasing the size of the adaptation: we can either increase the training load or change the nature of the session being conducted.

Table 8.1: The laws and adaptations to training

Principle	Overview
Overload	Refers to the size or magnitude of the applied stimulus, i.e. the size of the training load.
Specificity	This is the principle of fundamentals and refers to the fact that training specifically for one component of fitness will enhance that component but not necessarily another.
Accommodation	Refers to the body's natural response to the same level of stimulus over a prolonged period of time.
Distinctiveness	This law governs the fact that we are not all the same and that how one athlete responds to training may not be the same for another.

By changing the training load we can induce a stress on that system that exceeds its current capacity. If on the other hand we were to change the nature of the session or exercise being conducted, overload would also be induced, although this approach is only effective if the drill is new and the athlete is unaccustomed to the exercise.

Activity 8.1: Overload training

Consider ways in which you could induce overload for an athlete during training by examining your own sport and current training status.

1. For your sport, attempt to develop a sample training session that will be used on a regular basis.
2. Devise a training session which will bring about an overload through manipulating the training load.
3. Devise a training session with which you are unaccustomed but which would be relevant to your sport and would induce a training overload. For each sample session, you should consider:
   - The components of fitness within the session;
   - The variables of the training load (intensity, frequency, duration) and their relative weightings for the particular session;
   - The purpose of the training session.

In Chapter 7 we referred to the levels of training load and addressed the differences between the levels of training. We explained that if the training load used over a prolonged period of time does not increase, the athlete will experience a plateau effect: they will neither gain nor lose their adaptations. If the load is too low they will experience a loss of adaptations.

The loss of physiological adaptation becomes far more profound as the induced level of adaptation becomes greater. Therefore trained athletes will experience more noticeable loss of adaptation than those less well trained. There is strong evidence from the literature base to suggest that an athlete can experience a decrease in maximal aerobic power (VO_{2max}) of between 4 and 14 per cent following 4 weeks of training cessation (Houmard et al, 1992; Coyle et al, 1986).

Training that does not provide an overload or have a purpose (ineffective load) does not contribute to athlete development and so could be considered in a similar light to a period of complete training stoppage.

A common question asked by coaches and athletes is how do we know when to increase the training load to induce the overload? Although several responses may be given, in essence there are two answers: first, experienced coaches and athletes instinctively know when to increase the training load, either through tried and tested methods or because of the use of regular monitoring and feedback from the athlete which helps inform the coach when it is time to make the change and second, the training load is programmed into the plan using mesocycle planning whereby there is a pro-gressive, increasing load through each microcycle followed by a recovery microcycle. The subsequent mesocycle begins with a higher training load than for the previous cycle. For a more in-depth explanation of training programme planning, refer to Chapter 9.

Specificity

The principle of specificity tells us that training for one component of fitness could be detrimental to another component of fitness (Cronin et al, 2001; McArdle et al, 1978), as discussed in Chapter 7. There is another way of at looking at this relationship, which has been termed 'transfer of training' (Tanaka, 1994; Millet et al, 2002; Robinson et al, 1995). In principle, transfer training refers to the gain in one component of fitness as a result of training for another.

Imagine a young athlete who has started to train as a road cyclist and has developed a strong aerobic base, with a reasonable VO_{2max} of 58ml·kg^{-1}·min^{-1}. At this point, all he has done is cycle work. His coach wants him to develop and recognises that in order to be a good cyclist you not only need a well developed aerobic base but also good sprint speed, muscular strength and power. The coach therefore devises a set of tests to see where the athlete stands in terms of their ability in these three areas.

The tests used are a vertical jump for lower limb power, a leg press for muscular strength and a 6 second maximal cycle sprint for sprint speed. It is conceivable that the athlete will do quite well in the 6 second cycle, reasonably well in the vertical jump test and not particularly well in the leg press.

This is an example of training transference because although the athlete has not trained directly for speed, strength and power, there has been some physiological adaptation/development in these components as a result of trying to develop the aerobic base.

There are two further points to recognise at this stage. First, the degree of transference from one component of fitness to another is not universal across all components. Second, not all athletes are the same and so, although the order of transference will be the same across all athletes the degree of transference will be dependent on many factors external to the training plan, such as genetics and previous sporting background.

As with any scientific principle, we would like to be able measure and quantify the degree of transference, for then we can begin to estimate how much of the change in athlete performance is as a result of training a specific component of fitness and how much is due to transference. If you wish to know more about how to measure, record and quantify the training response, refer to the *Concept box* below.

Concept 8.1: Quantifying the training response

First, we face a problem in that different performances in different exercises are quantified in a variety of forms. Where possible SI units should be used, so speed would be quantified by m·s^{-1}, time by second (s), strength by the mass moved in kg and force by N. This clearly poses us with a problem in that how do you transfer a gain in, say, force development (N) to a gain in running speed (m·s^{-1})?

Clearly this is not easy, therefore we need to have a unit-less value that can be monitored.

So let us consider a scenario. We have a group of gymnasts who have been training for a prolonged period of time and part of the training plan is regular assessment of the key components of fitness. For each component the coach

Concept 8.1: Continued

uses a standard test and records the result for each athlete; they also consult their records and calculate the delta value (Δ) or change in a parameter. At this stage you should note that the change can be either an improvement (positive) or a decrease (negative) in that performance.

Let us now consider the results (Table 8.2) that the coach noted for this group of athletes in one test: the sit-and-reach test, for a simple and basic measure of lower limb and back flexibility.

Table 8.2: Results of sit-and-reach-test

Athlete	Results from current test		Trials (cm)	Mean (cm)	Previous test (mean) (cm)
1	44	45	46	45.0	42.0
2	38	38	39	38.3	38.0
3	56	54	55	55.0	57.1
4	40	41	43	41.3	40.9
5	44	44	44	44.0	44.0
6	43	45	44	44.0	39.2
7	48	49	49	48.6	48.0
Mean				45.2	44.2
Standard deviation (SD)				5.01	6.16

On initial inspection, the mean result for the group has improved, but what about on an individual basis. This is where we introduce the use of the result gain calculation (Zatsiorsky and Raitsin, 1974) which can be summarised by the following formula:

Result gain = Gain of a performance/SD of performance

So let us consider one of the gymnasts. Athlete 6 has a mean score for the current test of 44.0cm and a mean score from the previous assessment of 39.2cm. Therefore we can calculate that their gain of a performance is 4.8cm (44.0 – 39.2). The standard deviation (SD) of the group performance for the current test is 5.01cm. Therefore, using the formula we can calculate that the result gain for this athlete is 0.95 SD.

This is a useful way of quantifying the degree of change in an individual athlete's performance in relation to the overall group change. Of course what we

Concept 8.1: Continued

also want know is how much of the resultant gain is due to training response and how much is due to the transference of adaptation from another component of fitness. To do this, the coach would follow exactly the same approach as for the sit-and-reach test, only this time they would be collecting and analysing data for a separate exercise, such as one repetition maximum (1RM) in the squat exercise.

Now we have two sets of result gain data, one from the sit-and-reach and one from the 1RM for each athlete. Therefore we can calculate the degree of transference from the 1RM (strength) to the sit-and-reach (flexibility) through the use of the transfer of performance formula:

Transfer of performance = Result gain from non-trained exercise (1RM)/ Result gain from trained exercise (sit-and-reach)

Given that both result gains in the formula are SDs, we are technically calculating a ratio between the results for the trained and non-trained exercise. So the greater the deviation (higher ratio) the greater the transference of training and vice versa, thus low ratios indicate greater specificity of training.

Another problem is that we cannot use this approach with an individual athlete, as it only applies to athletes who work/train as a part of a group. Remember that we need to generate a SD score from the data, which can only reliably come from group data collection. Clearly, this is a problem for individual athletes where performance gains can be witnessed but not so easily quantified.

In previous chapters, we have referred to skill and task mastery, especially in relation to issues such as skill acquisition (Chapter 3). We can extend this understanding to the physical development of the athlete by recognising that there is an interesting relationship between specificity of training and the level of athletic mastery of the individual, which indicates why athletes at different stages of development respond differently.

Let us consider elite athletes who have a high level of mastery. These individuals have very specific training in order to take into account the accommodation principle and as a result adaptations to training become more specific and rarefied. Therefore we can observe an important aspect of the training response: the fitter or more developed the athlete is, the more specific the adaptations to training become and the smaller the level of adaptation becomes. By extension, the transfer of training in elite athletes is low because transference infers a lack of specificity, something not conducive to elite athlete development.

Conversely, for athletes just beginning the training process, the transference from training is very high, as any exercise performed at this stage will promote some form of performance gain and physiological adaptation. The level of specific adaptation will be low and will only become more specific as the athlete develops and is introduced to more specialised training methods.

This is why the development of the elite athlete is slow: any physiological/ performance gains will take a considerable amount of time, whereas the beginner will advance quickly and develop very rapidly. Therefore coaches should always take into account the specificity of training and the transference of the training gain.

Accommodation

If an athlete continues to use the same training load over a prolonged period of time, they will start to experience a decrement in performance. According to Zatsiorsky (1995) this principle of accommodation is an artefact of the biological law of accommodation, which suggests that the response of any biological organism to a constant stimulus will decrease over time. In terms of training, the stimulus is the physical activity and the decrease in the biological response is accommodation.

Therefore, if the applied stimulus remains constant over a protracted period of time (weeks and months), the athlete starts to lose the benefit of that stimulus. So when we first introduce any athlete to a new training stimulus (which could come in the form of a different exercise and/or skill or an increase in the training load) they will experience an initial surge in the level of physiological adaptation. We can characterise this initial gain as the athlete being highly susceptible to the stimulus and so the adaptation response is high.

However, if we now continue to apply the same stimulus in the form of the same training session the athlete will still initially gain (adapt) from the work, but over time the amount of adaptation will fall and as the body starts to become accommodated to the applied stimulus, the level of gain starts to decline. Therefore the training which initially produces the surge in adaptation could be viewed as being trainable load, but as the biological systems start to become accommodated the training becomes maintenance. If the imposed training load remains constant there will be no long term improvement, merely a short-term gain.

This poses the coach and athlete with a number of problems, especially when dealing with elite, well-trained individuals. The principle of accommodation states that we need to keep altering the stimulus in order to generate the adaptive response and avoid the onset of accommodation. Therefore, we will need to regularly adjust the imposed training stimulus and not use a standard set of training methods over a prolonged period of time.

At the same time however, we recognise that specific training sessions (exercises or loads) produce specific adaptations and responses and that we need to use training sessions that best mimic the demands of the sport. In other words we need a training programme that allows for change and variability but at the same time takes into account that the best physiological adaptations arise from a stable plan which uses specific exercises to meet the demands of the sport.

Distinctiveness

All individuals, and so by implication, all athletes are different. Even within a group environment, athletes will respond quite differently to training, with some showing rapid development, some slow and some not developing at all.

Coaches would be unwise to treat all athletes in the same way by giving all athletes the same annual training plan and the same work schedule for a training session. A generic training programme is by implication an average training programme, and therefore will not benefit athletes at the extremes of the development spectrum.

Activity 8.2: Athlete distinctiveness

1. Consider the sport that you are involved in and make a list of the key physical and psychological traits that you consider are important for success in that sport.
   - Once you have done this you should reflect on your own performance in the sport and complete the next task.
2. Next to each trait that you listed in task 1, indicate whether you possess that trait and crucially the degree to which that trait has responded to training (fast, medium, slow).
   - Now think about other team-mates, members of your training group or other athletes that you coach and complete the next task.
3. For each trait listed in task 1, indicate whether team-mates or training partners have shown athlete development as you did for yourself in task 2 (slow, medium, fast)
   - Reflect on the differences between yourself and other team-mates and how as a coach you would deal with these differences in relation to the laws of training and getting the most out of all the athletes in the group.

In a recent review, Smith (2003) presented a classification system for the different types of athlete that we come into contact with as both coaches and fellow competitors. If you want to know more about this rather unique approach refer to the *Concept box* below.

Concept 8.2: Athlete types

When you think about athletes you have competed against or those you have coached, you will probably recognise that there are two generalised classifications of athletes: those who are naturally gifted and talented and for whom achievement comes with minimal effort and those who have to work exceedingly hard to achieve any form of performance. Although these are rather broad classifications, they do generally hold true.

We should also recognise however, that there are athletes who do not naturally fall into these groupings but still need some form of classification. The reason for classifying athletes is quite logical: by appreciating the underlying make up of the athlete we can begin to tailor the training and support best suited to their needs. Pyne (1996) classified athletes based on the recognition that all athletes possess some level of speed and endurance. The classification system that was developed uses the analogy of racehorses as presented in Table 8.3.

Concept 8.2: Continued

Table 8.3: Classification of athletes

Classification	Characteristics
Wooden horse	These athletes have low levels of fitness and speed. Therefore performance-wise they may not be able to contribute much. This classification could apply to athletes who are just beginning training, or returning to training following a period of injury or illness.
Bolter	These athletes are characterised as having low levels of fitness but high levels of speed. They possess high levels of 'natural' speed and so may not complete as much training volume as their team-mates or peers. This type of athlete may have short-term success due to their natural speed but long-term elite level performances will be limited.
Workhorse	These individuals possess high levels of fitness but low levels of speed. They are training 'monsters', in that they are extremely dedicated training specialists. Furthermore, they are extremely consistent in completion of their training. However, this type of athlete tends to struggle in translating their training performances to competition. A number of reasons have been proposed for this, such as excessive training load, insufficient recovery or simply lack of speed.
Thoroughbred	These athletes exhibit high levels of both fitness and speed. They possess the physical capabilities required to excel in a particular sport.

Adapted from: Pyne D (1996) Designing an endurance training program. *Proceedings of the National Coaching and Officiating Conference*, Brisbane, Australia; also cited in Smith, D J (2003) A framework for understanding the training process leading to elite performance. *Sports Medicine*, 33: 1003–26.

All coaches dream of working with the thoroughbred athlete, the individual who is going to excel in competition; fine examples being Lance Armstrong in cycling and Michael Johnson in track and field.

However, the coach should not dismiss the importance of the workhorse athlete. A training group needs a workhorse, the athlete who can push the thoroughbred during training, especially when training becomes difficult and fatiguing. The workhorse is also a role model for training who can be used by the coach to show the dedication that is needed. It should also be recognised that with proper training and structured work, a workhorse can move closer to the thoroughbred and may even become competitive.

We now have in place the basic laws of training and in conjunction with an understanding of the variables and components of training we are in a position to begin to understand how training works; in other words how the body responds to training and at a broad level why and how athletes adapt to training.

The training response

Supercompensation

If we apply a training stimulus in the form of trainable load we will create a disturbance in the homeostasis of the body due to the imposed load exceeding the current physiological/metabolic level of the athlete.

According to the theory of 'supercompensation' and training overload this stimulus (training load) induces a physiological fatigue as a result of depleting or reducing the levels/concentrations of those biochemical substances that were taxed as a result of the training session, as highlighted by point A in Figure 8.1.

Trainable load is fatiguing and caused by the fall in biochemical substances below their pre-existing level. Once the athlete stops training and the fatigue stimulus is removed, the body will begin to remove the manifestations of fatigue and restore the biochemical substances that were depleted or utilised during the training session. This restoration of the body is the recovery phase of training. What Figure 8.1 demonstrates is that as the duration of the rest period increases so does the degree of restoration of the biochemical substances and hence the reduction of fatigue.

What makes the supercompensation theory so compelling is that this restoration process can continue beyond the pre-existing level therefore the biochemical substance levels increase, implying a physiological adaptation to training as demonstrated by point

Figure 8.1: Supercompensation model of training. An applied training load induces a physiological fatigue to a depletion of metabolic and physiological substances utilised during the training session. During the recovery period these substances are restored up to and slightly beyond the pre-existing biological level. It is this gain in the metabolic and physiological substances that is defined as supercompensation

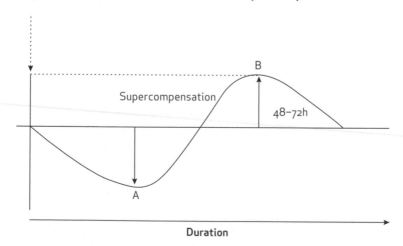

B on Figure 8.1. The levels of biochemical substances (and by implication, levels of associated fatigue) have been used to project a term of 'athlete preparedness' (Zatsiorsky, 1995).

Preparedness quite simply means the degree to which (physiologically, metabolically and psychologically) an athlete is ready to either compete or train again. At the start of the training session (highlighted by the dashed arrow) we could assume that the athlete is ready to train, but once the training session is over their level of preparedness is low; they are fatigued and tired and have suffered a depletion of biochemical substances, therefore they are not in the best shape to train again at point A.

However, as they go through the recovery process, their preparedness to train again increases until at point B it has reached an optimal state; the athlete is now fully prepared biologically to train again. Given this situation we can recognise two important implications that must be addressed: what happens when the athlete is optimally prepared (point B) and what happens if the athlete leaves the time to train longer than is optimal.

We shall consider the latter first as this helps to explain a basic principle of training.

Figure 8.1 demonstrates that if the coach and athlete were to delay the next training session or competition until a point after achievement of the optimal level of preparedness (point B), the athlete starts to lose the optimal preparedness level because they are losing the supercompensation (adaptation to training) induced by the previous session. The longer the athlete leaves between attaining optimal preparedness and training, the fewer adaptations they maintain until eventually they will fall back to pre-existing levels and all gains will be lost.

The time that we should apply the next training stimulus or competition is when the athlete is optimally prepared (point B). In both cases we will once again induce a state of fatigue and assuming that the training is trainable load and now exceeds the new homeostatic level (as shown by the dashed line in Figure 8.1) they will experience depletion followed by regeneration and supercompensation. Of course this makes training planning and programming appear rather easy when actually it is far from it.

To best understand the complexities surrounding the development of supercompensation common questions are addressed in the *Concept box* below.

Concept 8.3: Commonly asked questions and beliefs

How long should I rest between training sessions in order to be as prepared as possible?

This is a very complicated question with the answer in many parts. First, you should leave the next training session until you are optimally prepared. However, this is not always feasible due to the nature of recovery and the removal rate of fatigue in various biological systems. For example endurance-based training may lead to a supercompensation period of between 6 and 12 hours, whereas power or sprint training (which imposes significant strain on the central nervous system, CNS) may lead to a supercompensation period of between 36 and 48 hours. The average is generally 24 hours.

Concept 8.3: Continued

I am coaching an elite athlete; we cannot afford 24 hours of recovery between training sessions, what should we do?

Many elite athletes complete at least two sessions a day thereby reducing the amount of time for recovery between sessions and affecting their ability to be optimally prepared.

However, we recognise from both the literature base and coaching feedback that the frequency of the training units is a primary stimulant for an overall training response and long-term adaptation. The key here is to ensure that the athlete is not training prior to supercompensation and is not coming off supercompensation. On the other hand if the athlete undertakes training less frequently, they will still show signs of long-term adaptation but to a lesser degree.

My athletes are training frequently with less than 24 hours between sessions but rather than improving they seem to be going backwards, why would this be the case?

This is a common problem with training programme design and stems from a poor understanding of the relationship between programming the training, the training load and the desire to generate physiological adaptations. In order for athletes to adapt we need them to recover in order to respond to the next training stimulus. Therefore, it is very difficult for an athlete to keep training at high loads for a long period of time. This is commonly what happens when coaches misinterpret the laws of training and just keep applying frequent high intensity training sessions.

What is needed is a balance, in other words the coach creates a block of training containing some intense units of work, followed by a block of units which are less intense. So overall, although the adaptive gain is not as much as there is still more gain, the athlete will not be suffering high levels of fatigue and incomplete regeneration. This stems from our understanding of how we programme training with short supercompensation periods such as endurance and cardio-respiratory work, with training that has much longer supercompensation periods e.g. explosive strength training.

We can sequence the training to overlap the supercompensation components between sessions. Indeed, given that the recovery period for explosive training is so long it would not be wise to work that component on two consecutive sessions, therefore we could rest that component and work on developing another. The sequencing of the training sessions (units) is discussed in greater detail in Chapter 9.

Does this mean that there is an association between the intensity of training and the degree of supercompensation?

Absolutely. The higher the training intensity, the greater the inducement of fatigue and therefore the greater the degree of supercompensation. However, we also need to recognise that with more intense training, longer periods of

Concept 8.3: Continued

supercompensation are required, which is why coaches should always alternate periods of intense and less intense training.

Supercompensation provides a unique way of addressing the relationship between the training load, recovery and adaptation to training and can be used to identify the level of preparedness of the athlete. From this initial knowledge base many coaches recognise the association between training load, fatigue and hence supercompensation. If they were to maintain an increased training load for a specified period of time and then follow with a protracted block of recovery, the degree of supercompensation should be much larger than would normally occur during a standard training block.

This is the theory behind crash training, also referred to overloading microcycle training. However, before we explore this concept further we should address the levels of adaptation that occur in response to training and so further understand the training response. These are presented in Table 8.4.

Table 8.4: Training effects and responses

Training effect	Training response.
Acute effects	Training effects occurring during the actual training session.
Instantaneous effects	Training effects occurring in response to a single training session (unit) and becoming evident almost immediately.
Collective effects	Training effects that develop over a prolonged period of time.
Deferred effects	Training effects which result following a single training session (unit) after a given period of time.
Incomplete effects	Training effects resulting from a single training exercise (such as squats or bounding).
Residual effects	Training responses which only manifest after the cessation of training.

Crash training

In the crash training approach (as shown in Figure 9.4 in Chapter 9), we introduce a number of sessions prior to the athlete attaining the pre-existing physiological/ metabolic level. In so doing each session is performed by an athlete who is not fully recovered and in a state of physiological fatigue, but the overall result is a much higher level of fatigue compared with that generated from a single fatiguing session.

Once the final session has been completed, the athlete must recover; remember however, that the amount of fatigue and depletion of the biochemical substances dictates the amount of time taken to recover. The athlete may have to either completely stop training or undertake light recovery work; either way, the time taken tô reach optimal preparedness and hence supercompensation will be much longer.

Although the gains are appealing to coaches and athletes, there are obvious pitfalls to the approach. The most obvious problem is that many athletes simply cannot tolerate such a prolonged and excessive increase in training load. As a result, many athletes simply cannot complete the training required to induce the crash in fatigue, primarily because they are too fatigued from the previous training session.

The second factor to address is the association between increased levels of both peripheral and central fatigue and the risk of injury as we become more susceptible to sustaining an injury the more fatigued we become.

The third factor is that if the athlete is not allowed sufficient time to recover following the crash block they will re-commence training still in a fatigued state and will not be at all optimally prepared.

The final factor is a combination of all the above. If we push an athlete too hard with insufficient recovery and beyond their normal capabilities for too long, the chance of athlete burnout, overreaching and possibly even UPS increases. Therefore the secret of crash training is to use it cautiously and not become drawn into the gains at the expense of the potential cost.

We now have a solid understanding of the process of athlete adaptation and response to training and how we must carefully programme training load and recovery to best engender this response. You should also recognise that there are some negative aspects or consequences to training which should be addressed before establishing a training plan.

Many of these factors came under the banner heading of 'overtraining syndrome', but this broad term has now been given a slightly more ambiguous but far more appropriate title of 'under-performance syndrome' (UPS).

Under-performance syndrome

Throughout this book we have alluded to the concept of under-performance syndrome (UPS) and asserted that this condition can result from poor training, poor training programming, inadequate rest or excessive training load. Before exploring the nature and associated physiological and immunological factors associated with UPS, we should take a moment to conceptualise this as a factor.

Limited data from the literature base suggests that the prevalence of UPS and associated forms of UPS is high among well-trained athletes, with values reported anywhere between 20 per cent and 60 per cent (Lehmann et al, 1997). Indeed, the data suggests that this group of athletes experience a decrease in performance despite maintenance of a high training load for longer than two weeks. The overwhelming contributing factor to the prevalence of UPS was considered to be an excess of training volume.

Within the literature base, UPS has been consistently referred to as 'overtraining' or 'overtraining syndrome' which implies that the primary cause of decreasing performance is due to excessive training load. These terms do not take into account other factors contributing to the performance responses of the athlete such as psychological stress, malnutrition and lifestyle issues (Budgett, 1990).

Whichever primary term you choose to follow, all are characterised by a prolonged period and sensation of fatigue and a decrement in both training and competition performances, despite maintaining a high training load. The conditions experienced by the athlete may also be described by such terms as staleness, overreaching, burnout and chronic fatigue. In the classic scenario the athlete reports or shows signs of decreasing performance, so either alone or with the coach they increase the training load to combat this performance response. The result is of course increased fatigue and worsening performance and so the ever decreasing spiral continues.

In such cases, the primary combination contributing to UPS is an excess of training load with insufficient recovery. We thus have a condition which is debilitating to performance and the 'athlete lifestyle'. Yet at this point we should consider the different forms of UPS, which range from acute or short term through to chronic or long term.

The short-term response is defined as overreaching and is commonly experienced by athletes following an excessive period of training load, such as that associated with a crash cycle or overloading period of training. Overreaching is easily characterised in Figure 8.1 at point A as a period of fatigue followed by a period of supercompensation. Generally, this period of overreaching lasts for around 72 hours and is followed by full recovery of the athlete.

The complication lies where overreaching ends and overtraining or UPS begins. So we have a spectrum of response beginning with overreaching, which if not controlled (through the use of recovery) will extend into the full condition of UPS.

Perhaps where this issue has become clouded in the literature is through the use of the terminology to describe the same condition, or the various symptoms on a theme. Indeed staleness or being stale as an athlete would appear to be a term used quite often to describe UPS but according to Raglin (1993) is very different to athlete burnout.

An athlete who is experiencing burnout will display signs of de-motivation and withdrawal from the training and competing process, whereas the stale athlete is one who remains highly motivated despite the ever increasing fatigue build up and may independently increase their training load to combat the performance decrement. Either way, both burnout and staleness conform to the general description of UPS and/or overtraining syndrome.

Symptoms of UPS

The symptoms of UPS are varied with data from the literature base reporting over 200 possible symptoms associated with the syndrome. Table 8.5 lists some of the most commonly reported symptoms associated with the overtraining and under-performance syndromes, many of which appear to have a common theme of immunological suppression, which has led many researchers to believe that monitoring immunological or biochemical markers can be used to track and identify the onset of UPS.

Table 8.5: Commonly reported symptoms associated with unexplained UPS

Under performance
Muscle weakness
Chronic fatigue
Sore muscles
Increased perceived exertion
Reduced motivation
Sleep disturbance
Increased resting heart rates
Altered mood states
Loss of appetite
Gastrointestinal disturbances
Recurrent infection

Cited from: Gleeson, M (2003) Biochemical and immunological markers of overtraining. Journal of Sports Science and Medicine, 1: 31–41.

Let us briefly consider why some of these could be associated with a decrement in performance and increased levels of fatigue.

Recurrent infection is associated with a suppressed immunological response to fight infection and as a result there is a transient increase in the incidence of infections and illnesses, the mostly commonly reported being upper respiratory tract infection (URT).

At this point we should address why an athlete who is well trained can be more susceptible to infection and illness, for one would normally presume that the fitter and more trained an athlete is, the stronger their immune system and response to infection. This concept is explained by the model commonly known as Nieman's (Nieman, 1994).

This model is rather compelling in that it proposes that a moderate level of physical activity increases and enhances the functional capability of the immune system and response, whereas individuals engaged in high volume training may well be compromising their immune function. This is because data shows that conditions of intensified training are associated with suppressed leukocyte (white blood cell) numbers, which are the cells that help fight infection.

Peters (1996) found that further periods of moderate intensity training were associated with increased leukocyte numbers and a 29 per cent decrease in the risk of developing URT following 2 hours of moderate intensity training per day. In contrast, the well-trained athlete exposed to intensified training has a 100–150 per cent increased chance of developing URT.

Muscle soreness and weakness are commonly associated with UPS and are characterised by increased muscle stiffness, decreased range of motion, loss of strength, heightened blood lactate and rating of perceived exertion and a decreased rate of fore production (Jones et al, 1986). These symptoms have been associated with elevated levels of creatine kinase (CK), lactate dehydrogenase (LDH) and myoglobin; all associated with muscle contraction dynamics. Indeed high levels of CK have been associated with delayed onset muscle soreness (DOMS), which results from excessive eccentric muscle activation.

It also becomes apparent that induced muscle damage and soreness is associated with a reduced ability to restore the intramuscular stores of glycogen (O'Reilly et al, 1987). This is a direct result of an impaired functional capacity of the damaged muscle to take-up glucose from the blood for conversion to glycogen. If we follow this physiological chain of events, we could determine that a reduced ability to re-synthesise intramuscular glycogen will result in a decreased capacity for substrate provision in subsequent bouts of training.

Along with these more generic responses, there is data that reports decreased VO_{2max} scores along with altered maximum and submaximal lactate scores.

Sympathetic and parasympathetic UPS

Perhaps where the concept of UPS becomes less clear is through the recognition that there may be two distinct forms, which have been termed sympathetic and para-sympathetic UPS (Budgett, 1990).

The sympathetic form of UPS is characterised by an increased level of sympathetic activity at rest, such as increased resting and exercising heart rates, while the parasympathetic form is associated with a heightened level of parasympathetic activity (decreased resting and exercising heart rates) in conjunction with a suppression of sympathetic activity.

Identifying the onset of UPS

There are myriad responses that occur, all of which could be associated with an increased training load rather than being a prelude to the onset of UPS. Therefore initially the prognosis is not good in terms of observing markers and symptoms of UPS, especially as the responses can be different depending on whether we are observing sympathetic or parasympathetic UPS. Perhaps the answer lies else-where and why considerable attention has been paid to the use and monitoring of the psychological status of the athlete. Numerous methods have been proposed of which the most commonly cited is the assessment of athlete mood states through the use of the 'profile of mood states' (POMS) questionnaire (McNair et al, 1992).

This approach aims to assess the mood of the individual by subdividing the overall term into six subsets of tension, depression, anger, vigour, fatigue and confusion. Under 'normal' conditions, mood state profiles for non-fatigued performance athletes are characterised by the 'Iceberg' profile, where there would be a profound spike in a particular parameter such as vigour.

According to this model, athletes would normally show decreased mood scores for tension, depression and confusion but when experiencing the symptoms of UPS would show elevated values for fatigue, confusion, tension and a depressed score for vigour. However, we should err on the side of caution with the use of POMS as an assessment tool, for many researchers have suggested that it provides only limited means of distinguishing between athletes and non-athletes (Terry, 1995).

CASE STUDY: TRAINING PROGRAMME DESIGN – APPLIED TO CYCLING
Barney Storey

Training programme design is a process which should be undertaken carefully, considering several factors to achieve results.

It is important to understand as much as possible about the athlete you are coaching. What is the rider's motivation for training and what do they want to achieve? The rider must have realistic goals for training time and training performance. It is important for the coach to quickly establish what time the rider can set aside for training and if the time allocated is achievable in terms of their recovery.

When designing a cycling programme it is important to pinpoint the exact phase or date at which the rider must peak. Once established, the coach can work backwards to the current time and day. Helpful information during this initial planning phase will include any previous training history the rider may have. Even if the rider is considering a change of direction in terms of event, the history they have in cycling, or any other sport, will still help a coach to establish certain parameters.

These parameters include but are not exhaustive of: training load capacity, training load variety and the ability to cope with differing lengths of training time. Even if the rider has not previously trained in cycling, the hours spent on a different sport will give a good indication for a starting point and help the coach understand the rider far more quickly. If the rider doesn't have this information, it is still possible to design a training programme, but it may need adjusting far more frequently due to the changing needs of the rider in terms of recovery, training frequency, workload and overall intensity.

Regardless of which cycling discipline the rider wishes to train for, the overall plan for training programme design should remain fundamentally quite similar. The range of events available to a cyclist, from track cycling through to road racing or road time-trialling, all require the same base in terms of physiology and skills.

Throughout the process of training programme design, it is important to establish that the rider has a good basic understanding of the sport of cycling and the prescription in their programme. Fundamentally, they must understand all aspects of their event, including areas such as cadence requirement, heart rate response, recovery, bike position and the use of gears.

From a coaching perspective, the areas covered under this heading must be established early on and the coach should ensure the rider fully appreciates their role in understanding and carrying out the training required. Much time will be lost if the rider cannot understand the basics, especially in a sport like cycling, where much of the coaching is done remotely via e-mail and the coach does not always have the luxury of seeing the training performances of their athlete on a weekly or even daily basis.

It is therefore important for a coach to establish strong and very open lines of communication for feedback and other tools for measuring and monitoring progress. It is also imperative that the rider is fully apprised of their own

CASE STUDY: Continued

responsibility within the process. A rider should be fully consulted to establish their basic knowledge, giving them the opportunity to highlight where they lack confidence and would welcome further information or assistance.

Cycling programme design is helped by valuable training aid tools such as power measuring cranks, heart rate monitors and speed measuring computers. The minimum requirement for training programme design is the heart rate monitor. Scientific testing prior to writing the training programme will allow the coach to establish benchmark fitness levels, followed by periodic testing and close monitoring once the programme starts. The testing can be useful from amateur through to elite international level.

Equipment can be a factor requiring consideration in training programme design. Early establishment and constant review of equipment availability for any athlete is vitally important and the coach and rider should always seek ways to improve the current set-up where finance and time permits.

The equipment cyclists have at their disposal should ideally include, but is not restricted to, a road bike (imperative for all cyclists whether or not they race on the road), a track bike (low-profile for pursuiting, upright for bunch racing and sprints), a road time-trial bike or equipment to adapt the road bike (specific to those riding road time-trials).

In addition to these basic requirements it would also be advisable for the rider to have a turbo trainer and set of rollers to use during bad weather and for warm-up/cool down during competition. In order to maintain the rider's interest, the training programme will include a variety of different training exercises and with a greater range of equipment, the more options a coach will have in writing training programmes. In addition to the cycling equipment, it would be useful to establish whether the rider has access to a gym and if so, the style of the facility and the available resources there.

Establishing and developing a rider's skills is a fundamental consideration for training programme design. The types of training and levels of intensity will vary according to the ability of the rider. Drills and skill development sessions can be included early in the season to ensure the rider gains as much as possible from this area.

For example, it would be a waste of time getting a road time-trial bike rider to the point where they are physically capable of winning races, if their cornering skills loses them considerable time at road junctions and roundabouts. Underpinning the entire skills philosophy must be the safety considerations of good bike handling skills. It would be unethical for a coach to allow any rider to compete in an event if their skills meant doing so would be dangerous. If a rider has the physiology for an event, the skills can easily be worked on to make it safe.

Throughout the process of writing a training programme, a coach must always consider the end goal of their rider and justify any aspect of the programme aimed at reaching that goal. The programme will include smaller stepping stones, known as training cycles, in order to make the main goal more manageable and to provide checkpoints to mark progress along the way.

CASE STUDY: Continued

The best programmes will also always allow for contingencies should any aspect of the smaller goals be underachieved. Within the smaller stepping stones to the major goal, consideration must be given to basic training, skills training, specific training, competition training and interim competitions to aid race development. The balance between racing and training must be established with flexibility to change at a later stage should a rider find they are racing too often (usually the case) or too little.

Within cycling, it would be easy to race year round, however consideration must be paid as to whether this approach will give the optimum result for the main goal of the season. Riders may need to peak several times during the year, or may be targeting a season of road racing of several months. This should all be carefully considered during initial planning and constantly reviewed throughout the training and racing phases. This approach is more likely to ensure that form can continue to the very end of the race period.

Coaches should always be confident of their chosen approach and the programme should always reflect a certain amount of the rider's input, even if they have a limited knowledge of their sport. It is important the riders feel valued in this process, as ultimately they will gain greater understanding of their sport and feel in control of their goal. If the athlete is at elite level, their input may increase to greater levels and at certain times of the year they may wish to take full responsibility for certain aspects of their programme. This is a proven approach at Olympic and Paralympic level and enables the riders to understand their bodies more and ultimately provide more feedback to aid both coach and riders achieve the performance goals.

In conclusion, the coach must be something of a juggler and remember that no two riders will ever be the same, even if they compete in the same events. Managing the ups and downs of a training and racing season requires careful planning and good communication.

Barney Storey MBE
Sprints coach
GB Paralympic Cycling Team

Take home message

When constructing a training plan we must follow the basic principles of training and follow a plan that is sensibly and systematically structured to meet the overall goal of the athlete. In so doing, we must recognise the role of training overload and the associated physiological responses, especially in the context of the training effects.

Within this domain, we have to respect both the individual nature of the athlete and their sport but also the specific nature of the required training and it is this latter concept that poses us with the considerable problem of trying to balance a programme between specific and variable requirements. Perhaps the most compelling part of the training response is the development of training adaptations, therefore we have examined the supercompensation theory and shown how there is an association between the degree of adaptation and the size of induced fatigue. We must recognise, however, that this model, although demonstrated in relation to glycogen super-compensation, has not consistently been shown in relation to other biological markers.

Given the association between training stimulus, development of fatigue and the degree of adaptation we have explored the concept of UPS or overtraining syndrome and shown how the development of this syndrome is related in part to training load and insufficient recovery but also to other factors such as lifestyle and wellbeing. Overall, in order to get the best out of an athlete, we need to develop adaptation, while at the same time avoiding the negative consequences of training.

Further study

In order to assist with your understanding and application of the material covered within this chapter the following list of material has been complied. This list contains literature sources related to overload, supercompensation, UPS and training timing.

Budgett, R (1998) Fatigue and underperformance in athletes: The overtraining syndrome. *British Journal of Sports Medicine*, 32: 107–10

Fry, R W, Morton, A R and Keast D (1992) Periodisation of training stress – A review. *Canadian Journal of Sports Science*, 17: 234–40

Fry, R W, Morton, A R and Keast D (1992) Periodisation and the prevention of overtraining. *Canadian Journal of Sports Science*, 241–8

Fry, R W, Morton, A R and Garcia-Webb, P (1992) Biological response to overload training in endurance sports. *European Journal of Applied Physiology*, 64: 335–44

Herberger, E (1977) *Rudern*. Berlin: Sportverlag

Houmard, J A, Hortobagyi, T and Johns, R A (1992) Effect of short term training cessation on performance measures in distance runners. *International Journal of Sports Medicine*, 13: 572–6

Keul, J, Konig, D and Huonker, M (1996) Adaptations to training and performance in elite athletes. *Research Quarterly for Exercise and Sport*, 67: S29-S36

Matveyev, L (1981) *Fundamentals of sport training* (translated from the revised Russian edition). Moscow: Progress Publishers.

Morton, R H (1997) Modelling training and overtraining. *Journal of Sports Science*, 15: 335–40

Zatsiorsky, V M (1995) *Science and practice of strength training*. Champaign, IL: Human Kinetics.

www.bases.org.uk/newsite/home.asp – British Association of Sport and Exercise Sciences: National body for sport and exercise science within the UK. Useful contacts and documents related to physiology, psychology, biomechanics, health and coaching.

www.athleticscoaching.ca/default.aspx?pid=7&spid=35 – Canadian Athletics Coaching Centre: Site containing information relating to coaching and sports science. This link relates to training loads and structuring.

www.elitetrack.com – Elitetrack: A website which houses both peer reviewed and lay articles. All papers are referenced and are either written by coaches or sports scientists. A very good resource for all disciplines within coaching.

www.eis2win.co.uk/gen – English Institute of Sport: National organisation who support and work with elite athletes in England.

www.everythingtrackandfield.com/catalog/matriarch/OnePiecePage.asp_Q_PageID_E_350_A_PageName_E_ArticlesGeneralCoaching – Everything Track and Field: Articles related to coaching and training.

www.mysport.net – My Sport: An online community for coach education and discussion.

www.sirc.ca – SIRC: Sport, Research, Intelligence, Sportive: An international database which lists articles and publications related to coaching. Also has links to International Governing Bodies of sport and Sport Institutes.

www.uksport.gov.uk – UK Sport. National body supporting elite world class performers. Useful resources related to coach education and drug free sport.

www.verkhoshansky.com – Verkhoshansky: Site of Professor Verkhoshansky, which contains articles and data relating to training methods and responses.

Chapter 9

Training planning and structuring

The purpose of this chapter is to introduce you to the concepts and science of training programme design and construction, providing you with detailed analysis of the physiological and metabolic consequences of using correctly or incorrectly designed training plans. Upon completion of this chapter you will have:

- understood how the training year is divided into specific phases of work;
- examined the principles of periodised training;
- grasped the concept of training chapters and training chapter construction;
- explored the physiological and metabolic consequences associated with correct and incorrect planning;
- addressed key issues such as tapering and de-training;
- applied these concepts to your own sporting pursuits.

Introduction

> I am playing all the right notes, but not necessarily in the right order
>
> *(Eric Morecombe – Comedian)*

A former coach of mine once described the training of an athlete as being very similar to baking a cake. He suggested that to bake a cake you needed to know all the ingredients before starting and what quantities you will need. Then you need to establish the order in which you add each ingredient to the mix and how long and at what temperature you allow the cake to bake before serving.

This analogy summarises the design and success of a training plan quite succinctly. First, we need to know what the demands of the event are, which therefore dictates the fitness components that we need to work on (ingredients). Next we need to know how much of each fitness component we need to work with, classifying the components in order of functional importance (quantity of ingredients). Then we can begin the actual training of the athlete ensuring best results by adding the components and working on them in the correct order (order of ingredients). Finally, we need to ensure that our athlete peaks optimally to produce the best performance (temperature and duration of baking).

Structuring training to meet the overall goal is indeed like cooking: for many it is a daunting and often complex task, which can be viewed as both a science and an art. A common approach is to assume that if the athletes train in all the fitness components, they will produce an optimal performance, yet as can be seen from our cooking analogy, even with the right components in place, the outcome for both the cake and the athlete might not be optimal.

We need therefore to develop a structured training plan which allows us to introduce the fitness components in the correct quantities at the correct times, with the aim of producing an optimal performance at a specified day or timeframe.

This is the art of training programme design and although there is a scientific background to the methods used, the interpretation can be subjective and influenced by the nature of the coach and athlete. This chapter will explore the design, construction and implementation of a fully developed training programme to best meet the needs of our athlete.

Periodisation of training

The structuring of the training year is termed 'periodisation' and will be the term used from now on to describe the overall structure and format of the training programme. Technically there are two forms of periodisation: that which describes the overall planning and structure of the annual plan and that which defines the structuring of the specific components of fitness. Figure 9.1 shows that the training year is divided up into phases and sub-phases which describe that current segment of the training cycle.

The three man phases identified are Preparatory, Competition and Transition, with both the Preparatory and Competition phases being sub-divided into two smaller sub-sections. These sub-sections define specific outcomes or goals for that part of the training phase, so in the preparatory phase we have general and then specific preparation and in the Competition phase the sub-divisions are for pre-competition and competitive.

The plan can be altered to meet the needs of the athlete and the demands of the sport, therefore coaches may adjust the plan according to the number of major competitions or in relation to the capability and developmental status of the athlete. For the latter refer to Chapter 15.

Figure 9.1: Structure and divisions of a periodised training plan

Training phase	Preparation		Competition		Transition
Training cycles	General preparation	Specific preparation	Pre-competition	Competitive	Transition
Mesocycles					
Microcycles					

We should also appreciate however, that not all athletes are the same (see Chapter 8) and so any plan has to reflect an individual's requirement. A classic example is the scheduling of more than one competition period. This is often seen in sports such as track and field, where athletes have both indoor (winter) and outdoor (summer) competition schedules, both requiring the athlete to be at peak athletic capability.

An annual plan with one competitive block is termed a monocycle training plan; those with two competition seasons or phases are termed bi-cycle plans and a plan that structures three competition phases would be referred to as a tri-cycle plan. An important point to consider is that the gap between competition phases in either a bi- or tri-cycle plan should be at least 4 months, to allow for suitable training adaptation between competitions.

To understand how we mesh the training cycles (microcycles, macrocycles) and the training phases (Preparation, Competition and Transition) we will address each separately.

Training phases of the annual plan

Preparation phase

This phase is the most important component of the annual plan because here we establish the foundation upon which we build the rest of the season's athletic performances. The phase is used in order to 'prepare' the athlete for the competition phase and competitive season. The primary focus across the whole of this phase is development and enhancement of the endurance, technical and tactical components of the sport.

For a monocycle structured plan, the preparation phase is usually of 3–6 months duration with variations depending on the nature of the sport and the athlete's needs and should be designed to be approximately twice as long as the competition phase.

Within the preparatory phase we have two main sub-blocks: the General and Specific preparation components. These blocks focus on different aspects of the athlete's development.

General preparatory phase

The general sub-phase is primarily devoted to developing wide-ranging physical fitness and is very much about laying foundations and getting the athlete fit to train. In this sub-phase, the training load varies from medium to high or maximal intensity depending on the sport. At the same time a high training volume is encouraged to promote development of the components of fitness without inducing excessive stress on the athlete through overly high-intensity training.

Let us first consider the duration of the phase: given that we have between 3 and 6 months of preparatory training and that the primary focus of this phase is to develop specific training adaptations, the general phase should constitute no more than one-third of the total duration (1–2 months). This has to be viewed in the context of the current status of the athlete (level of mastery). A well-trained athlete will not need to expend so much time within the preparatory phase on developing general fitness, as this should already be well established, whereas our novice athlete will need to spend as much time as can be afforded on developing their fitness foundation before progressing to more specific preparatory training.

There would appear to be a strong relationship between the amount of work conducted (volume) in the general sub-phase and the consistency of performance within the competition phase. Indeed a lack of emphasis on the conditioning of an athlete during this initial phase may lead to poor quality work in the competition phase and a decrement in competition performances as the duration of the competition phase increases.

Specific preparatory phase

This phase follows the general preparatory phase and it is worth noting that some coaches divide this phase into blocks; one regarding specific training and one regarding training that will prepare for competition. Here, we will consider this sub-phase as one block.

This phase will last between 2 and 4 months depending on the overall structure of the annual plan or the level of mastery of the athlete. It encourages high load training, primarily through an increase in training intensity compared with the general preparation phase, but also through maintenance of high training volume.

The emphasis here is development of technical components of the sport through training and exercises that promote the use of primary muscle groups and energy systems related to the actual discipline. Indeed, evidence from coaches would suggest that the use of non-specific exercises within this phase should be dramatically reduced to no more than 30 per cent of the total.

As this phase progresses closer to the competition phase, there is a shift in the nature of the training conducted, with the volume being reduced to facilitate an increase in intensity of training. It has been reported that for sports governed by high intensity efforts, total training volume could be reduced by between 60 and 80 per cent of that seen at the onset of the specific phase, but always in a progressive manner.

Competition phase

The primary aim of this phase is to develop optimal performance; in essence, we are aiming for a peak in athletic capability. Referring back to the supercompensation theory (Chapter 8), we recall that the primary factor requiring monitoring and consideration is the level of athletic preparedness; therefore we are aiming to ensure that the athlete is optimally prepared for their most important competition. Throughout both sub-sections of the competition phase the primary stimulus is training intensity and depending on the sport, the training volume can be dropped by varying degrees to accommodate the increase in intensity.

Pre-competition phase

The primary objective of this phase is to act as an assessment tool for both coach and athlete through the participation in regular competitions. These competitions do not form the primary goal of the athlete for the season, but are lower echelon meetings that allow the coach and athlete to assess current performance capability under competition conditions.

It is very easy to make a mistake with the structuring of the training plan within this phase, by merely introducing competitions without recognising their contribution to the overall stress and hence fatigue of the athlete. The training plan should therefore reflect this increased physiological cost and competitions should be scheduled in relation to the training load.

Competitive phase

The primary aim of this sub-phase is the main competition or competition block. Interestingly, it is associated with a high level of induced fatigue, which at first glance would appear contradictory to what is required in order to compete.

However, we must recognise that during this phase there is increased intensity of training, as well as heightened intensity due to competitions. An important point to remember is that the overall fatigue profile during this phase should not be a plateau but rather should be an undulating form, reflecting the changes in intensity associated with both training and competition but also the reduction in intensity as a result of the recovery process. So overall intensity is high but there are deviations either side of the mean value. Also remember that with increased amounts of induced fatigue, recovery times must also be longer.

When constructing the training plan, competitions should be ordered by their level of importance, beginning with the least important and culminating in the pinnacle or main competition. Imagine that your main competition is the Olympic Games. This is the biggest competition for many athletes; therefore it should be the pinnacle competition of the plan. It is also not logical to expect an athlete to compete or produce a high level of performance soon after such a stressful competition.

In order to bring about optimal performance and have the athlete in an optimal state of preparedness, we need to ensure that they have reached a performance peak, which is simply optimal physical development with little residual fatigue being present.

PEAKING AND TAPERING

The athlete's peak is brought about by use of a 'taper', which can be summarised as a training phase prior to competition containing a progressive reduction in training load to allow for optimal physiological and psychological recovery. Tapers vary between 7 and 21 days in length, during which time the training load is reduced but training intensity remains at around 90 per cent of the pre-taper value. As a result, the primary factors requiring manipulation are training frequency and duration.

The literature base informs us that in order to optimise the taper, a high training frequency must be maintained; indeed in trained swimmers around 80 per cent of peak values have been reported (Mujika and Padilla, 2003) although in less well-trained individuals, the frequency of training can be decreased to around 30–50 per cent of the pre-taper value and still allow maintenance of performance. If you wish to know more about the physiological mechanisms and programming of the taper component refer to the *Concept box*.

Concept 9.1: Tapering theory and practice

The taper has been defined in the literature as a progressive reduction in training load in order to reduce fatigue and bring about physiological and psychological optimisation. We should therefore examine more closely how a taper is constructed and what the physiological rationale is behind this approach to training and training design. In order to do this we will address a series of key questions.

Why must training intensity be maintained during the taper?

The overwhelming reason is because the intensity of training acts as the primary stimulus for maintaining the physiological and biochemical adaptations gained during the previous phases of the training plan. Hickson et al (1985) demonstrated that physiological adaptations gained during a 10-week intensive training block could not be maintained during a subsequent 15-week period of training, where intensity was reduced by two-thirds with training volume remaining constant (Mujika and Padilla, 2003). Further studies have demonstrated that when training volume is decreased there needs to be maintenance of training intensity at around 90 per cent of the pre-taper value (Houmard and Johns, 1994).

Why does there need to be a reduction in training volume during the taper period?

The role of the taper is to bring about a recuperation and recovery process in response to a period of intense training. One of the primary components of training that can be controlled is the volume of work done. Shepley et al (1992) suggested that using a reduction in training volume of ~62 per cent during a 7-day taper resulted in no change in performance, however when a reduction in volume of 90 per cent was used over a 7-day period there was a 22 per cent increase in exercise time to exhaustion.

We can conclude therefore, that a substantial reduction in training volume in conjunction with maintained exercise intensity is needed to induce recovery and the so-called tapering rebound effect.

Given that training volume is a manifestation of training frequency and duration, which of these variables should be altered in order to optimise the taper?

The main finding from the literature base is that training frequency should be reduced by around 50 per cent during the taper phase; however, Houmard and Johns (1994) suggest a conservative estimate of only a 20 per cent reduction as being more realistic. So, why the discrepancy?

We need to decipher information from the literature base and in doing so we see that the size of the frequency reduction is dependent on the ability of the athlete. Novice athletes show signs of recovery following a larger reduction in the frequency of training sessions, whereas the well-trained athlete appears to need a much higher training frequency, with a reduction of no more than 20 per cent being recommended (Mujika and Padilla, 2003).

The duration of the taper has been well investigated in the literature and the consensus from the data suggests an optimal duration of 7–21 days (Mujika and

Concept 9.1: Continued

Padilla, 2000). Any longer and the data suggests performance maintenance rather than further improvement.

There is also evidence to suggest that power athletes benefit from shorter duration tapers whereas endurance-based athletes respond better to a longer taper.

What kind of taper should be used?

The literature base defines four types of taper, highlighted in Table 9.1.

Table 9.1: Summary of the four tapering approaches

Taper format	Outline of the taper
Linear	This approach has an overall higher training load for the duration of the taper than either of the exponential models.
Exponential (slow)	The overall training load is lower than experienced during the linear approach but higher than for the fast exponential decay. Note that the decline in training load is progressive but extended over the taper duration.
Exponential (fast)	This is associated with lower training loads for the duration of the taper than is associated with either the slow exponential or linear decay approaches. There is an initial rapid decay in training load followed by a gradual levelling out towards the end of the phase.
Step	This is defined as being a non-progressive reduction in training load where the training load is reduced by around 30% from the pre-taper value and is maintained at this level for the duration.

The table highlights the use of the linear, exponential (fast and slow) and the step reduction approaches. Adapted from: Mujika, I and Padilla, S (2003) Scientific basis for pre-competition tapering strategies. *Medicine and Science in Sports and Exercise*, 35: 1192–87.

Zarkadas et al (1995) suggest that an exponential decay taper is more beneficial to performance improvement than a step reduction, with the latter producing non-significant results following a 10-day taper. They also inform us that a fast exponential decay taper is more beneficial compared with a slow decay with the former showing a 6.3 per cent improvement in run time for 5km compared with 2.4 per cent for the latter.

What are the potential physiological and performance responses to a taper?

This issue is confused by the various factors listed previously so any analysis can only be viewed as average and may not apply to all models and athletes. We recognise however, that a taper can create significant performance responses, such as increases in exercise time to exhaustion, faster running, swimming or cycling times, with a range of between 0.5 and 6.0 per cent.

A performance response will only occur in response to a psychological and/or physiological improvement or adaptation; for example, between 2.0 and 9.0 per cent improvements have been demonstrated for VO_{2max} and gains of between 0.3 and 15 per cent have been reported for haemoglobin concentration, coinciding with 0.2 and 15 per cent increases in red blood cell production. Interestingly, maximal, sub-maximal and resting heart rates, cardiac dimensions and blood pressure are shown not to change in response to a taper.

Reported metabolic responses include increases in muscle glycogen in the order of 15–34 per cent during the period and increases in peak blood lactate concentration. Two markers of considerable interest that have been monitored in studies during the taper period are creatine kinase (CK) and cortisol.

During a taper period there is a progressive decline in the concentration of CK, reflecting reduced stress on the muscle and increased levels of restoration. A decrease of 70 per cent has been reported during the taper period however most studies report decreases in the region of 20–30 per cent.

Cortisol has been described as a stress hormone and elevated levels are associated with heightened levels of metabolic and psychological stress. Initially, the scientific community tracked cortisol concentrations during the taper on the premise that as the level of stress within the body starts to fall, so too will cortisol concentration.

This approach proved inconclusive but more success was found when tracking the resting concentration of cortisol rather than the exercising value. The suggestion is that there is a significant relationship between resting concentration and performance in anaerobic based sports (Bonifazi et al, 2000).

How can we summarise the principles of tapering?
The list below, adapted from the work of Mujika and Padilla (2003) summarises the currently acknowledged thinking on taper design.

- Maintain a high training intensity during the taper;
- Reduce the training volume by between 60–90 per cent;
- Maintain training frequency; do not decrease by more than 20 per cent;
- Design the taper specifically to meet the needs of the athlete with duration of between 7 and 21 days;
- Use progressive non-linear taper designs (exponential decays);
- Expect a performance improvement in the order of ~6 per cent;
- Use the taper to minimise fatigue and enhance athletic recovery.

Transition phase

This part of the annual plan is often referred to as the 'off-season' – a time when athletes can rest and in essence, not engage in training. This assertion is partly correct, for the transition period is a time of recovery from training and competition, as well as a time to prepare for the forthcoming training cycle.

The transition phase should not be used however, as a complete cessation of training. The focus of this phase is what I refer to as 'assisted recovery', where the athlete gains maximal regeneration and removal of fatigue but not by just stopping training; we want to assist the process through the use of exercise.

The transition phase normally lasts between 2 and 4 weeks, with a maximal timeframe of 5 weeks during which time the athlete reduces their level of physical preparation to between 40 and 50 per cent of that expressed in the competition phase. This phase is often misunderstood and ill-conceived, in many cases being tagged onto the plan without consideration of the phasing and cycling of the training. This raises a number of common questions which are presented in the *Concept box* below.

Concept 9.2: Transition phases: concerns and beliefs

Why is the transition phase so long?

The literature base suggests that peripheral fatigue will have been removed within a matter of days. However a significant contributing factor to the fatigue process is that of fatigue to the CNS (central fatigue); indeed this has been shown to remain for considerably longer than the peripheral form.

We also need to recognise that the more intense the competition phase in terms of training and competing, the longer the timeframe required for physiological and psychological regeneration of the athlete.

A track and field coach reported in conversation that when the transition phase is used correctly, the athlete recovers and is 'chomping at the bit' to start training again; this desire to re-commence the training is a good indication that the central fatigue has dissipated and the athlete is fresh for the onset of the new annual plan.

Why do my athletes need to remain active during the transition phase?

Given that by investing a considerable amount of time in their training the athlete has developed physiological responses, it would be rather unfortunate if they immediately ceased training at the end of the competition phase. If this was to happen, rather than inducing a period of recovery and regeneration they would promote the de-training response, through which the previous training year's physiological gains would start to be lost.

There is strong evidence to suggest that prolonged periods of training abstinence not only lead to the de-training effect and loss of physiological adaptation, but can induce symptoms of insomnia, loss of appetite and mood swings.

Concept 9.2: Continued

Given that there is a reduction in training volume during this phase, how many times a week should my athletes train?

The reduction in volume during this phase of the annual plan is substantive and is reflected in the reduction in training frequency. The general consensus is to reduce the number of training sessions to 2–4 per week, depending on the fitness level of the athlete and how often they were training prior to the transition phase.

There is an old saying that applies to the transition phase: 'the bigger they are the harder they fall'. In translation, this means that the more well-trained the individual, the quicker and more noticeable the loss of training will be if the athlete does too little work and starts to de-train. On the other hand, when they do too much training in this phase they simply slow the rate of fatigue dissipation and recovery.

The specifics of training during this phase are very much at the discretion of the athlete, with guidance from the coach. The emphasis should be on active work but simultaneously doing exercise that is fun and perhaps different from that worked on during the rest of the training process.

Some athletes express the need for complete rest following a hard year of training and competing; if this is the case, it should be programmed into the first week of the transition phase followed by resumption of training at a reduced volume. If this complete cessation is not used the athlete should progress immediately from the competition phase to the transition phase as though it were an unloading or recovery part of the training plan.

The overriding aim of this training phase is therefore to prepare the athlete for the next training year, simultaneously avoiding loss of training adaptations developed during the previous season. If you want to know more about the loss of training adaptations, refer to the *Concept box* below.

Concept 9.3: De-training: the loss of training adaptations

In a seminal review paper Mujika et al (2000) stated that the principle of training reversibility is associated with a loss of the physiological and metabolic adaptations associated with the previous period of training. Given that there is a loss of the training response during this period, we can define reversibility as a de-training response. At this stage, we must recognise the difference between de-training and reduced training.

De-training is usually associated with complete abandonment of the training plan and complete cessation of training. It is important to apply this to a timeframe in order to make interpretable comparisons; therefore the general consensus is that de-training is associated with a cessation of training for more than four weeks.

Conversely, training reduction is associated with reduced training volume and/or load over a prolonged period of time, however unlike de-training it is associated with either maintenance of training adaptation or a further enhancement of these responses as evidenced during the taper period. Table 9.2 presents some of the fundamental responses associated with a period of training cessation.

Table 9.2: Values and classification of physiological responses to training cessation

Physiological variable	Response
Maximal oxygen uptake (VO_{2max})	Following a period of de-training it has been shown that there can be a decline in VO_{2max} in the order of 4–14% in trained athletes; in less well-trained athletes the reduction has been shown at between 3–6%.
Total blood volume	A period of training cessation in excess of four weeks has been associated with a reduction in blood volume in the order of 5–12%. Plasma volume has been shown to fall within the first two days of training cessation.
Heart rate	Following a period of de-training heart rate has been shown to increase both during sub-maximal and maximal intensity exercise. The degree of this change is in the order of 5–10%. Resting heart rate also increases back to pre-training levels.
Stroke volume	Reductions in stroke volume have been reported following a period of training cessation of 10–21 days, of about 10–21%. These reductions in stroke volume are associated with the reduction in total blood volume.
Heart size	Training has been associated with increases in both left ventricular mass and size, both of which decrease in response to a period of training cessation. Indeed the left ventricular mass and size reduce by 25% and 19%, respectively following three weeks of training cessation.
Substrate usage and availability	A period of training cessation is associated with a shift in substrate usage with greater reliance on carbohydrates at both sub-maximal and maximal work rates in the order of a 10% change. Concurrently there is associated decline in lipolysis and fatty acid metabolism.

Concept 9.3: *Continued*

Table 9.2: Continued

Physiological variable	Response
Blood lactate responses	A period of training cessation of a matter of days in swimmers is associated with increase in the lactate concentration at both sub-maximal and maximal exercise intensities. Similar results have been seen in endurance runners and cyclists. The lactate turn-point has been shown to occur at a lower percentage of VO_{2max} or exercise intensity following training cessation, apparently related to a reduction in the oxidative capacity of the muscle by as much as 50%.
Intramuscular glycogen	There is a clear association between training cessation and muscle glycogen levels with a reduction of 20% being reported following just seven days of de-training. This rapid reduction has been associated with a decline in the rate of conversion from glucose to glycogen.
Muscle fibre characteristics	A period of training cessation has been associated with a decrease in the muscle fibre cross-sectional area particularly in type II fibres. There are however no reported changes in the muscle fibre type distribution patterns.
Performance responses	Following a period of training cessation there will be a reduction in athletic performance in the region of 2–25% depending on the nature of the athlete and the mode of performance assessment.

Adapted from: Mujika, I and Padilla, S (2000) De-training: Loss of training induced physiological and performance adaptations. Part 1: Short-term insufficient training stimulus. *Sports Medicine*, 30: 79–87.

From our understanding of both training and de-training responses we observe that a period of training cessation can be detrimental to athletic performance and that the onset of this decline can manifest within a matter of days of stopping training and removing the stimulus for adaptation.

Structuring the phases of the annual plan

Training chapters

We now need to consider how to structure each component in order to produce physiological adaptations and lead the athlete to the point of peak performance. To do this we need to reflect on the use of training chapters which help to define both training cycles and phases, as shown in Figure 9.1. There are three types of training chapter as highlighted in Table 9.3.

The way to think about these training chapters is to view them as a Babushka or Russian Doll. Each chapter sits inside the previous larger chapter, with macrocycles being the largest followed by mesocycles, microcycles and then individual training units. The way in which we construct the annual plan is dependent on the ordering and sequencing of the training chapters. The Russian doll concept of annual plan design is highlighted in Figure 9.2, which shows how each of the small components sits within a larger more generalised format.

Table 9.3: Classification of the training chapters within an annual training plan

Chapter	Classification
Microcycle	Characterised as being made up of a series of training units and usually of one week's duration.
Mesocycle	The general construction of a mesocycle is four weeks, i.e. four microcycles. The length and general construction will change depending on the athlete and the training phase.
Macrocycle	Generally constructed from a series of mesocycles and therefore a macrocycle will define each of the training cycles.

Why use the phrase 'training chapters' to describe the structure of the phases? Let us for example consider the structure of this textbook. The content of each chapter leads you, the reader, into the next section or chapter. The knowledge gained in one chapter is used as the building block for the next chapter and so on, which is very much the way of training programme design.

There are broad contextual chapters which set the tone for the work to be carried out (macrocycles), within which we reveal the sub-chapters or sub-sections of the mesocycles. Within each of these we find further sub-sections of microcycles and the training units of sessions.

Macrocycles

The term macrocycle is used to define the greater training objective; in other words, we are using a broad brush to define a specific component of the plan. We have previously encountered the macrocycle when studying training phases and cycles, for it is these cycles of the plan that are our macrocycles.

Figure 9.2: Schematic of a section of an annual training plan showing the training phase (Preparation), the Macrocycles (General preparation and Specific preparation), a series of three Mesocycles within the specific preparation macrocycle and the four microcycles that make up one of these mesocycles

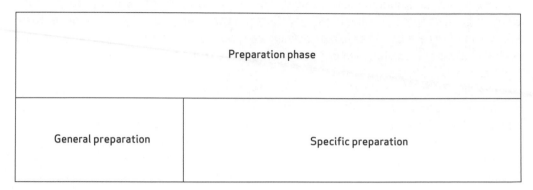

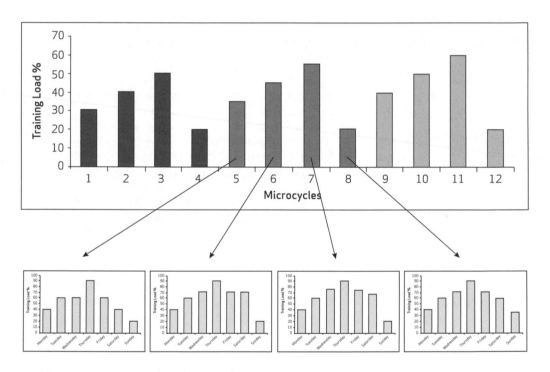

Macrocycles have a broad emphasis, as seen when discussing the construction of preparation, competition and transition phases. Yet by using macrocycles we can establish the emphasis of the work to be completed. It should be noted that there are some general rules to consider when establishing the composition of the macrocycles as shown in Table 9.4.

Mesocycles

The common length for a mesocycle is four weeks, as this fits neatly into a calendar month. However, many coaches and athletes use longer mesocycles of up to 6 weeks,

Table 9.4: Macrocycle rules of construction

Point of consideration	Reasoning
Ability of the athlete	Will in part dictate the duration of each macrocycle. A novice athlete will have a much longer general preparation macrocycle to help with base fitness development, whereas an elite athlete will require a shorter block of training.
What are the objectives?	For each phase there will be objectives designed to allow athlete progression. They form the framework of both microcycle and mesocycle construction, which in turn establish the duration of the macrocycle.
How much time does the athlete have for training?	This is often overlooked and yet is key to training programme design. For full-time athletes the macrocycle objectives can be detailed and there is greater opportunity to train a number of fitness components within a microcycle block. For time-limited athletes the focus of the plan changes, with the objective being to train the key components of the event or areas of weakness. Either way the number of training units – as dictated by athlete availability – will determine the duration of each macrocycle.
How flexible are you as the coach?	The coach must be flexible and recognise that there will be times when they have to deviate from the plan and re-adjust the training strategy. This is quite common when athletes do not respond to the training load as expected. This need not be a negative as there may be occasions where the coach simply misjudges the degree to which the athlete will respond to the imposed load and they develop at a faster rate than expected. In this case, be prepared to alter the design of the plan to best serve the athlete's needs. We also have to be flexible when planning an athlete's return from injury or illness, as a lay off will reduce the amount of training time left prior to a competition and will also reduce the athlete's physiological and psychological level of preparedness.

There are many points to consider when constructing the annual plan and in particular the cycles for each of the training phases.

especially in the preparation phase, with shorter ones being employed in the competition phase, especially when entering the tapering component.

Whichever way the mesocycle is constructed, its duration will reflect the number of microcycles being employed, so a six-week cycle will usually contain six microcycles and a four-week mesocycle will comprise four microcycles. The aim of the mesocycle is to identify the athlete's load progression through the use of a variety of mesocycle constructions.

There are four basic forms of the mesocycle: developmental, crashing, peaking and maintenance/regeneration. What is clear from the literature base is that there should be a degree of athlete regeneration from one mesocycle's-worth of training before progressing to the next block as highlighted in Figure 9.3 below.

Figure 9.3: Progression of three successive mesocycles highlighting the need for a period of regeneration prior to a slight increase in training load

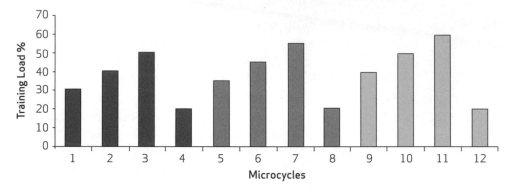

The degree to which regeneration is utilised depends on the status of the athlete and the objective of the next mesocycle. If you wish to gain a greater insight into mesocycle construction refer to the *Concept box* below.

Concept 9.4: Mesocycle design and utilisation

The construction of each mesocycle is dependent on the objectives of the macrocycle and also the way in which the microcycles have been developed. For instance, we cannot have a mesocycle whose overall aim is athlete development if all the contributing microcycles are focused on athlete regeneration.

Development mesocycle:
These cycles are constructed to allow for a uniform increase in training load throughout the block of work. Although we are encouraging progressive training overload we are not inducing severe states of fatigue in the athlete. An example of this approach is shown in Figure 9.4, highlighting the stepwise increase in training load through three successive microcycles, followed by a recovery or regeneration microcycle.

A variation on this theme is when we have a series of developmental microcycles followed by a non-uniform increase in training load (crash microcycle), as highlighted in Figure 9.5.

There will be a period of supercompensation during the recovery microcycle of this training block, but because imposed load is low, the degree of supercompensation will also be relatively low. Developmental blocks of training are composed of relatively low loads but high volumes of training, therefore we tend to use these more in the preparation phase of the annual plan where we aim to

Concept 9.4: Continued

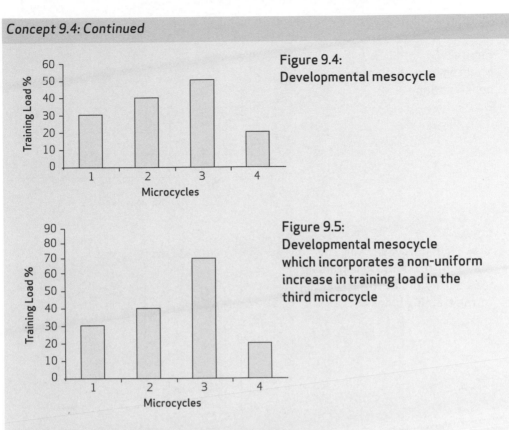

Figure 9.4:
Developmental mesocycle

Figure 9.5:
Developmental mesocycle
which incorporates a non-uniform
increase in training load in the
third microcycle

develop the athletic foundations on which we can build the subtleties of competition performance.

Maintenance/regeneration mesocycle

These blocks are used to maintain the adaptive state of the athlete while simultaneously ensuring that the athlete is not pushed too hard. This form of training is used when specific components require longer work, while recognising that the athlete may struggle if there was an increase in training load.

Given that there is little emphasis on adaptation and hence little induced fatigue, it may not be necessary to use a recovery microcycle at the end of this type of mesocycle, as shown in Figure 9.6.

These training blocks will allow the athlete some recovery from the previous period of training but will also encourage some regeneration of physiological and psychological preparedness. They tend to be used in the specific preparation phase rather than in competition phases where we require higher intensity training.

Crash or shock mesocycle

As shown in Figure 9.7, a crash cycle is composed of a series of high load microcycles (the crashing effect) followed by a sudden non-uniform decrease in training load. As previously discussed, this form of training brings on a

Figure 9.6:
Maintenance mesocycle
construction

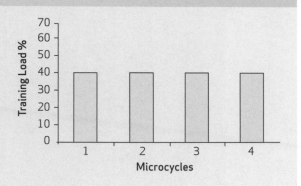

Figure 9.7:
Crash mesocycle showing the
non-uniform increase in training
load during the third microcycle
of the training block

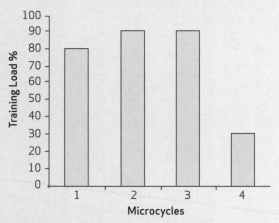

higher degree of supercompensation than just developmental work, but can be associated with an increased risk of athlete burnout and fatigue.

As shown in Figure 9.7 the training load is consistently high throughout the mesocycle with only the final microcycle being associated with a reduction in training load. This form of training is actively encouraged in the preparation phase as a means of bringing on the adaptive response of the athlete.

Such programming should not be used in the competition phase where the fatiguing effects and prolonged recovery periods will prove detrimental to competition performance.

Peaking mesocycles
These blocks are incorporated into the annual plan to bring about peak athletic preparedness. Quite simply a peaking mesocycle will unburden the athlete of training induced fatigue whilst simultaneously prompting a period of super-compensation; this is very much our formulisation of the tapering component within the annual plan as shown in Figure 9.8.

Concept 9.4: Continued

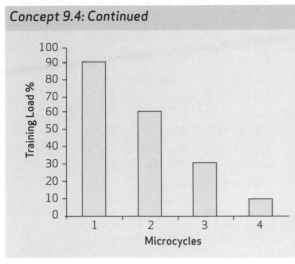

Figure 9.8:
Peaking mesocycle showing the progressive decline in training load so as to promote athlete recovery and preparedness. Although the load is falling the intensity of training will remain at ~90% of peak values but there will be a progressive decrease in the training volume, for more detail refer to the section on tapering design

As considered previously, the overall outcome of the mesocycle (developmental, crashing etc) is very much dependent on the nature and construction of the micro-cycles used; therefore we will now consider the role and design of the microcycles of the annual plan.

Microcycles

We have already discovered that a mesocycle is constructed through a series of training microcycles and that each microcycle usually refers to a week's worth of training.

However, at this point, we need to appreciate that each day's worth of work is a compilation of the number of training units used on that day. So for an athlete who trains twice a day, the reported training load will represent the average load between the two sessions, so although they have seven days of training in the plan we need to recognise that in this example there may be up to 14 units worth of training.

Each microcycle is therefore designed as part of the overall jigsaw of training. By itself a single microcycle will not meet the training goal of the athlete, but if constructed correctly a series of microcycles will allow the athlete to meet the overall goal.

There is a need for balance between training load and recovery and this balance can induce different levels of physiological adaptation. In order for the athlete to prosper effectively, there must be correct sequencing of the training units within a microcycle. This approach to unit sequencing dates back to the 1970s and a piece of literature that came out of the former Soviet Union, and although perhaps scientifically old, the justifications and applications still hold true today and are presented in the Table 9.5.

Table 9.5: Optimal sequencing of training units within a microcycle

Component	Training intensity
Learning and perfecting technique	Medium intensity
Perfecting technique	Sub-maximal to maximal intensity
Developing short-term speed	Maximal to supramaximal intensity
Develop anaerobic endurance	Sub-maximal to maximal intensity
Improve muscular strength	Maximal intensity (90–100% of maximal lift)
Develop muscular endurance	Low to medium intensity
Develop muscular endurance	Medium to maximal intensity
Develop cardio–respiratory endurance	Maximal intensity
Develop cardio–respiratory endurance	Sub-maximal intensity

Adapted from: Ozolin, N G (1971) *Athletes training system for competition*. Moscow: Phyzkultura, I Sports; also cited in Bompa, T O (1999) *Periodization: Theory and methodology of training*. 4th edition. Champaign, IL: Human Kinetics.

Activity 9.1: *Sequencing of training within a microcycle*

Consider your own sport and then compile a list of training exercises that could be conducted to meet each of the components highlighted by Ozolin (1971). For each component, think of a training session that could be used and indicate in the boxes examples of the intensity of the session.

Component	General training intensity	Example training session	Specifics of the session (repetitions, sets, etc.)
Learning and perfecting technique	Medium intensity		
Perfecting technique	Sub-maximal to maximal intensity		
Developing short-term speed	Maximal to supra-maximal intensity		
Develop anaerobic endurance	Sub-maximal to maximal intensity		
Improve muscular strength	Maximal intensity (90–100% of maximal lift)		
Develop muscular endurance	Low to medium intensity		
Develop muscular endurance	Medium to maximal intensity		
Develop cardio–respiratory endurance	Maximal intensity		

Activity 9.1: Continued

A second component of this task can be a group exercise. We have been presented with an order for each microcycle – what you should now consider and discuss is why this order is as proposed. Think about:

* the type of training encountered within each component;
* the amount of induced fatigue;
* the physiological components recruited during each form of training;
* the intensity of training conducted.

Each microcycle can be classified in relation to the level and sequencing of the applied load using the same terminology previously encountered, i.e. developmental, regeneration, crashing and peaking microcycles. If you wish to gain a further level of understanding of microcycle design and structure refer to the *Concept box* below.

Concept 9.5: Microcycle structuring

Each microcycle is established against training goals and objectives and the amount of applied load. The load is a reflection of the load for that day's work and may be a combination of two or even three unit's worth of work.

The difference between mesocycle and microcycle design is that with microcycles, as long as the load conforms to the overall training objective, we can use various forms of design to meet the needs of the athlete and annual plan. For example, Figure 9.9 highlights a microcycle construction where the overall training load is medium but with a single high intensity day in the middle of the week.

We may however be looking for a more intense block of training and so we can use two peaks or days of very high intensity training as shown in Figure 9.10. Again, observe the association between high intensity and low intensity blocks of training.

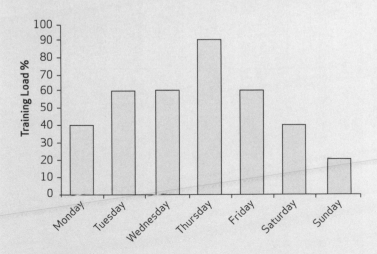

Figure 9.9:
Single peak microcycle design with an overall medium intensity training load

Concept 9.5: Continued

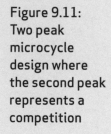

Figure 9.10:
Double peak
microcycle
design with an
overall high
intensity
training load

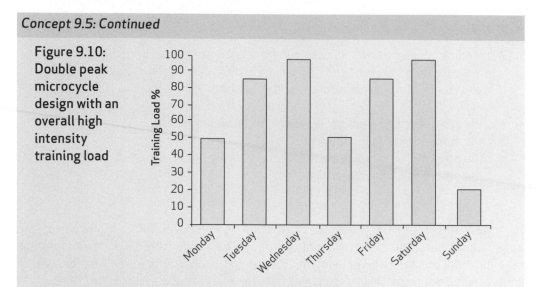

The key to microcycle design and structure is the alternation between levels of training intensity. The general rule of thumb is that the major training peak should occur in the middle of the week and depending on the overall objective of the microcycle and mesocycle, the remaining days can be slotted in accordingly. A final consideration is that if a competition occurs within a microcycle, it should be counted as training and constitute maximal load work, therefore training intensity both pre- and post- this competition should be reduced as shown in Figure 9.11.

Figure 9.11:
Two peak
microcycle
design where
the second peak
represents a
competition

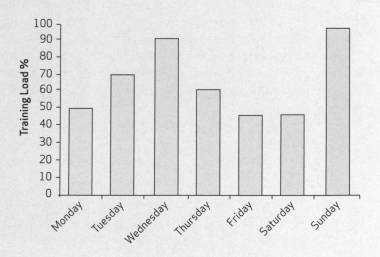

CASE STUDY: TRAINING PROGRAMME DESIGN FOR 800M RUNNERS   Phil Hayes

Overview

Each year, towards the end of the transition phase, I sit down to plan the next year's training. Four items I have with me are my coaching philosophy, my coaching diary from the previous year, my evaluation on the various phases of the previous year and each runner's goals for the coming year. I start by reading my coaching philosophy to give myself a good sense of perspective. Using my coaching diary and notes from the previous year I decide which aspects worked and will be kept and one aspect I would like to change and how this will be evaluated. I try and change only one aspect each year so that I can evaluate its effect. At this point I am ready to begin planning. A mnemonic that can be used to sequence the planning of a training programme is: *Ah So No-one Is Perfect Eh?*. This stands for Aim(s), Sub-objectives, Needs, Initial evaluation, Plan and Evaluation.

The aim(s) are the priority target(s) for the athlete. At the very least these are annual goals, for example to make the final of the AAA. It is also important to have long-term goals as they provide the context within which any annual plan operates. Without knowing the final destination how can you possibly navigate your way there? Before setting the aims I consider the athlete's training age and where they are on the long-term athlete development scale. Sub-objectives are next and take a variety of forms, from specific race goals such as winning the North of England Championship, to running specific times at different points in the season; set times for 'benchmark' training sessions or even improvements in physiological tests.

There are well-documented but differing models of endurance running performance, with both neuromuscular (Paavolainen et al, 1994) and predominantly metabolic (Hill, 1999; Midgley et al, 2007; Spencer, 2001; Wood, 1999) models proposed. It is important to recognise that ultimate performance should be used to determine the needs, not the next season. The focus must remain on long-term development, even at the cost of short-term success. Where possible, the initial evaluation will involve physiological testing. When this is not possible I use race times, analysis of race performances, benchmark training sessions and the runner's perceptions.

The plan is the main part of the process, but it is worth noting how much work has been completed prior to this point. Writing out some training is easy, but developing a well-reasoned plan is different and requires time and thought. The details of the plan will be covered separately in the next section. Evaluation is the final step and is primarily conducted at the end of the year prior to the next plan. It should also be conducted at the end of each training cycle with notes made for the subsequent year's plan. Good record-keeping is essential; records of every training session, coaching course and any thoughts about the process need to be continually documented.

Planning the programme

The starting point for my plan is the year's peak from which I work backwards, planning out the duration of each phase. For each phase I identify key race dates, set aims and outline the main training methods to be used. Verkoshansky (2007a) suggests that periodisation is outdated and that a blocked approach should be employed. The method I use began as a traditional periodised approach, but overtime I have experimented with different methods. I have used four-week blocks with a different main emphasis in each block to good effect, but now use longer phases.

Programme content
Throughout the year the runners complete strength and conditioning work, although I will not detail it here. This should not presuppose a lack of importance, far from it, strength and conditioning is an intrinsic part of the programme.

Foundation stage
Currently the year begins with a 6–10 week foundation stage. This consists almost exclusively of steady state running, a considerable proportion of which is in the heavy domain (Jones and Poole, 2005), i.e. between lactate threshold and lactate turnpoint. The duration of this phase depends upon training age, being longer for those with a younger training age. There is no interval training for at least the first four weeks, after which one interval session is introduced with the aim of developing max. This foundation stage is essential for stable race performance and coping with higher intensity work later in the year.

Four-week cycles
This idea is a mix of two approaches, those of Lydiard and Gilmore (1962) and Labuschagne (1994). Lydiard proposed one easy (recovery) week in every four. Labuschagne used variable intensity four-week cycles consisting of a week each of high volume, a high intensity aerobic work, speed and recovery. Some athletes like to begin the cycle with the high volume week and get faster; others prefer to do their speed week first when they are fresh. It's a question of what works best for each individual. The term 'speed' week can be misleading. For me, speed is relative to the time of year. For example, in the winter 20 x 200 (200 jog recovery) at 1,500m pace is speed work, however in the summer it is slower than many of the sessions and is therefore used as an extensive interval session (Schmolinsky, 1983). Within speed weeks the goal is to recruit fast twitch fibres but avoid high lactate levels. This means repetitions are relatively short with recoveries being reasonably long. Throughout the winter, each type of week progresses in terms of volume, and to a lesser extent intensity.

Throughout this phase, 'benchmark' training sessions are employed. These are fixed sessions and feature once every two cycles. The advantage is that this provides a regular benchmark by which to judge progress, for both coach and athlete. The sessions cannot be repeated too frequently (2–3 sessions in an eight-week period) otherwise the training becomes too psychologically stressful. Some sessions feature each year, others vary from year to year; different runners may have different benchmark sessions. By and large, the runners are unaware of the benchmark sessions.

Concurrent themes

The four-week cycles run from October/November through to March/April. At this point, weekly training becomes a little more homogeneous. From the beginning of this block through to nine weeks before the main peak, two themes run concurrently. One increases the running velocity without developing too much lactate and the other maintains aerobic fitness.

The increase in speed comes from using short repetitions at often faster than race pace with long recoveries. It may seem odd that in an event where high levels of lactate occur that there is an avoidance of too much lactate in training. From experience I know that athletes get stale with too much of this type of training and race performance becomes less stable. It is important to remember that an 800m race is predominantly aerobic, therefore aerobic fitness must be sustained or race performances drop off towards the end of the summer and it becomes hard to peak. Early season races are included in this phase, but not too many.

Lactate tolerance and peaking

Nine weeks before the main peak, a six-week lactate tolerance phase is completed. During this block two, occasionally three, sessions per week involve high levels of lactate. This approach was pioneered in cyclists (Lindsay et al, 1996; Westgarth-Taylor et al, 1997) and shows increased muscle buffer capacity. This is a very tough phase but links speed and aerobic fitness to develop event-specific speed endurance. Most sessions are at 800m pace or faster. At the end of this phase a three week peaking phase aims to maintain the level of fitness.

Putting the plan into action

Having a plan and putting it into practice are very different entities. Two principles that I use are: (1) never write too far in advance, (2) why am I doing this? Over a number of years I have tried writing weekly schedules or having months at a time mapped out. Neither of these two extremes worked very well. They were either too inflexible or I easily lost sight of the overall goal. For several years I have used four-week schedules. In practice this provides time to have a theme and plan progression without losing flexibility. The second principle was adopted to prevent myself just lazily writing schedules. Every single training session must have a purpose. If you cannot answer the question 'why is this athlete doing this training today?' then it should not be in their schedule. Each session must be justifiable.

Conclusion

On the surface, this case study has covered a lot but provided very little specific detail. At coaching conferences and talking to athletes and coaches I find them obsessed with sets, reps, recoveries and speeds. Most athletes have many, if not all, the correct ingredients within their schedule. The most common error that I come across is that schedules are not planned and structured in a way to get the most out of the athlete. Success therefore becomes a matter of chance rather than a planned activity and very few sportsmen and women become consistently successful by chance. As Henry Ford once said, 'Before everything else, getting ready is the key to success'.

Phil Hayes
UK Athletics Level 3 Coach
Senior Lecturer Exercise Physiology – University of Northumbria at Newcastle
BASES accredited Exercise Physiologist (support)

Take home message

We began this chapter with a quote from Eric Morecombe about playing the right notes in the right order. I hope that you have by now discovered how true that statement is. There are myriad of different notes available to us but only by sequencing them in a structured manner will we produce a symphonic sound rather than a loud drone.

However, despite being able to play all the right notes in the right order we also need to recognise the need for being flexible in our role as a coach and training co-ordinator. There will be occasions when you have to improvise and move away from the grand plan but still have the overall training objective in place. So although you will produce an annual plan on paper which ticks all the boxes in terms of athlete development, remember that you must always bear in mind the overall training goal and the level of preparedness of your athlete.

Further study

To support your studies in relation to planning and structuring training a list of suitable learning resources has been compiled here, which contains both peer reviewed articles and textbooks. Within the list there is material related to the methods of periodisation, physiological factors associated related to periodisation, tapering and performance and consequences of poor training planning.

Banister, E W, Carter, J B and Zarkadas, P C (1999) Training theory and taper: Validation in triathlon athletes. *European Journal of Applied Physiology*, 79: 182–91

Costill, D L, Flynn, M G, Kirwan, J P, Houmard J A, Mitchell, J B, Thomas, R and Park, S H. (1988) Effects of repeated days of intensified training on muscle glycogen and swimming performance. *Medicine and Science in Sports and Exercise*, 20: 249–54

Costill, D L, Bowers, R, Branan, G and Sparks, K (1971) Muscle glycogen utilisation during prolonged exercise on successive days. *Journal of Applied Physiology*, 31: 834–8

Fleck, S J (1999) Periodized strength training. A critical review. *Journal of Strength and Conditioning Research*, 13: 82–9

Fry, R W, Morton, A R and Keast D (1992) Periodisation of training stress – A review. *Canadian Journal of Sports Science*, 17: 234–40

Fry, R W, Morton, A R. and Keast D (1992) Periodisation and the prevention of overtraining. *Canadian Journal of Sports Science*, 241–8

Graham, J (2002) Periodization research and an example application. *Strength and Conditioning Journal*, 24: 62–70

Kremer, W J, Ratamess, N, Fry, A C, Triplett-McBride, T, Koziris, P L, Bauer, J A, Lynch, J M and Fleck, S J (2000) Influence of resistance training volume and periodisation on physiological and performance adaptations in collegiate women's tennis players. *American Journal of Sports Medicine*, 28: 626–33

Kraemer, W J, Ratamaee, S S and Nicholas, A (2004) Fundamentals of resistance training: Progression and exercise prescription. *Medicine and Science in Sports and Exercise*, 36: 674–88

Matveyev, L (1981) *Fundamentals of sport training* (translated from the revised Russian edition). Moscow: Progress Publishers.

Morton, R H (1997) Modelling training and overtraining. *Journal of Sports Sciences*, 15: 335–40

Mujika, I, Padilla, S, Pyne, D and Busso, T (2004) Physiological changes associated with the pre-event taper in athletes. *Sports Medicine*, 34: 891–927

Mujika, I, Padilla, S and Pyne, D (2002) Swimming performance changes during the final 3 weeks of training leading to the Sydney 2000 Olympic Games. *International Journal of Sports Medicine*, 29: 582–7

Noakes, T D (1991) *Lore of running*. 3rd edition. Champaign, IL: Human Kinetics

Pyne, D (1996) The periodisation of swimming training at the Australian Institute of sport. *Sports Coach*, 18: 34–8

Stone, M H, O'Bryant, H S, Schilling, B K, Johnson, R L, Pierce, K C, Haff, G G, Koch, A J and Stone, M (1999) Periodization: Effects of manipulating volume and intensity. Part 2. *Journal of Strength and Conditioning*, 21: 54–60

Westgarth-Taylor, C., Hawley, J, A., Rickard, S., Myburgh, K, H., Noakes, T, D., Dennis, S, C. (1997) Metabolic and performance adaptations to interval training in endurance-trained cyclists. European Journal of Applied Physiology. 75: 298–304

Willoughby, D S (1991) Training volume equated: A comparison of periodised and progressive resistance weight training programs. *Journal of Human Movement Studies*, 21: 233–48

Zatsiorsky, V M (1995) *Science and practice of strength training*. Champaign, IL: Human Kinetics

www.bases.org.uk/newsite/home.asp – British Association of Sport and Exercise Sciences: National body for sport and exercise science within the UK. Useful contacts and documents related to physiology, psychology, biomechanics, health and coaching.

www.athleticscoaching.ca/default.aspx?pid=7&spid=34 – Canadian Athletics Coaching Centre: Site containing information relating to coaching and sports science. This link relates to periodisation of training.

www.elitetrack.com – Elitetrack: A website which houses both peer reviewed and lay articles. All papers are referenced and are either written by coaches or sports scientists. A very good resource for all disciplines within coaching.

www.eis2win.co.uk/gen – English Institute of Sport: National organisation who support and work with elite athletes in England.

www.everythingtrackandfield.com/catalog/matriarch/OnePiecePage.asp_Q_PageID_E_350_A_PageName_E_ArticlesGeneralCoaching – Everything Track and Field: Articles related to coaching and training.

www.mysport.net – My Sport: An on-line community for coach education and discussion.

www.sirc.ca – SIRC: Sport, Research, Intelligence, Sportive: An international database which lists articles and publications related to coaching. Also has links to International Governing Bodies of sport and Sport Institutes.

www.uksport.gov.uk – UK Sport. National body supporting elite world class performers. Useful resources related to coach education and drug free sport.

www.verkhoshansky.com – Verkhoshansky: Site of Professor Verkhoshansky, which contains articles and data relating to training methods and responses.

Chapter 10

Endurance training

Introduction

The success of any training programme and therefore overall performance of the athlete is dependent not only on playing all the right notes in the right order (Chapter 9), but also on actually knowing which tune has to be played.

The tune in the case of training can be viewed as a symphony where lots of instruments in the orchestra contribute at various stages of the piece to produce the overall result. A composer needs to know what sound each instrument makes and how each combines with another, for clearly there are certain instruments that complement each other well to produce a harmonious sound and those that when combined either grate on the hearing or generate a sound where one instrument drowns out the other.

The methods and modes of training are very much like conducting the orchestra to get that perfect tune. The coach needs to know what tune to produce; there are many different types of music and symphony and so this forms the structure of the training or tempo of the tune. Next, just as the conductor needs to know which instruments to use, the coach needs to recognise what methods of training are at their disposal. Perhaps most importantly, the coach must understand what adaptations will occur in response to the various forms of training available, just as the conductor must appreciate and recognise the different sounds that can be produced from each instrument and how they combine to produce the overall sound.

In essence, we must be fully aware of not just how to train the athlete but also the athlete's responses as a result of that training. Once these responses – both positive and negative – are appreciated, the ordering can be placed into the programme.

The following chapters will explore factors that contribute to the components of fitness, the physiological responses to training each of the components and how we actually go about training each of the components.

This chapter will introduce you to the principles of endurance training and its associated physiological responses. This chapter will give you the opportunity to focus on the components of endurance, the indices of endurance performance and how an athlete can train in order to develop endurance. These will all be related back to the annual training plan. Therefore upon completion of this chapter, you will have:

- evaluated the factors contributing to endurance performance;
- discussed the physiological and metabolic adaptations and responses occurring as a result of endurance training;
- explored the levels of training intensity in relation to endurance training;
- become acquainted with the modes of endurance training;
- determined how to programme endurance training within the annual plan.

Endurance

According to Professor Andy Jones, who has been the physiologist to the athlete Paula Radcliffe among others for the past 15 years, we can express endurance as the capacity to sustain a given velocity or power output for the longest possible time (Jones and Carter, 2000).

Yet we need to be slightly cautious with this definition in that there is interplay between exercise intensity and the ability to sustain that intensity. Therefore we must set upper and lower thresholds for our definition. Referring to the work of Jones and Carter (2000) the suggested lower threshold value is of five minutes and the upper threshold of 240min

The logical explanation is that any work conducted at the highest sustained intensity for less than five minutes would incur a high level of anaerobic metabolism. Although initially being associated with endurance, sustained work for greater than 240min would be limited by factors which reflect exercise duration rather than the physiology of the athlete.

Now we have a definition and timeframe we can appreciate the metabolic demands associated with endurance performance and training. A very simple way of expressing endurance metabolism is to think that we need to re-synthesis ATP by aerobic means, signifying the need for an adequate supply of oxygen from the atmosphere to meet the metabolic demands of the engaged muscles and muscle groups. Therefore the primary metabolic substrates for this form of training will be in the form of carbohydrates and fats, but there will still be contributions from lactic and alactic sources.

Physiological components of endurance

Given that we have a framework from which to begin (aerobic metabolism) it is not surprising that the factors contributing to aerobic substrate utilisation contribute to endurance performance. In order to best understand the underlying physiological mechanisms we will sub-divide the components into two categories: those that contribute to oxygen delivery and those which contribute to oxygen utilisation.

Oxygen delivery

Oxygen delivery is primarily dictated by the heart, therefore we see that endurance trained athletes have enlarged hearts, especially in relation to the left ventricle where these athletes show signs of eccentric and concentric hypertrophy of the left ventricle. As a result of these and other physiological adaptations, endurance athletes have an increased cardiac output (Q_{min}) when compared to a sedentary individual. Indeed output values of 40l·min^{-1} of blood have been reported during maximal intensity exercise compared to around 25l·min^{-1} in the un-trained individual. Coupled with this there is increased maximal heart rate and decreased sub-maximal and resting heart rates when comparing endurance trained to non-trained athletes.

Endurance athletes have increased levels of red blood cells (RBCs) and haemoglobin (Hb). As Hb is the carrier for O_2 and also removes of CO_2, the increased levels improve the efficiency of the cardiovascular response to exercise.

Coupled with these cardiovascular and haematological factors, endurance training results in an increase in the capillary to muscle fibre ratio, indeed we see that endurance training results in an increase in the number of capillaries to each muscle fibre, thereby facilitating an increased rate of O_2 delivery to the muscle.

Oxygen utilisation

In terms of O_2 utilisation there is strong evidence from the literature base to suggest that endurance athletes have an increased a-vO_2 difference (arterial-venous difference) within the muscle. This is a measure of the rate at which O_2 can be extracted and used in the process of energy supply. Endurance training results in a greater extraction rate and therefore less O_2 appearing in the venous blood.

Endurance training also results in an increase in the size and density of mitochondria in the muscle along with increased amounts of aerobic enzymes such as lactate dehydrogenase (LDH) and succinate dehydrogenase (SDH). Metabolically we see a reduction in the rate of glucose and glycogen metabolism for the same relative exercise intensity, along with decreased lactate production and concentrations at sub-maximal workloads and increased lactate concentrations at maximal workloads.

Table 10.1 highlights the major physiological and metabolic adaptations that occur in response to a period of endurance training.

Table 10.1: Primary physiological responses to endurance training

Parameter	Adaptation
Mitochondrial density and size	Increase
Capillary density	Increase
Aerobic enzymes	Increase
Glycogen storage	Increase
Red blood cell count	Increase
Haemoglobin	Increase
VO2max	Increase
Lactate turnpoint	Rightward shift in relation to exercise intensity
Lactate threshold	Rightward shift in relation to exercise intensity
Submaximal lactate concentration	Decrease
Running economy	Decreased O2 cost for same relative exercise intensity
vVO2max	Increase
Submaximal heart rate	Decrease
Heart size	Increase in left ventricular size and mass
Maximal cardiac output	Increase
Neural recruitment	Enhanced recruitment of primary movers
Muscle fibre type	Enhanced efficiency of both type I and type II fibres

Activity 10.1: Reflecting on the adaptations to endurance training

The physiological and metabolic responses to endurance training are well documented and summarised in Table 10.1. From your current understanding you should reflect on the following.

To what degree does endurance play a part in your own sport? Think about the association between velocity and duration and the type of metabolic substrate that would predominate.

If you would like to know some more about the balance between oxygen delivery and utilisation and the factors which contribute to these processes then refer to the *Concept box* below.

Concept 10.1: Oxygen delivery and utilisation

The processes of oxygen delivery and utilisation are described according to the Fick principle which is summarised as follows:

Oxygen delivery = $Q\ CaO_2$ and
Oxygen utilisation (extraction) = $a\text{-}vO_{2dif}$

where Q = cardiac output ($l\cdot min^{-1}$) and CaO_2 = arterial oxygen content. By combining these two expressions we generate the following equation:

$$VO_2 = Q(a\text{-}vO_{2diff})$$

This equation suggests that the volume of oxygen uptake is dependent on both the amount of blood that can be pumped from the heart in one minute and the amount of oxygen that can be extracted from the circulation at the muscle. However it also worth noting that this principle merely defines for us the ability to deliver the required oxygen to the muscle and not the ability to extract this bound O_2 from its carrier and get it into the mitochondria. This process is explained for us in a second equation which has been termed Fick's law of Diffusion:

$$VO_2 = DO_2\_PvO_2$$

where VO_2 = oxygen uptake, DO_2 = diffusion capacity for O_2 and PvO_2 = partial pressure of O_2 in mixed venous blood. Therefore the VO_2 at any given workload is dependent on both the ability to deliver and extract the bound O_2.

The overall contribution of these and other adaptations are for a decreased oxygen cost (VO_2) of exercise at sub-maximal workloads, an increased maximal rate of oxygen uptake (VO_{2max}) and an increase in the exercise intensity at which blood lactate shows a dramatic rise: the lactate-turn-point. If you wish to know more about the indices of endurance performance refer to the *Concept box*.

Concept 10.2: Indices of endurance performance

These indices are important to coaches and athletes alike as they can be measured in a clinical or field setting and used to either describe the physiological responses of the athlete to training or to establish a set of training zones from which all sessions can be planned.

Maximal aerobic power (VO_{2max})

Of all of the measures used to define and describe endurance performance it is VO_{2max} that has received the greatest attention, not surprisingly given that early applied physiological studies show significant correlations between VO_{2max} and endurance performance (Hopkins and McKenzie, 1994; Coyle, 2005).

VO_{2max} reflects the maximal rate at which an individual can take up and consume oxygen from the atmosphere for aerobic respiration, therefore representing the maximal rate of aerobic energy expenditure.

As a unit it is measured in absolute terms as litres per minute ($l \cdot min^{-1}$) and in relative terms as millilitres per kilogram of body mass per minute ($ml \cdot kg^{-1} \cdot min^{-1}$). VO_{2max} values for sedentary individuals are in the order of $40–42 ml \cdot kg^{-1} \cdot min^{-1}$ compared to elite endurance athlete scores in excess of $65 ml \cdot kg^{-1} \cdot min^{-1}$.

As an endurance index the literature base informs us that VO_{2max} is limited by the rate at which oxygen can be delivered to the working muscles, therefore is directly related to the pumping variables established in the Fick principle ($VO_{2max} = Q_{max} \times a\text{-}vO_{2diffmax}$).

The higher the VO_{2max}, the greater the cardiac output of the heart. As a result of endurance training there is a decrease in the requirement for blood flow through the muscle due to the increased $a\text{-}vO_2$ difference. Further there is reduced heart rate during sub-maximal exercise primarily as a result of increased stroke volume of the heart, which is a response to the changes in left ventricular size and functioning.

During maximal intensity exercise the increased Q and $a\text{-}VO_2$ difference leads to an increase in VO_{2max}. However as with any physiological parameter the increases in VO_{2max} start to become smaller and less overt with well-trained athletes. This notwithstanding, VO_{2max} still provides us with a measure of cardio-respiratory performance and can also be used an indication of de-training.

Performance economy (sub-maximal cost of exercise)

This has been defined as the oxygen uptake (VO_2) required at a given absolute exercise intensity (Jones and Carter, 2000). In its broadest sense running performance economy expressed as the oxygen cost of running ($VO_2 ml \cdot kg^{-1} \cdot min^{-1}$) or ($ml \cdot kg^{-1} \cdot km^{-1}$) is lower at the same relative exercise intensity in an economical athlete compared to a less economical athlete.

Athletes can become more economical following a prolonged period of endurance training, however in order to best understand what drives the physiological adaptations we should consider some of the factors contributing to the economical status of an athlete. Performance economy is an interesting index reflecting the association between the biomechanics and physiology of performance.

Concept 10.2: Continued

In runners (where this component is assessed most widely) running economy is associated with the oxidative capacity of the muscle, neural recruitment patterns, muscle fibre typing, flexibility, substrate use, running gait, force generation and elastic potential of the muscle. Further, di Prampero et al (1993) suggested that a 5 per cent increase in running economy would result in a 3.8 per cent increase in running distance and that running economy distinguishes between the ability of runners for distances greater than 5,000m better than VO_{2max}.

Velocity at VO_{2max} (vVO_{2max}):

This parameter expresses the association/interaction between performance economy and VO_{2max}. Figure 10.1 highlights this relationship for us, demonstrating how the interaction of the two parameters helps to define this composite measure of the highest sustainable aerobic speed or workload, which is highly predictive of endurance performance from 3,000m to 10,000m.

Longitudinal studies have demonstrated that vVO_{2max} is a reliable and sensitive measure of endurance capability fitness. An increase in vVO_{2max} reflects an increased ability to sustain a higher percentage of VO_{2max}. It is further suggested that vVO_{2max} is the ideal exercise intensity for interval training.

Lactate kinetics: lactate threshold and lactate turnpoint:

The blood lactate response to exercise represents changes in the metabolic cost of exercise and thereby reflects the relative demands placed on aerobic and anaerobic sources. As exercise intensity increases so does the blood lactate response as a result of an increased demand on anaerobic glycolysis.

The lactate turnpoint is identified with the dashed arrow in Figure 10.2, representing a sudden and continual rise in blood lactate levels. Studies have

Figure 10.1: Graph showing two athletes with different combinations of economy and VO_{2max}. Despite Athlete B having a higher VO_{2max} than Athlete B, Athlete B has a better combination of economy and VO_{2max} and hence a higher calculated vVO_{2max}

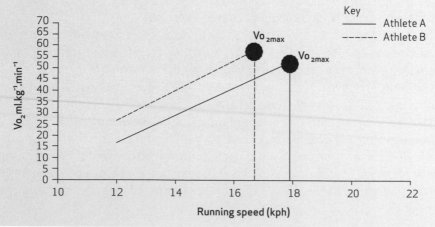

Concept 10.2: Continued

suggested that the lactate turnpoint is a powerful predicator of endurance performance and a sensitive indicator of the aerobic response to training.

Exercise conducted at intensities in excess of the lactate turn-point is associated with a pronounced onset of metabolic acidosis and peripheral muscular fatigue as well as being associated with physiological factors such as capillary density, percentage of type I and type II muscle fibres, the onset of type II fibre type recruitment, mitochondrial density and concentrations of key aerobic enzymes. The onset of fatigue at exercise intensities beyond the lactate turnpoint is either the consequence of acidosis impairing muscle contractile dynamics, or through a depletion of intramuscular glycogen stores.

The preceding point on the blood lactate kinetic curve is less well appreciated but has significance especially for endurance athletes and in our appreciation of recovery training. This first point identified on the curve in Figure 10.2 is defined as the lactate threshold and represents the first initial rise in blood lactate above baseline values. It has been widely associated with the velocity of marathon performance and occurs at a heart rate corresponding to between 50 and 80 per cent VO_{2max}.

Perhaps what makes the blood lactate response to exercise so compelling is that not only does this profile respond to training and detraining, but by identifying these two points the coach is able to identify a series of heart rate training zones for almost all sessions. An example of this is shown in Figure 10.3.

Other factors associated with endurance performance include haematological factors such red blood cell count, haemoglobin concentration and haematocrit. There are obvious associations between endurance performance and respiratory function, with lung capacity volumes in elite athletes being recorded in excess of 8l compared with around 4l in the sedentary population.

Figure 10.2: The blood lactate response to exercise during an incremental treadmill test. The solid line shows the lactate response the dashed line shows the heart rate response. The dashed arrow = lactate turn-point and the solid arrow = lactate threshold

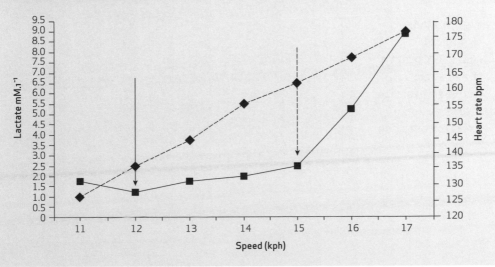

Figure 10.3: Heart rate training zones determined in relation to the blood lactate response to incremental exercise. E = Easy training, S = Steady training, T = Tempo training and I = Interval training

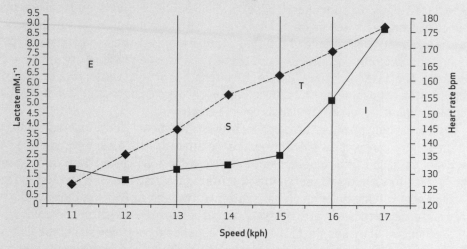

The highlighted examples of indices of endurance performance can easily be applied to sports such as cycling, running and rowing; but what about with swimming where the use of equipment to assess the oxygen cost of exercise is highly impractical? Again, coaches tend to use blood lactate data, with the swimmer completing a series of step-wise increments in the pool, but another method that is widely used and is less invasive is that of determining critical speed. This concept is based on the association between exercise intensity and time as demonstrated in Figure 10.4. The actual concept describes a relationship between speed and time (Monod and Scherrer, 1965) and has been discussed in considerable depth in the literature (Hill, 1993). The swimmer would complete a series of maximal effort swims over a range of distances from 25m through to 400m. This data can the be plotted on a graph very much like that in Figure 10.4

Figure 10.4: Graphical representation of the association between exercise intensity and exercise duration

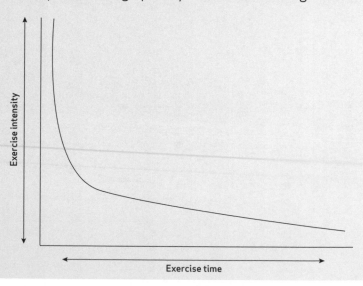

Concept 10.2: Continued

and used to generate the measure of critical speed (highest sustainable speed). The simplest approach is to calculate the inverse of time and plot this against speed and the intercept on the y-axis will equate to the critical speed.

Principles of endurance training

Now we have some appreciation for the underlying metabolic and physiological factors contributing to and adapting from endurance training we should begin to consider how we actually train to develop endurance. Previously we have defined levels of intensity ranging from low to supra-maximal intensity training, the so called spectrum of intensity. Through our understanding of the physiological responses to increasing exercise intensity we have come to appreciate that we can plan a series of training zones which can be both monitored and controlled, conforming to our appreciation of the spectrum of intensity. An overview of these zones is presented in Table 10.2.

Table 10.2: Endurance training zones established through the use of heart rate and blood lactate data

Training zone	Heart rate (bpm)	Blood lactate (mM·l−1)	Intensity
Easy	<140–150	1.0–1.5	Low
Steady	140/150–170	1.6–4.0	Medium
Tempo	170–180	4.0–6.0	Sub-maximal
Interval	>180	>6.0	Maximal/ Supra-maximal

Note that four zones have been identified which is common when profiling endurance runners, however sports such as cycling and rowing use a similar approach but have more zones identified.

Using these zones we should now explore the different forms of endurance training that can be programmed into the annual plan. When constructing an endurance training programme it is important to remember that there needs to be a solid foundation on which all other training is built.

Low intensity (easy zone training)

Many athletes and coaches make the mistake of dismissing this zone out of hand when in fact it is very useful in the development of the athlete. It is conducted at an intensity which will not induce any undue physiological stress, but is associated with the promotion of training stress reduction and removal.

This zone is associated with recovery training and can be used either as a specific unit's worth of training incorporated into the microcycle structure, or as the intensity during a session where multiple repetitions of training have to be conducted, such as interval and repetition training. If you wish to gain a greater appreciation for the physiological rationale of recovery work during training refer to the *Concept box*.

Concept 10.3: Physiological basis of recovery

A common approach to training is to use multiple repetitions of work at high intensity as a means of promoting and developing VO_{2max} and lactate tolerance (Billat, 2001). For the athlete to sustain this high intensity training, there must be a period of recovery programmed in between both repetitions and sets to allow the athlete some physiological respite and at the same time promote some level of physiological recovery.

A parameter associated with the recovery process is that of blood lactate concentration which in high concentrations, is linked with an impairment of excitation contraction coupling in the muscle (Stephenson et al, 1998) and the onset of local muscular fatigue.

Studies have demonstrated excessive levels of lactate in the blood following 10s of supra-maximal work and that following ~60s of maximal intensity training the athlete may encounter blood lactate scores in the region 8–10mM·l^{-1} (Billat, 2001). Such an increase in lactate and thereby muscle fatigue is associated with a decrease in performance velocity and an increased metabolic cost of the exercise. If not controlled, this will result in the athlete either dropping out of the training session, or through reducing the performance velocity, changing the nature of the training session.

We need to consider a recovery process which promotes a reduction in the metabolic consequences of fatigue, and so helps to maintain the integrity of the training session.

In addressing the recovery period between multiple bouts of work, we need to consider two key factors: the intensity of work that should be conducted and how long the recovery intervention should be.

Belcastro and Bonen (1975) inform us that the optimal recovery intensity is between 35–40 per cent VO_{2max} which equates to a heart rate of around 140–150bpm. So why such a specific intensity of effort? The key to understanding lies in our appreciation of blood flow dynamics during exercise and the availability of oxygen for metabolism. There is a balance between supplying enough oxygen to meet demand within the working muscle and witnessing the systemic rise in blood lactate concentration when supply can no longer meet demand.

The supply of oxygen to the working muscle is dependent on blood flow to the muscle, dictated and regulated through cardiac output and heart rate. In other words if the exercise intensity in recovery is too high we would start to see an increase in lactate concentrations and if too low we would not be promoting an active rate of removal of lactate from the muscle through the circulation, or delivering an optimal supply of oxygen to the muscle to promote the oxidation of lactate back to pyruvate. This informs us as to why a passive recovery would not be the optimal form of recovery during training.

We also need to appreciate that the recovery process in terms of lactate removal is muscle fibre type specific, with the greatest proportion of lactate being oxidised in the slow twitch type I fibres. They have an abundance of aerobic structures such as mitochondria, capillary networks and enzymes such as Lactate Dehydrogenase (LDH), which promotes the conversion of lactate back to

Concept 10.3: Continued

pyruvate. Indeed these muscles seem to contain more heart specific LDH than muscle specific LDH, which is important because heart specific LDH is more effective at promoting oxidation of lactate than the muscle specific form.

The duration of the recovery period is partly dependent on the fitness of the athlete and the nature of the training session. If we are trying to develop lactate tolerance, a shorter recovery period may be employed; if on the other hand we are aiming to develop top end speed, perhaps during the competition phase of the annual plan, we may incorporate longer rest intervals to keep the quality of work high. In order to understand this association we must again consider the relationship between the supply and demand of oxygen. During the actual training bout, there is an increase in oxygen uptake (VO_2) in order to meet increased demands from the exercising muscle. The degree to which exercise VO_2 increases depends on the intensity of the exercise. However, during the subsequent recovery period, VO_2 does not immediately return to resting levels but rather follows a slower decay pattern over time.

This slow return back to resting values for VO_2 during recovery has been termed excess post exercise oxygen consumption (EPOC) and highlights the interplay between exercise intensity, recovery duration and the restoration of physiological and metabolic homeostasis. In other words EPOC reflects the excess oxygen consumed beyond resting values to enable recovery and regeneration to occur.

If we study the time course of VO_2 in recovery we see that there are two very distinct components to the EPOC phase and a less clear, but still important, third component. The first phase in recovery has been termed the ultra-fast component and is evidenced by the very rapid decline in oxygen uptake within the first few minutes post exercise. The second phase has been defined as the fast component of EPOC and can last for approximately 1 h with the final phase being termed the slow component of EPOC and lasting for several hours. Each phase highlighted in Table 10.3 is associated with the restoration and recovery of specific physiological and metabolic parameters.

Other factors attributed to EPOC are the elevation in core temperature, ventilation rate and heart rate also as result of the training bout. Therefore we must recognise the association between exercise intensity and the rate of physiological and metabolic recovery. A high intensity bout of exercise will incur a much larger EPOC than a low intensity bout, at the same time we must consider how much recovery we want from the athlete.

A short recovery encompassing only the ultra-fast phase may be suited to training where intensity is very high and of short duration, whereas a longer period of recovery may be used when we are aiming to train VO_{2max} or lactate tolerance and so need to remove some of the residual fatigue in order to maintain form during subsequent bouts of training. The longer the recovery period the greater the restoration, which may be useful when explosive 'all out' efforts are required, but we should also ensure that periods of recovery are not too long, which can reduce the effectiveness of the session due to the athlete 'cooling down'.

Concept 10.3: Continued

Table 10.3: Physiological and metabolic responses during a period of recovery from exercise

EPOC Phase	Physiological and metabolic responses
Phase 1: Ultra-fast (15–20min post-exercise)	Often termed the alactacid component of the recovery because this initial rapid phase is not associated with glycolytic or lactate-based recovery. We witness a rapid restoration of high energy phosphates (ATP-PC) and simultaneously a restoration of the O_2 stores that are bound to myoglobin. Studies have revealed that there is approximately 50% restoration of ATP-PC within the first minute of recovery (Tesch and Wright, 1983).
Phase 2: Fast (60min post-exercise)	Often referred to as the lactacid component primarily because the increased oxygen cost above resting values is associated with removal of lactate from within the cell and the blood, a re-establishment of both blood and cellular pH through the dissipation of H^+ ions and the onset of restoration of intra-muscular glycogen stores. Literature informs us that there is approximately 85% removal of lactate from the cell within the first six minutes of recovery (Belcastro and Bonen, 1975).
Phase 3: Slow (>60min up to 24h)	This phase is very slow and is associated with only slightly elevated EPOC scores, but reflects the raised metabolic rate as a result of the preceding bout of exercise. During this phase there is a continuation of the restoration of muscle glycogen and repair to muscle tissue.

Referring back to Chapter 9, we described alternations of training load throughout a microcycle's worth of work, where generally, one session is defined as a recovery day or recovery unit. This form of training promotes supercompensation, helping to encourage the decline in both peripheral and central fatigue.

This training should not lead to any significant increase in blood lactate concentration as this would imply intensity that is too high. At the same time, it should not be of excessive duration; it is usual for this training to be around 30–60min. The athlete should feel as though they are recuperating from the demands of the previous sessions.

The mistakes often made with this zone are that coaches either misinterpret the intensity, programming this form of training for the development of aerobic capacity, or they consider the intensity of effort to be too low to be of discernable benefit to the athlete and classify it as ineffective load training. In respect to the latter, this is not the case as recovery is needed in the overall development of the athlete and without it the athlete will not develop and grow. This form of training can also be of some benefit during the transition phase of the annual plan.

Activity 10.2: Recovery training

Recovery training is an integral part of all training for all sporting disciplines. This is a reflective exercise to allow application of your acquired knowledge to your own sport; in so doing you should:

- think about how you currently recover from training, or programme recovery into a session;
- consider how you could apply the knowledge of recovery or low intensity training to sports such as ice hockey and American football, where players come on and off the sidelines during a game.

Medium intensity (steady zone training)

I often refer to this as aerobic base training as it is used to establish the base or foundations on which all other endurance work is established. So if you are working with a novice athlete it will form a considerable part of their annual plan, but is also a crucial component of the well-trained athlete's plan.

This form of training promotes the development of aerobic capacity and is associated with high volume sessions where a single session could last for up to 2h. This level of training is normally associated with continuous training, whereby the athlete maintains the desired intensity without alternating or changing pace for a prolonged period of time.

It is possible to mix up the training a little in this zone by using what is known as variable pace training. Remember that this is a big training zone, as highlighted by the wide range in heart rates at the upper and lower ends, and should be used to its maximum. Variable paced training allows the athlete to maintain a constant period of work but within this session we could alternate the pace perhaps using a pyramid format of training as shown in the examples below.

Examples of medium intensity training

We have an athlete with a steady zone of between 141–170bpm (14–16 kph). Here are two types of 60min training sessions:

- Continuous session: HR of around 155bpm for 60min @ constant pace.
- Variable paced session: 5min @ 140bpm, 10min @ 150bpm, 10min @ 160bpm; 5min @ 170bpm, 10min @ 160bpm, 10min @ 150bpm, 10min @ 140bpm.

The average HR for the two sessions is very similar (155bpm for continuous, 153bpm for variable paced); the metabolic cost would therefore be very similar between the two.

Variable paced training is useful because it promotes change of pace within the session and helps to break the monotony of completing high volume training such as that completed by marathon runners, where they could be running anything up to 160 km/week.

Something that is common in this zone is to sub-divide it into two smaller zones referred to as long and short steady training. The long steady training would be associated with HRs at the lower end of the zone and a high duration (up to 2h), while the short steady zone is associated with work in the order of 60min. This form of medium intensity training would predominate in the preparation phase of the annual plan but would still form part of the plan in the competition phase but to a lesser degree.

Activity 10.3: Medium intensity training

The examples provided are generic in nature. Use this task to detail TWO types of medium intensity training that you either currently use or could use within your chosen sport. For each session suggest the mode of training to be conducted (variable, continuous), and the duration of each session/repetition.

Sub-maximal (tempo zone training)

This level of training is often referred to as threshold training. In this zone we are prompting training associated with elevated blood lactate levels and hence increased oxygen demand. It is used to promote higher intensity training and so has a much shorter duration than that performed in the medium intensity zone.

There are actually two forms of sub-maximal training: the classic tempo session where the athlete exercises continuously for between 20–30min and cruise training or cruise intervals (Daniels, 2005). Again the athlete is completing training in the Tempo zone but this time the session is broken down into a series of efforts interspersed with a block of active recovery.

By breaking the session down like this the athlete can accomplish more work than would be completed using the Tempo method. The work to rest ratio in this zone is 5 min exercise to around 1 min rest. Because rest blocks are incorporated into this training, the total duration of the session can be longer than that for a tempo session, reaching up to 60min. This form of training is used in both specific preparation and competition phases of the annual plan, with the emphasis generally being on shorter recovery work in the preparation phase.

Examples of sub-maximal intensity training

We have an athlete with a Tempo zone of between 171 and 178bpm.

- Tempo session: 20–30min session @ 171–178bpm.
- Cruise interval session: 4 × 3000m @ ~510s per 3000m with 120s rest (running) or 8 × 20min @ ~175bpm with 5 min rest (cycling).

Activity 10.4: Sub-maximal intensity training

The examples provided are generic in nature. Use this task to detail TWO types of sub-maximal intensity training that you either currently use or could use within your chosen sport. For each session suggest the mode of training to be conducted (tempo, cruise intervals), and the duration of each session/repetition.

Maximal/supra-maximal (interval zone training)

Maximal intensity training is often referred to as VO_{2max} training as this is the primary factor stressed during this form of high intensity work. Because the intensity of effort is so demanding there must be an interchange between work done and recovery. The duration of effort for maximal intensity work is between 30s and 5min.

When establishing interval training sessions a number of points require consideration, as follows: We must ensure that the duration of the repetition is between 30s and 5min; any shorter and we drift into the supra-maximal domain, any longer and the effort will be unsustainable, in which case the athlete will back off in terms of pace and fall back into the Tempo zone, or they will just stop the effort. Next we must ensure that the recovery time employed is equal to or shorter than the training repetition and that work conducted in the training repetition is of high quality. Then we encourage an active recovery period with the HR for the athlete at the upper end of the Easy zone.

Finally the athlete should not be overloaded with excessive amounts of interval training in a microcycle as it is highly demanding, therefore we should try to ensure that the total amount of interval work constitutes no more than 8 per cent of the total training in a single microcycle (Daniels, 2005).

This form of training is used during both the specific preparation and pre competition phases but more sparingly during the competitive phase. We should not ignore the supra-maximal workouts that fall within this zone. These are used either to promote training at race pace in order to encourage biomechanical development at race speeds, or for the use of over-speed training.

Over-speed training encourages the athlete to train at speeds in excess of their race pace, in order to develop faster and more efficient muscle contractions through enhanced neural recruitment patterns. For an endurance athlete, both forms of training would be short in duration with reasonably long recovery to ensure sufficient restoration of high energy phosphates and significant reduction in peripheral fatigue. If you want to learn more about interval training review the *Concept box*.

Concept 10.4: Examples of maximal (interval intensity training)

We have an athlete with an Interval zone >178bpm

- Interval session: $6 \times 1500m$ @ ~300s/1,500m with 300s recovery *or* $8 \times$ 3min @ 90–95 per cent maximal power output with 3min recovery (cycling).

Activity 10.5: Maximal/supra-maximal intensity training

The examples provided are generic in nature. Use this task to detail TWO types of maximal/supra-maximal intensity training that you either currently use or could use within your chosen sport. For each session suggest the mode of training to be conducted (interval), the duration of each session/repetition and the amount of recovery to be included between sets and repetitions.

Understanding intervals

The secret to understanding intervals is recognising that they allow the athlete to complete more total work than they could complete if the session was continuous in nature. Furthermore, we recognise that the degree of physiological adaptation is greater through interval training than from continuous, indeed studies show that interval training is a primary stimulus for the development of VO_{2max} (Helgerud et al, 2007), but that the stress placed on the athlete is far greater.

We must recognise however that, especially for maximal intensity intervals, there is interplay between the duration of the interval and the overall development of the athlete. This is exemplified for us by Jack Daniels in his book the Running Formula (2005). We recognise that when undertaking aerobic training (<VO_{2max}), it will take approximately 2min for the athlete's oxygen consumption to reach VO_{2max} levels. Therefore, if the session to be completed is 4×5min at VO_{2max} the athlete will spend only 3min of each repetition completing interval (VO_{2max}) training. This equates to 12min out of the 20min session being conducted at the desired intensity.

Daniels expands on this further by asking what would happen if the session was 7×3min runs. The session duration as a whole looks pretty similar to the 4×5min, however using the 2min rule, the athlete would complete only seven minutes at the actual interval/VO_{2max} intensity. Furthermore, if we were to ask the athlete to complete 20×1min repetitions at maximal intensity pace, they would in fact accomplish no work that develops VO_{2max} as they will not have spent sufficient time during each bout of training to stress this component of fitness.

Indeed this form of training would be better classed as supra-maximal work and would be of more benefit if the training speed or pace were increased.

Anaerobic endurance

This may seem to be an illogical training parameter to reference in relation to endurance/aerobic training, however we must recognise that the relative contribution to many endurance exercises from anaerobic metabolism is considerable, therefore this key component must be both acknowledged and trained.

When we refer to anaerobic endurance we are in fact referring to the anaerobic capacity of the athlete which is best defined as 'the maximal amount of ATP re-synthesis via anaerobic metabolism (by the whole organism) during a specific type of short duration maximal intensity exercise' (Green, 1994). Given the nature of this parameter (anaerobic) it is not surprising that the most suitable training method is through the use of intervals of duration between 60 and 240s and at about 90–95 per cent of peak speed. Therefore many of the interval sessions employed in the development of endurance or team athlete will be for the development of anaerobic capacity.

Despite the considerable relationship between the anaerobic capacity and events such as 800m (63 per cent aerobic, 37 per cent anaerobic) and 1,500m running (73 per cent aerobic, 27 per cent anaerobic) a word of caution must be applied. Although it would seem that the anaerobic capacity is a discriminating variable between trained and less well trained athletes in these disciplines (Gastin and Lawson, 1994), we should not ignore that this capacity is built on a solid aerobic foundation, indeed those athletes who exhibit the largest anaerobic capacities also show the largest VO_{2max} scores (Gastin and Lawson, 1994), suggesting that the anaerobic capacity can neither be developed at the expense of aerobic base work or without having already established a firm aerobic foundation from which to begin.

CASE STUDY

Gender: Male
Age: 42
Mass: 61.5kg
Height: 1.70m
Event: Paralympic Games, 5,000m T46 (Arm Amputee), Athens, September 2004

This athlete was a marathon runner, who 18 months before the Paralympic Games in Athens was forced to change his event to 5,000m due to the marathon being cancelled from the programme. The athlete's current strengths and weaknesses therefore needed reassessment and a training programme prepared for the 18 months ahead. Therefore this case study focuses on the preparation of the plan for the final year.

Prior to preparing the plan, the coach and athlete reviewed the previous year's training and competition. An essential part of the review was to analyse the results of the latest physiological test.

REVIEW OF THE PREVIOUS YEAR

The review of the physiological test indicated the following key points:

Vertical jump
(35cm) A little low for a 5,000m runner so could benefit from introducing more circuits, weights and additional hill work.

CASE STUDY: *Continued*

Treadmill test

- *Running economy (VO₂):* $-55.0\text{ml·kg}^{-1}\text{·min}^{-1}$ at 16.0km·h^{-1}. Is more important for a marathon runner but should be maintained at this level by training at relatively higher speeds
- VO_{2max}: $65.0\text{ml·kg}^{-1}\text{·min}^{-1}$
- vVO_{2max}: 19.5km·h^{-1} (74s/400m lap). These are considered most important for a 5,000m runner therefore focus on improving if possible by running 800–1,200m reps at 3k/5k pace. A positive test result for competing in the future over 5000m
- *Lactate threshold:* 14.0km·h^{-1} @ -142b·min^{-1}
- *Lactate turnpoint:* -16.0km·h^{-1} @ -154b·min^{-1}

Lactate threshold was not particularly high (speed) and could be improved by introducing more tempo runs just above the lactate turnpoint. This data also provided the information determining the heart rate zones for training.

The review of the previous years training and competition programme indicated the following key points:

Tactical awareness

The athlete is not confident when performing in this event. Concern over lack of basic finishing speed encourages the athlete to front run almost from the start.

Injuries/illness

The previous year's injuries and illnesses coincided with phases of high mileage. A number of factors may have contributed to this, including the athlete's age and certainly the nature of his disability.

Training

The athlete did not always stick implicitly to the training plan. This in itself is not a particular problem as he has many years experience and will make changes according to how his body responds to training and other personal commitments. However, it is essential that the athlete convey these changes to the coach so further adjustments to the programme can be made as necessary.

To make the transition from marathon and road running into 5,000m running, more track sessions will be required.

Competition programme

The previous year's track programme did not include many track races, particularly over the shorter distances of 1,500m and 3,000m. A more focused approach to the track season is required and it is necessary to stop competing in road races once this season commences.

Following the review, it was now possible to construct the yearly plan, outlining the different phases of training for the year and also to set personal targets.

CASE STUDY: Continued

Set targets

To run 15:15–15:20min in order to medal at the Paralympic Games (Athens) in September 2004. At the time of planning his PB was 15:27min. Target required an improvement of 7–12s.

The qualifying time for the games was already achieved so the athlete only needed to prove fitness and show good form prior to the team selection in June. Therefore only one peak was required in the annual training plan.

THE TRAINING PLAN

Figure 10.5 provides an overview of the annual training plan used for this athlete in their build-up.

Aerobic conditioning: November to February

The main objective of this phase was to develop a good endurance base and improve general strength. The athlete had to gradually increase mileage until conditioned to run 80 miles/week without undue stress whilst ensuring easy runs were run at an easy pace.

Hill training commences in November with one session per week, increasing the distance of each effort or number of efforts every four weeks. One longer session per week on grass or road if possible. In order to induce continued overload recovery time would be reduced or speed increased every four weeks, but two weeks after hills have been increased.

Typical sessions on grass: 8 × 2min 1 min recovery or 4 × 1mile (5min, 2min recovery).

At weekends the athlete completed long runs of up to 15 miles, conducted according to their heart rate within the steady zone. Rest days were very easy 5–7 miles at 7-min mile pace. Looking to run strongly in cross country season, mostly local races but no easing down. Circuit training session once per week.

Competition targets: Lancashire CC champs, Northern CC, Portugal CC, National CC.

Speed endurance phase 1: February to April

During this phase there would be a move towards two interval sessions per week along with one hill session. Track work would be introduced later with a simultaneous slight reduction in mileage.

Intervals consist of one long session between 600m and 1,500m (total 15–20min). To ensure progression the speed would be maintained but the duration of the recovery between repetitions would be decreased. Volume also increased as the phase progressed.

Introduce the key session which is 10 × 400m, with 1 min recovery, followed by 1,000m. This is to gain confidence in using the race tactic of running a fast last 1k.

CASE STUDY: Continued

WORLD CLASS PERFORMACE PLAN

ATHLETE TRAINING & COMPETITION PROGRAMME

ATHLETE ....

EVENT (1) 5000m

COACH(ES) ....

PERFORMANCE TARGET 15m15s

DATE	NOV				DEC				JAN					FEB				MAR				APR				MAY				JUNE				JULY				AUG				SEP			
WEEK No	1	2	3	4	5	6	7	8	9	10	11	12	13	14	15	16	17	18	19	20	21	22	23	24	25	26	27	28	29	30	31	32	33	34	35	36	37	38	39	40	41	42	43	44	45	46	47	48
TRAINING EMPHASIS																																																
Aerobic Conditioning																																																
Strength Endurance																																																
Speed Endurance																																																
Speed																																																
Competition Preparation																																																
Holding Camp																																																
Olympic Village																																																
TRAINING SESSIONS/WK	9	9	9	9	10	10	10	10	10	10	10	10	12	12	12	12	12	12	12	12	12	12	9	9	9	9	8	8	8	8	8	10	12	12	12	12	10	10	8	8	8	8	8	8	8	8	8	8
ESTIMATED MILEAGE/WK	70	70	70	80	80	80	80	80	80	80	80	80	80	80	80	80	80	80	70	70	60	60	60	60	55	50	50	50	55	50	60	70	70	60	60	60	60	55	55	55	50	50						
MAJOR COMPETITIONS																											DSE									5k											
MINOR COMPETITIONS						CC									CC	CC			1/2				10k	5k									1500				1500				3k	5k						

TRAINING NOTES – to show the MAIN training emphasis during each period

Figure 10.5: Example annual training plan for Athens 2004 Paralympic Games

---

CASE STUDY: Continued

Some shorter sessions would also be introduced such as 20 × 200m, not fast 200m but at 5,000m pace. Circuit training would continue as per aerobic conditioning phase.

We would target a few road races over 10km just to keep competitive but not tapering prior to these.

Competition preparation phase 1: May

In this phase weekly mileage would reduce to ~60 miles/week with a 4-day sharp taper at the end, prior to proving fitness over 5k at the Disability Sport England (DSE) championships. During this race the athlete would try new race tactics. Target 15:35–15:40min.

As the phase progressed there would be an introduction of shorter reps with focus on improving leg turnover speed but without sprinting. The athlete would feel strong but not necessarily sharp. This phase would also include two short track races.

Typical sessions: 4 × 10 × 100m, 3 × 6 × 200m, 10 × 400m plus 1 × 1,000m.

Following the DSE championship the athlete would have a few days rest prior to the big physical push towards Athens.

Speed endurance phase 2: June to July

First half of this phase included hills for form and leg speed. The focus was on 5k pace sessions such as 10 × 400m plus 1k. This key session was completed every week up to the final preparation phase. The athlete was encouraged to start running at 15:15min pace in key sessions, gradually reducing recovery time and increasing speed. However, they were advised that they did not need to get faster than 70s/400m. During this phase there would be one long session (e.g. 5 × 1,000m) every other week. Half-way through this block of training, circuit training would be phased out. The athlete was encouraged to enter a decent 5k race and a few shorter distance races. The main focus of the phase was to reduce recovery time and so develop both aerobic capacity and lactate tolerance.

Speed: August to September

In this phase recovery is at its minimum. Running speed was increased by using one short recovery strength endurance session and two speed sessions. The speed sessions were based around 200m and 300m reps with a typical session being 2 × 8 × 200m @ 33s with 40s recovery between reps and 5min between sets, relatively quick but not sprinting. Every two weeks a fast session was introduced, typically 3 × 4 × 200m @ 31s with 1min recovery and 5min between sets.

Competition preparation: final two weeks

The athlete would run a 5k session once per week with the last key session occurring 1 week before the Paralympic Games. Other sessions would be short, sharp track sessions. During this final phase there would be a further slight reduction in mileage with a taper occurring in the last four days prior to competing.

SUMMARY

The year's training went well and confidence was gained in the event with new tactics being applied successfully in warm-up competitions. The athlete avoided major injuries and arrived at the games fit and healthy along with a good clear mental approach to the event. The race itself was faster than expected and was won inside 15min. The athlete held onto the pace until the last 1k and finished a good 5th place in a personal best of 15:21.56min.

By focusing solely on the Paralympic Games and using every other event as part of the preparation the athlete was able to produce a personal best at the age of 42.

Wayne Buxton
Endurance performance coach UK Athletics disABILITY Programme 1998–2004

Take home message

The ability to develop endurance through training is a complex process and one which is dependent on the nature of the training being undertaken and the ability of the athlete. There are profound physiological and metabolic adaptations which occur in response to endurance training which can be classified as being oxygen utilisation or oxygen supply responses.

The nature of the adaptation is therefore dependent on the form of training being undertaken; therefore we must be conscious of the way in which we programme endurance training within the annual plan, ensuring a balance is achieved between the desire for athletic advancement and optimal work to rest rates for the athlete.

Endurance is common to almost all sporting pursuits and it is the function of the coach to ensure that the type of training undertaken therefore matches both the needs of the athlete and also the demands of the sport.

Further study

The following is a list of peer reviewed publications and boos which will aid you in your understanding and appreciation for the principles of endurance training. There are articles related to interval training, VO_{2max}, physiological responses to endurance training and principles of recovery training.

Achten, J and Jeukendrup, A E (2003) Heart rate monitoring: applications and limitations. *Sports Medicine*, 33: 517–38

Billat, V L, Flechet, B and Petit, B (1999) Interval training at VO_{2max}: Effects on aerobic performance and overtraining markers. *Medicine and Science in Sports and Exercise*, 31: 156–63

Bogdanis, G C, Nevill, M E and Lakomy, H K A (1996) Effects of active recovery on power output during repeated maximal sprint cycling. *European Journal of Applied Physiology*, 74: 461–9

Bonen, A, Campbell, C J, Kirby, R L and Belcastro, N (1979) A multiple regression model for blood lactate removal in man. *Pflüger's Archive*, 380: 205–10

Daniels, J (1985) A physiologist's view of running economy. *Medicine and Science in Sports and Exercise*, 17: 332–8

Dodd, S, Powers, S K, Callender, T and Brooks, E (1984) Blood lactate disappearance at various intensities of exercise. *Journal of Applied Physiology*, 57: 1462–5

Hickson, R, Hagberg, J and Ehsani, A (1991) Time course of the adaptive responses of aerobic power and heart rate to training. *Medicine and Science in Sports and Exercise*, 13: 17–20

Holloszy, J O and Coyle, E F (1984) Adaptations of skeletal muscle to endurance exercise and their metabolic consequences. *Journal of Applied Physiology*, 56: 831–8

Kubukeli, Z N, Noakes, T D and Dennis, S C (2002) Training techniques to improve endurance exercise performances. *Sports Medicine*, 32: 489–509

Myburgh, K H (2003) What makes and endurance athlete world-class? Not simply a physiological conundrum. *Comparative Physiology and Biochemistry* Part A, 136: 171–90

Noakes, T D (1991) *Lore of running.* 3rd edition. Champaign IL: Human Kinetics

www.everythingtrackandfield.com/catalog/matrlarch/OnePiecePage.asp_Q_PageID_E_ 350_A_PageName_E_ArticlesGeneralCoaching – Everything Track and Field: Articles related to coaching and training.

www.bases.org.uk/newsite/home.asp – British Association of Sport and Exercise Sciences: National body for sport and exercise science within the UK. Useful contacts and documents related to physiology, psychology, biomechanics, health and coaching.

www.mysport.net – My Sport: An online community for coach education and discussion.

www.elitetrack.com – Elitetrack: A website which houses both peer reviewed and lay articles. All papers are referenced and are either written by coaches or sports scientists. A very good resource for all disciplines within coaching.

www.verkhoshansky.com – Verkhoshansky: Site of Professor Verkhoshansky, which contains articles and data relating to training methods and responses.

www.athleticscoaching.ca/default.aspx?pid=7&spid=34 – Canadian Athletics Coaching Centre: Site containing information relating to coaching and sports science. This link relates to periodisation of training.

www.athleticscoaching.ca/default.aspx?pid=7&spid=35 – Canadian Athletics Coaching Centre: Site containing information relating to coaching and sports science. This link relates to training loads and structuring.

Chapter 11

Strength and power training

Strength is a key aspect of all sporting pursuits. The problem lies in that the strength required for sports such as power lifting for example, is very different to that of a marathon runner. This chapter will introduce you to the concepts of strength and power training and show how the athlete adapts to the various modes of training that are available. Discussion will also consider when and how to programme strength as a component of fitness in the annual plan. Therefore upon completion of this chapter you will have:

- understood the difference between strength and power;
- examined the physiological and mechanical factors within the muscle contributing to the development of muscular strength and power;
- addressed the different types of muscular contraction and how to tailor them to specific strength and power requirements;
- evaluated the physiological responses occurring in response to strength and power training;
- considered how to programme strength and power work into the annual plan.

Strength and power

Strength can be viewed as an integral part of most athletes' training programmes, yet there is considerable confusion surrounding the concept of strength development and its relationship to performance.

In order to best understand the principles of strength training we should begin by defining this as a concept. Strength can be defined simply as 'the ability to apply force'. This is a good way to view strength for it allows us to break down strength into its key constituents of force and direction (application). In so doing, we apply Newton's second law of motion:

Force (F) = mass (m) × acceleration (a)

Consider this statement of motion in relation to an athlete developing strength while training in a gym. They are aiming to enhance the amount of force (F) that they can produce and this development is a product of either the amount of load (resistance) moved (the mass (m) component of the equation), or the rate at which they move the load (acceleration (a) in the equation).

The relationship between the amount of force produced and the rate at which the mass moves to produce this force is inverse, as highlighted in Figure 11.1 which shows the classic force velocity curve. If the aim of a training session is to produce high amounts of force (F), it can only be achieved at the expense of movement (a) which has to be slow. Given the association between mass and acceleration the load (m) which the athlete will need to move will be high.

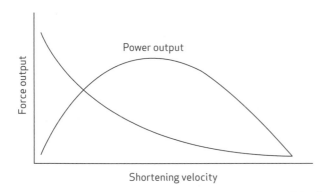

Figure 11.1:
Force velocity relationship of the muscle. As the force generated increases the velocity of movement or muscle shortening decreases, whereas if the applied force decreases the velocity of shortening and speed of movement increases

On the other hand, if we wish to develop rapid movements there will be a low rate of force development accompanied by a low load to be moved. It is the relationship between these three variables which helps define the form of strength development to be undertaken.

Components of strength

The ability to generate force is dependent on the length of the lever that is involved, in other words the length of the limbs involved in the action, given that longer levers generate more applied force.

There is also the issue of the degree to which muscles are innervated or recruited. Do we need to recruit lots of muscle fibres to generate the desired force, or do we need to recruit smaller amount of fibres more rapidly to generate the desired level of force production?

Finally, there is the issue of the amount of muscle mass involved. Are we recruiting large muscle groups for the development of force?

Muscle actions and contraction

In order to appreciate how the three factors can be linked to the development of strength and the force/velocity relationship, we should briefly consider factors accounting for the generation of movement within the muscle. At a very simple level, the generation of muscular force is dependent on the principle of feedback.

Imagine that you are in the gym performing a knee flexion/extension movement against a fixed resistance. As soon as you attempt to apply the force against the weights machine, a signal (afferent) is sent from the muscle via neural pathways to the brain, resulting in the recognition of the signal and promoting a response which is propagated back along on the neural pathways (efferent signal) to the muscle, initiating the muscle contraction. The efferent signal determines the degree to which muscle fibres are recruited and also the rate at which they are recruited in order to perform the specified action.

Because it is the contraction and innervation of muscle fibres that generates movement and ultimately the development of force, development of muscular actions and the rate of force development are dependent on the level of neural recruitment and the magnitude of muscle fibre involvement. Should you wish to gain a greater understanding of the role of neural recruitment in muscle contractions refer to the *Concept box* below.

Concept: 11.1: Neural control of force development

At this point it is prudent to discuss another key aspect associated with the development of the muscular force, that of the role of the central nervous system (CNS) and the neural control of force development. When we consider a muscle contraction, we tend to think about the mechanisms involved in the muscle fibres themselves, however we do need to address how these chemical processes within the muscle fibre are initiated to generate the desired amount of force.

The term used to describe the association between the CNS and the actual fibre is the motor unit which categorises all the constituent components involved in the generation of force, which are the motor neuron, the axon of the nerve, the motor endplate and the muscle fibre. The initiation of the contraction process (voluntary or involuntary) causes a change in the ionic potential at the motor endplate. The ionic potential can be best summarised as a chemical balance between the inner and outer membrane of the muscle fibre.

The innervation of the motor neuron generates a wave of excitation across the nerve cell with the subsequent spreading of this excitation across the motor endplates. This excitation occurs through a dynamic changing in the ionic potential with the chemical environment, thereby changing from negatively to positively charged. In other words there is a period of depolarisation followed by an almost immediate re-polarisation as the chemical balance is restored.

If the signal dispatched across the motor endplate exceeds the ionic threshold (baseline value) a further wave of excitation spreads across the muscle fibre as a whole, stimulating the release of calcium ions (Ca^{2+}) from the T-tubules within the fibre. It is the release of these Ca^{2+} ions that triggers the processes leading to the release and subsequent utilisation of ATP for the generation of the power stroke within the muscle cell and the generation of force. Therefore we have described the propagation of an electrical signal into a chemical signal and the subsequent development of force, which can be summarised by a term that is consistently used in the literature of excitation-contraction-coupling. Should you wish to gain a more detailed understanding of these processes you are referred to the book by Jones et al (2005).

A primary factor to consider when addressing the development of muscular force is that of the length/tension relationship of a muscle. This is directly associated with the ability of the muscle to produce optimal force and states that there is an optimal length at which the muscle must be held in order to produce its optimal tension and therefore optimal amount of force. If you wish to know more about the length/tension relationship of a muscle refer to the *Concept box* below.

Concept: 11.2: Length/tension relationship of muscle

Within the muscle there are muscle fibres, the number of which depends on the type of fibre and size of the muscle. This helps explain why there are around 172,000–418,000 muscle fibres in the biceps brachii compared with around 20,000 in the muscles of the finger. Each muscle fibre is composed of a series of myofibrils and each myofibril is composed of sarcomeres laid in series.

Sarcomeres vary in length from between ~1.2 μm and ~3.6 μm. The difference in lengths can be explained in relation to the muscle either being in a state of shortening (~1.2 μm) or lengthening (~3.6 μm). This state of contraction (relaxation through to full contraction) is associated with the amount of tension generated by the muscle. The tension in the muscle is directly related to the amount of force that can be generated by the muscle; optimal tension = optimal force.

The development of tension in the muscle depends on the degree of overlap between the actin and myosin filaments in the muscle and the amount of cross bridge attachment between the myosin and actin.

The myosin filament is composed of a series of heads which protrude from the filament. When biochemical conditions are right, these heads move in a 'power stroke' causing them to attach, pull the actin filament and then detach, in other words going from a state of relaxation to contraction to relaxation.

When considering the development of tension we are referring to the degree by which the myosin filament can attach and thereby pull on the actin filament to generate a contraction. Our understanding of muscle function shows the optimal amount of tension being developed when there is an optimal degree of overlap between the actin and myosin filaments.

However, a loss of developed tension occurs as a consequence of too much overlap between the actin and myosin filaments, preventing the cross bridge attachment from occurring. At the other extreme, we see very little tension being generated in the muscle this time the decrease in tension development is due to the actin and myosin filaments being too far apart to allow for cross bridge attachment to occur.

Understanding the interaction between the length and tension developed in the sarcomere helps to explain how an optimal amount of force is produced, for what we see at this microscopic level can be magnified up to represent the functioning of the muscle as a whole.

Muscle contraction types

Given that we have some appreciation for the mechanics of muscle contractions we should now consider the types of muscle contraction that exist and can be employed as highlighted in Table 11.1.

Table 11.1: Types of muscle contraction and their associated action

Contraction type	Muscle action
Static contractions	
Isometric	An application of force during which the muscle neither lengthens nor shortens. Isometric contractions are associated with a high degree of neural recruitment primarily resulting from the need to maintain the desired force despite not generating changes in muscle length.
Isotonic contractions (dynamic)	
Concentric	Under conditions of concentric loading the muscle will produce force while shortening, sometimes referred to as myometric muscle contractions. Concentric contractions are typically preceded by an eccentric contraction (see below). Concentric contractions require the use of energy to generate the muscle shortening.
Eccentric	Under eccentric loading conditions the muscle will produce force while lengthening, sometimes referred to as a plyometric contraction. Eccentric contractions are used to store energy, which is released to generate the concentric phase of a movement. Eccentric contractions are associated with a minimal amount of energy usage.

Activity 11.1: Muscle contraction types

Table 11.1 lists the types of muscle contraction that can be encountered and trained. For this task, reflect on your own sport and consider the following:

- When would you encounter each of these muscle contraction types in your own sport? If there are multiple actions within the sport focus on just one of the actions.
- For each of the contraction types, consider how you would train using a specific exercise that is relevant to your sport.

The linkage between energy stored during an eccentric contraction (which we can consider as potential energy) and the subsequent release of energy during the concentric phase (kinetic energy) has been termed the stretch shortening cycle (SSC). Imagine this relationship between eccentric and concentric contractions as a rubber band. If you take a rubber band and hold it in the palm of your hand it is benign and exhibits no potential for energy release. However, if you start to stretch the band you are not releasing energy through the rubber but providing energy through application of the stretch. As the band stretches, its stored energy (potential) increases until you are ready to release it, at which point the potential stored energy is converted to movement (kinetic) energy and the rubber band recoils and flies out of your hand. As with muscle the band has lengthened and shortened.

Types of strength

Given the association between force, velocity and acceleration and the length/tension relationship of the muscle, there are a variety of levels of strength, all of which have some implication for the coach and athlete. These are summarised in Table 11.2.

Table 11.2: Types and components of strength

Strength classification	Strength components
Base strength	This establishes the foundations on which all other levels of strength development are built. This is a key factor to be addressed in the novice athlete, and for all athlete types would be programmed into the preparatory phase of the annual plan. Weak foundations lead to unstable construction further along the path of athletic development.
Action strength	Action strength is associated with the specifics of the sport in which the athlete is engaged (see Chapter 8). The aim is for the athlete to develop this to the optimum and should be introduced into the annual plan towards the end of the specific preparation phase.
Maximum strength	This is often referred to as one repetition maximum (1RM); terminology used to describe the maximal amount of force that can be produced by engaged muscles during a voluntary contraction. The reason for this distinction in terms of voluntary contractions is that under conditions of involuntary contraction, the amount of produced force can be substantially greater (St Clair Gibson et al, 2001)
Muscular endurance	This reflects the ability of the muscle to sustain a desired level of force output for a prolonged period of time. It is the combination of both strength (general and specific) and endurance capacity of the muscle.

Table 11.2: Continued

Strength classification	Strength components
Power	Power is a product of the strength of the muscle and the speed of the contraction (SSC). Therefore it is the ability to produce the maximum amount of force within the engaged muscle group in the shortest period of time. Given the association between speed of movement and strength, power training is introduced only within the specific preparatory phase and only when a suitable level of base general strength has been established.

Adapted from: Bompa, T O (1999) Periodization: Theory and Methodology of training. 4th edition. Champaign IL: Human Kinetics.

When you are structuring an annual plan and considering the place of strength within a training period you must obey three basic principles: ability of the athlete, the specific requirements of the sport and the training phase for which you are programming the strength training block. In relation to the ability of the athlete, refer to Chapter 15.

With respect to sport-specific requirements, we must consider the type of strength to be worked on. For example, muscular endurance may not be necessary for a volleyball player, whereas power development and maximum strength would be. Then again a middle distance runner requires muscular endurance but maximum strength is not as important to their performance. Also consider that an elite, well-trained athlete will need to focus on the intricate specific strength components of their event, whereas a novice athlete should focus more on a broad based development of strength.

The programming of the strength components is training phase specific but should begin in the general preparatory phase where, irrespective of the sport and ability of the athlete, the number of strength exercises performed would be high. As the athlete progresses towards the competition phase of the annual plan the number of exercises reduces in order to focus on the specific actions of the sport (Bompa, 1999).

Activity 11.2: Types of strength

This task is designed for you to assess the relevance of each strength type to your sport. Therefore you should consider each of the strength types in Table 11.2 and rank them in their order of importance in relation to your chosen sport, using a scale of 1 to 5 with 1 being the most important and 5 the least important.

Constructing the strength training session

Each strength training session is centred on the type of strength requiring development and the phase that the athlete has reached within the annual plan. Therefore we need to address how to construct a strength training session. To do this, we need to familiarise ourselves with the terminology of strength; namely the terms repetitions, sets and load.

Sets, reps and load

When constructing a strength training session we must think about how many times athletes should train the muscle groups without a prolonged rest period. This is the number of repetitions of an exercise. The sets within a session refers to the number of blocks of work the athlete should conduct, each set being interspersed by a period of rest or recovery. The load refers to the amount of resistance to be moved in the session and varies from quite low loads (20–80%1RM) used in the development of muscular endurance to extremely high loads (>100 per cent) used in the development of maximum strength. Table 11.3 highlights the basic principles of association between sets, repetitions and load in relation to the various forms of strength.

Table 11.3: Constructions and parameters for a strength training session

Type of strength	Training load (%1RM)	Number of repetitions	Number of sets
Muscular endurance	20–80	20–250	10–50
Power	30–80	5–10	3–5
Maximum strength	>80	1–3	1–5

%1RM reflects the percentage of the 1 repetition maximum of the athlete, i.e. what is the maximum load that they can move (1RM).

As the training load increases (as determined by the %1RM) the total amount of work that can be completed (number of repetitions per training session) decreases due to increased demand on both the muscles and also the CNS, resulting in local muscular fatigue and/or muscle damage.

A number of questions commonly asked by coaches and athletes are presented in the *Concept box* below.

Concept: 11.3: Commonly asked questions about the specifics of strength training

Is there a particular way I should construct a strength training session?

The literature suggests that when conducting a strength training session it should begin with an isometric contraction of the engaged muscle group. This is because under isometric conditions, the greatest level of neural recruitment is generated under voluntary conditions, the so called Maximal Voluntary Contraction (MVC). This means that as long as subsequent bouts of dynamic strength training occur within a 2–3 minute window of the MVC, they will be done so under conditions of heightened neural recruitment meaning more of the required muscle fibres will be engaged, thereby enhancing the development of strength.

Are there other exercises that I can use instead of the MVC?

Yes. Sometimes it is hard for an athlete to complete an MVC so they could complete any action requiring significant increases in neural recruitment, in other words, activities requiring rapid muscular contractions such as sprinting and plyometrics. Although neural recruitment will not be as high as that seen from the MVC it will be heightened enough to be of considerable benefit to the athlete. Indeed this form of training, where strength training follows neural innervation training, has been termed complex training.

Are there any negative consequences associated with sequencing the strength training session?

Coaches and athletes report decreased performance and increased susceptibility to injury when they programme a session beginning with strength work and followed by neural work, such as when the athlete may need to work on muscular endurance followed by a power training session.

The reason for these reports is that strength training invokes fatigue onto the engaged muscle groups, resulting in reduced or depleted stores of high energy phosphates, increased levels of fatigue metabolites (lactic acid, hydrogen ions), reduction in the intramuscular glycogen stores and inducement of fatigue within the CNS.

The implications of these responses for a subsequent power training session such as a plyometric session would be that the muscles will already be fatigued and there will be a weakened level of musculoskeletal co-ordination both of which contribute to decreases in the precision of the task being executed and also to the risk of injury.

An often suggested method is the use of repetitions which are greater than the athlete's 1RM, how can this be achieved?

Let us refer back to Table 11.1 and the nature of an eccentric contraction. These contractions produce significantly greater levels of force than those exhibited through concentric contractions.

However, in order for the athlete to perform this action we need to use what is called negative work. This is where the concentric component of the movement is not performed and the athlete engages in the eccentric, resistive part of the exercise. The concentric part of the movement is negated by the help of a partner assisted movement, where the load is controlled by a helper until the athlete is ready to resist the load during the eccentric phase.

Imagine an athlete performing a knee extension exercise on a weights machine. The concentric phase of the movement is the extension of the knee from an angle of around 90° in the relaxed, flexed state to around 170° in the extended, contracted state. This movement can be extremely difficult at high loads or it may be that we wish the athlete to develop their eccentric phase. Therefore their partner moves the load to the point of maximum extension without any assistance from the athlete. At this point the athlete takes the strain and resists the load as they move from a state of extension through to flexion; this is the eccentric phase and allows them to work at loads in excess of their 1RM.

Concept: 11.1: Continued

Which is better for strength development, free weights or machines?
Before we consider this, let us briefly debate the relative merits of the two approaches which have been defined in the literature as free form (FW) (free weights) and fixed from (FF) (machine-based). Free form strength training is associated with the development of balance and muscular co-ordination due to the movement patterns involved in multiple planes (Cotterman et al, 2005). On the other hand fixed form strength training devices allow the user to maintain the required pattern of movement for the full range of motion. So given that this is the case it is not surprising that coaches and athletes alike report greater degrees of strength development following free form training compared to fixed form. Free form training can be used to replicate the movement patterns of the sport (specificity of training) whereas fixed form devices limit the replication of the actual sporting movement pattern. The implications are considerable in that the free form of training engages more of the synergistic muscles through the need for greater balance than the fixed form, thereby developing overall strength across the required range of motion. However, do not fully discount the fixed from of training as this is obviously easily accessible for all athletes and perhaps crucially is safer when either working with novice athletes or when training on your own.

Plyometrics: a specific form of power training

An enhancement of the SSC is clearly important to any activity requiring rapid muscular contraction or development of a significant amount of power. Traditionally power has been derived through the use of resistance based training programmes where heavy loads are used to increase muscle mass; it is now recognised however that this form of training does not increase the power of the muscle, rather it enhances its strength generating capacity.

Referring to Table 11.2, we see that power is a function of both the strength of the muscle and the rate at which the muscle contracts. Plyometrics, or SSC training, is used to bridge the gap between strength development and the production of explosive power. To best understand how this form of training works we must refer to Figure 11.2.

Under conditions of eccentric muscle loading, the amount of force generated is highest at high velocities (in lengthened muscle) and declines with increasing velocities (in shortened muscle). Therefore plyometric training is used to develop the eccentric phase of the SSC, where potential energy is stored to be released in the subsequent concentric phase.

According to Chu (1998) the only pre-requisite for an exercise to be defined as plyometric is that a movement is preceded by an eccentric contraction. If we look at the long jumper who wants to generate force off the board at the point of take-off – as they hit the board there is a dip of the hips and flexion of the knee and ankle followed by a lengthening of the lower limbs. The ability to take-off is therefore a composite of the amount of energy that can be stored and subsequently released through the muscles.

Figure 11.2: Force velocity relationship for both eccentric and concentric muscle contractions with the point of 0 velocity showing an isometric contraction

Adapted from: Jones, D., Round, J. and de Haan, A. (2005) *Skeletal muscle from molecules to movement*. United Kingdom, Churchill Livingstone.

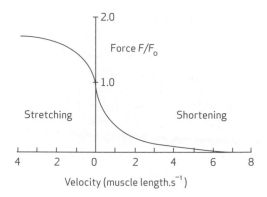

The more rapidly this energy can be converted from potential to kinetic the more powerful the muscular contraction will be.

The concept of association with time has been referred to as the amortisation phase, and it is this component that is developed through plyometric training. Given the nature of this form of training it is not surprising that the predominant physiological adaptation to training is enhancement of the neural recruitment of the muscle, therefore allowing for a decrease in the amortization phase.

A word of caution should be applied when using this from of training, for although there is enhancement of the SSC of the muscle, this can only be achieved when the muscle has well developed levels of both base and action strength. Remember that power is a combination of both rate of force development and strength of the muscle, therefore attempting to develop power without establishing a solid strength base is associated with reduced power development and increased risk of injury.

Examples of plyometric exercises

- *Depth jumps:* The athlete begins on a box approximately 50cm off the ground. They then step off the box, landing on both feet with the knees held at around 90°. As soon as this dip occurs they explode upwards onto a second box of approximately 50cm in height.
- *Overhead throw:* The athlete begins by holding a medicine ball (3–5kg) in the overhead position with straight arms. They then take a step forward at which point they bring their arms forward and release the medicine ball as hard and as far as possible.
- *Bounding:* The athlete is instructed to bound from one foot to the other over a distance of 20–50m. They should use an opposite arm to leg approach. The aim is to get distance rather than height on the bound.

Physiological adaptations to strength and power training

The purpose of training is to stimulate growth and thereby develop physiological adaptations which subsequently result in or contribute to an enhanced level of athletic performance. The primary adaptation occurring in response to strength training, such as that where the load is greater than 50%1RM, is muscular hypertrophy, the term used to describe the increase in cross-sectional area (CSA) of the muscle. The muscle fibre's response to training in terms of CSA development is associated with the magnitude of the applied load, therefore in order to move larger loads the athlete would recruit more type II than type I fibres, hence both would adapt but type II to a greater degree.

When considering the timeframe of strength development we see that the initial physiological response is neurological with increased levels of neural recruitment to the muscle. This is followed by a more gradual increase in CSA, but as CSA starts to develop, the neural recruitment development of the muscle starts to plateau (Hakkinen et al, 1985). These findings help to explain why athletes both report and show signs of strength development within the first few weeks of a strength training programme, despite showing no increase in muscle CSA. For a more in depth analysis of the physiological adaptations to strength training refer to Table 11.4.

Table 11.4: Morphological and neuromuscular adaptations to strength training

Parameter	Response
Cross-sectional area (CSA)	Following a period of strength training (>8 weeks) there is an increase in CSA of the engaged muscle. This response appears to be both gender (Cureton et al, 1988) and age specific. Females have approximately 60–80% of CSA, muscle fibre CSA and strength of men, while in relation to age there is a decrease in CSA. Increases of greater than 12% following nine weeks of training have been reported (Tracy et al, 1999).
Muscle fibre hypertrophy	Generally regarded as the primary adaptation to strength training. An increase in fibre size accounts for the increase in whole muscle CSA and is therefore associated with an increase in the number of cross bridges within the fibre, hence an increase in force production (Jones et al, 1989). There is however little evidence for a hyperplasic response.
Type II muscle fibre hypertrophy	A major factor in both the increase in CSA and muscle fibre hypertrophy is the increase in size of type II muscle fibres following a period of strength training. They are described as having a high level of plasticity and show a rapid response to training (6 weeks) when compared to type I fibres (Hakkinen et al, 1981). Hypertrophy is associated with the make-up of these fibres and has also been shown to relate to their high specific tension.
Myofibrillar responses	Strength training has been associated with both an increase in the CSA of engaged myofibrils and in the splitting of myofibrils, although there would appear to be no change in myofibril density (MacDougall et al, 1980). There is however data to support an increase in myofibril proliferation following training (Goldspink, 1974). There are a number of proposed mechanisms

Table 11.4: Continued

Parameter	Response
	responsible for these changes such as increases in satellite cell number and Z-disc spacing.
Muscle fibre typing	Following a period of strength training there is no change in the proportion of each muscle fibre type.
Myosin heavy chains (MHC)	Subtle changes have been observed in the expression of specific MHC isoforms following a period of strength training, with increases in MHC IIA and concurrent decreases in fibres expressing I/IIA and IIA/IIX (Williamson et al, 2001).
Tendons and connective tissues	There is no change in the proportion or arrangement of connective tissue following strength training but some evidence suggests an increase in tendon stiffness due both structural and hypertrophic responses (Kubo et al, 2001).
Neuromuscular	Neuromuscular responses are associated with enhanced co-ordination of muscle recruitment within the agonist and synergist muscles and decreased activation of the antagonist groups. The first few weeks of strength training are associated with increases in strength with little or no change in muscle CSA. This has been attributed to enhanced neural response. Specific neuromuscular adaptations include increased motor unit synchronisation and motor unit recruitment although there is no apparent change in firing frequency. Interestingly, a period of strength training has been associated with decreases in antagonist co-activation during the initial stages of a strength training period (Hakkinen et al, 1998).

There are some negative consequences to a period of strength training such as a decrease in mitochondrial volume and density and a concurrent decrease in the capillary network to the muscle (Chilibeck et al, 1999). This may not be viewed as significant for the pure strength athlete such as a body builder, but for sports with significant contribution from aerobic oxidative metabolism, this is a significant issue. There are however some studies (e.g. Hickson et al, 1980), which suggest that strength and endurance are mutually exclusive. Indeed more recent literature has suggested that a period of plyometric training rather than strength training can be beneficial to endurance performance through an enhancement of the performance economy of the athlete (Spurrs et al, 2003). The reasoning offered for this enhancement of economy and hence endurance performance has been associated with an enhancement in muscle tendon stiffness and resultant ability to store and utilise energy during the eccentric phase of the running cycle (Dalleau et al, 1998).

Activity 11.3: Strength training sessions

In relation to your own sport:

- Compile a list of strength exercises which are specific to the sporting action; your list should include exercise for training for power, maximum strength and muscular endurance.
- For each session, list the size of the load to be moved, the number of repetitions and sets and the recovery time between each set.
- For each session, provide a physiological justification as to why this session would be conducted.

Take home message

There is little doubt that strength is an integral part of almost all sporting disciplines. The fascination lies in determining which type of strength is important to which athletic event and how this strength can be trained. Strength must be programmed carefully within the annual plan ensuring that the correct form of strength work is undertaken at the appropriate time.

There are myriad physiological and mechanical adaptations which occur as a result of strength and power training, ranging from morphological responses through to neural and CNS responses. We must also ensure that when programming strength training we do so in an order which ensures the desired physiological adaptations but without causing undue stress on the athlete. Coaches need to be open to the need for strength training within almost all sporting domains whilst recognising that there is more than one type of strength.

Further study

The list below is a collection of assorted publications which have been selected to aid you in your understanding and appreciation for strength and power training. There are literature sources related to the physiological responses to strength and power training, physiological mechanisms of the stretch shortening cycle, plyometric exercises and periodisation of strength training.

Costill, D L, Coyle, E F, Fink, W F, Lesmes, G R and Wittmann, F A (1979) Adaptations in skeletal muscle following strength training. *Journal of Applied Physiology*, 46: 96–9

Folland, J P and Williams, A G (2007) The adaptations to strength training: Morphological and neurological contributions to increased strength. *Sports Medicine*, 37: 145–68

Hickson, R, C. (1980) Interference of strength development by simultaneously training for strength and endurance. *European Journal of Applied Physiology and Occupational Physiology*. 45: 255–263

Jones, D, Round, J and de Haan, A (2005) *Skeletal muscle from molecules to movement*. Edinburgh: Churchill Livingstone

Kawakami, Y, Abe, T, Kuno, S Y and Fukanaga, T. (1995) Training induced changes in muscle architecture and specific tension. *European Journal of Applied Physiology,* 72: 42–7

Lundinn, P and Berg, W (1991) A review of plyometric training. *National Strength and Conditioning Association Journal,* 13: 22–30

MacDougall, J D, Elder, G C B, Sale, D G, Moroz, J R and Sutton, J R (1980) Effects of strength training and immobilisation on human muscle fibres. *European Journal of Applied Physiology,* 43: 25–34

Nicol, C, Avela, J and Komi, P V (2006) The stretch shortening cycle: A model to study naturally occurring neuromuscular fatigue. *Sports Medicine,* 36: 977–99

Rahimi, R (2005) Effect of different rest intervals on the exercise volume completed during squat bouts. *Journal of Sports Science and Medicine,* 4: 361–6

Vernbom, M, Augustsson, J and Thomas, R (2007) The influence of frequency, intensity, volume and mode of strength training on whole muscle cross sectional area in humans. *Sports Medicine,* 37: 225–64

Young, W B (2006) Transfer of strength and power training to sports performance. *International Journal of Sports Physiology and Performance,* 1: 74–83

www.everythingtrackandfield.com/catalog/matriarch/OnePiecePage.asp_Q_PageID_E_350_A_PageName_E_ArticlesGeneralCoaching – Everything Track and Field: Articles related to coaching and training.

www.sportscoachuk.org – Sports Coach UK. National body responsible for regulating and overseeing coach education within the UK. Site contains information relating to coaching courses and contacts through to coaching resources and support.

www.bases.org.uk/newsite/home.asp – British Association of Sport and Exercise Sciences: National body for sport and exercise science within the UK. Useful contacts and documents related to physiology, psychology, biomechanics, health and coaching.

www.mysport.net – My Sport: An online community for coach education and discussion.

www.elitetrack.com – Elitetrack: A website which houses both peer reviewed and lay articles. All papers are referenced and are either written by coaches or sports scientists. A very good resource for all disciplines within coaching.

www.uksca.org.uk/uksca/Common/home.asp – UK Strength and Conditioning Association: Contains details of courses and coach education related to strength and conditioning.

www.sport-fitness-advisor.com/plyometric.html – Sports Fitness Advisor: Website related to the practical application of training techniques and principles. This link is directly related to the use of plyometric training and exercises.

Chapter 12

Flexibility training

For sports such as gymnastics and high board diving, flexibility is a key component of fitness within the annual plan. Yet we should also be aware of the integral place of flexibility within almost all sporting disciplines. This chapter will introduce you to the concept of flexibility training within the annual plan, focusing on factors such as the physiological adaptations to flexibility, modes of training and how to programme flexibility work within the annual plan. Upon completion of this chapter you will have:

- explored the factors contributing to the level of flexibility and range of motion within the limbs;
- examined acute and chronic physiological responses and adaptations occurring in relation to flexibility training;
- addressed performance responses associated with both acute and chronic flexibility training;
- considered the various modes of flexibility training and how the coach and athlete can adopt them;
- examined how to programme flexibility work into the annual plan of training.

Flexibility

The use of flexibility has become integral to the training process, both in terms of its use before and after a single training unit, or as a specific component within the annual plan. Previously we described flexibility as suppleness and can further define it as the range of possible movements in a joint or series of joints (de Vries, 1986).

As a fitness component, flexibility encompasses all the elements contributing to the whole musculoskeletal system, such as the muscles themselves, ligaments, tendons, bony structures, neural pathways, joints and even the skin. These factors which contribute to and also constrain muscle flexibility and subsequent range of motion (ROM) are highlighted in Table 12.1.

Table 12.1: Constraints to muscle stretch and flexibility

Component	Characteristics
Neurogenic	Factors governed by the neurological control of muscle stretch which can be either voluntary or through a reflex control.
Myogenic	Both the passive and active components of the muscle when being stretched.
Joint structures	Factors contributing to joint articulation such as the joint capsule, the ligaments and tendons. View these as being resistive components to the stretch.
Periphery	Encompasses structures such as the skin, subcutaneous fat and connective tissue around the muscle and joint

Adapted from: Hutton R S (1992) Neuromuscular basis of stretching exercises, in Komi, P V (eds) Strength and power in sport. Oxford: Blackwell Science, pp 29–38.

Activity 12.1: Flexibility within your sport

This exercise is designed to help you to consider the relevance of flexibility to various sporting disciplines. Using Table 12.2 fit the sports into the headings of 'Highly relevant', 'Relevant' and 'Not at all relevant'. Place a tick in the box of for each sport indicating the level of relevance.

Table 12.2: Relevance of flexibility to various sporting disciplines

	Highly relevant	Relevant	Not at all relevant
Boxing	❑	❑	❑
Swimming	❑	❑	❑
Cycling	❑	❑	❑
Marathon running	❑	❑	❑
Archery	❑	❑	❑
Gymnastics	❑	❑	❑
Ice skating	❑	❑	❑
Curling	❑	❑	❑
Diving	❑	❑	❑
Sprinting	❑	❑	❑
Rowing	❑	❑	❑
Canoeing	❑	❑	❑
Skiing	❑	❑	❑
Soccer	❑	❑	❑
Hockey	❑	❑	❑
Equestrian (rider)	❑	❑	❑
High jump	❑	❑	❑
Long jump	❑	❑	❑
Volley ball	❑	❑	❑
Sailing	❑	❑	❑

Although the aim of flexibility training/exercise is to enhance the range of movement of a joint or joint series, we should recognise that this flexibility is a composite of the factors which contribute to the whole musculoskeletal system.

The physiology of flexibility

The muscle stretch and response

As a muscle (sarcomeres) shortens there is an increase in the amount of overlap between the actin and myosin filaments (according to the length tension relationship), and when the muscle elongates (stretches) the degree of overlap between these filaments will decrease to allow for development of the increase in muscle length. What is fascinating about muscle plasticity is that once the muscle elongates and all the sarcomeres are at their maximum length (muscle stretch), any further stretch to the muscle complex comes through the connective tissues. These tissues also elongate and change their direction of orientation to that of the developed tension within the muscle.

So what prevents the muscle complex from continually elongating and in essence over-stretching and causing damage? The answer lies in the use of neural feedback and control which is regulated by proprioceptors located in both the muscle fibres and the tendons. The muscle proprioceptors are termed 'muscle spindles' and when the muscle elongates so do these muscle spindles. They are sensitive not only to changes in muscle length, but crucially also to the rate of change in the length of the muscle. Within the tendon are two more proprioceptors which are sensitive to both tension (Golgi tendon organ) and to pressure and position (pacinian corpuscles). So through the information garnered from these proprioceptors, CNS awareness is generated regarding the relative position and movement of the muscle groups and limb.

As has been mentioned the role of the Golgi tendon apparatus is to monitor tension across the muscle–tendon complex. For each muscle group there is a threshold value which, if exceeded during the elongation either due to the speed of the stretch or the amount of tension developed, is sensed by the Golgi tendon apparatus generating a direct response in the muscle termed 'autogenic inhibition'. This is very much a protective mechanism which results in an inhibitory response within the muscle, leading to relaxation and hence reduction in the amount of tension across the muscle.

So when a muscle is stretched this is sensed and recorded through the muscle spindle, which is also stretched and from the changes recorded signals are sent through the CNS. The result is the generation of a neural signal which causes the generation of the stretch-reflex in the muscle. The stretch-reflex is an involuntary response within the muscle unit which acts to resist the elongation of the muscle by attempting to generate a shortening of the muscle length. Interestingly, research has suggested that there are two components to the stretch reflex: a dynamic response which can be very strong but deteriorates over the course of the stretch and static which remains constant for as long as the muscle is elongated (Mathews, 1991).

So when we compare two athletes in relation to their flexibility, we are referring to their Range of Motion (ROM) and it is clear that the less compliant muscles or muscle groups will have smaller ROMs when compared to more elastic or pliable muscles. When considering the development of elongation in a muscle we recognise that the less pliable muscles will require a greater amount of applied external force to generate the stretch than more compliant muscles.

Performance benefits of flexibility training

There are many benefits resulting from a sustained period of flexibility training. Therefore we need to recognise the difference between short term or acute responses and those which are cumulative and therefore long term or chronic responses.

Acute responses

When referring to an acute response we are merely highlighting those responses which occur in relation to either a single stretch of the muscle unit or a non-progressive flexibility programme. Note that the acute responses are related only to the neurogenic and myogenic factors as listed in Table 12.1. In terms of acute responses to stretching it is advised that you refer to work such as Hutton (1992), however in relation to flexibility training we need to address the associated benefits which result from a chronic period of development.

Chronic responses

The benefits derived from a period of flexibility training are highlighted in Table 12.3.

An often-cited issue is that flexibility training is associated with a reduced risk of injury. This stems from the notion that the ability of a muscle to absorb energy during movement is dependent on both active and passive components of the muscle and the greater the ability of the muscle unit to absorb energy, the more compliant the muscle

Table 12.3: Possible benefits of long-term (chronic) flexibility training

Proposed benefit	Rationale
Increased ROM	The enhancement of ROM is associated with the development of either increased force or velocity of movement.
Increased ROM within a synchronous movement	Most sport activities require co-ordination of multiple joint articulations and muscle contractions. These movements are enhanced and level of skill increased when there is an increase in the ROM of the total articulating system involved. In other words performance becomes more technically proficient.
Increased contractile force	A pre-stretched muscle stores elastic energy which is released when the muscle contracts; this potential for elastic energy is enhanced with flexibility training.

Adapted from: Bloomfield, J (1998) Flexibility in sport, in Elliot, B and Mester, J (eds) Training in sport: Applying sport science. Chichester: Wiley.

must be. Therefore the ability of the muscle and tendon unit to absorb the energy is greater with more flexibility.

However, in a less compliant muscle (low flexibility) more energy will be absorbed by the contractile part of the muscle with little being absorbed by the tendon. On this logic we can suggest that in a more flexible muscle, there is reduction in the stress being applied to the muscle itself and hence less of a chance of suffering muscle trauma (injury).

It is this rather simple philosophy which has persuaded both coaches and athletes that flexibility exercises either as a pre-training session routine or as a part of a co-ordinated annual plan will help reduce the incidence of muscle based injuries.

However, the literature is not so clear in this regard with many conflicting studies either showing no benefits of flexibility training in the prevention of injury (van Mechelen et al, 1983) or a reduction in the incidence of injury through flexibility training (Witvrouw et al, 2004).

So why these contradictory findings? According to Witvrouw et al (2004) this inconsistency in findings may be explained by the nature of the exercise being performed. If the exercise is such that a high rate of stretch shortening cycle (SSC) is required then flexibility may help reduce the risk of injury, because these types of 'explosive' action require the muscle unit to be compliant enough to both store and release high amounts of elastic energy. Conversely, in activities that have a low rate of SSC, flexibility training may have no perceived benefits.

Flexibility training

Modes of flexibility training

When we consider flexibility and stretching work it is apparent that coaches and athletes use it as either as a pre-exercise warm-up/cool-down routine or as one of the components of fitness and hence to develop those physiological adaptations that have been highlighted in Table 12.3. There are two broad themes into which all flexibility training can be classified: general and specific. General flexibility relates to the overall mobility required for all movements and coaches and athletes recognise that some level of flexibility is required in order to perform any sporting action. Specific flexibility refers to a particular sporting discipline, for example that which is required for floor gymnastics is considerably different to that required for track cycling. Table 12.4 presents the various stretching modalities that are available for the enhancement of flexibility.

An issue that must be addressed is how to structure a flexibility session. There has been some considerable debate in the literature relating to the optimal duration for which a stretch should be held (Rubini et al, 2007). Indeed the range of stretch duration has been reported to be 10–480 seconds (s). This is a huge range and as a coach it is crucial to know where the truth lies. The problem is that the research in this area of training physiology is lacking and in many cases weak. The consensus from what literature there is suggests that a 10s stretch is as effective as a 20s stretch in improving flexibility. So how many repetitions of a stretch should be carried out? Again there is no formal agreement in relation to this so we have to appraise ourselves of both the limited literature and also with coaching practice. From both we can see that the consensus is three repetitions for each of the muscle groups to be worked but this could also be flexibility mode dependent.

Table 12.4: Methods for developing flexibility

Method	Description of the method
Passive	There are two approaches to this method, either using a partner or weights. In the partner assisted approach the limb to be worked on is moved by the partner without any involvement from the athlete to the maximum state of flexibility. This position is held for between 5–10s and then relaxed. The alternate approach is to replace the partner with weights but again ensuring that the athlete is passively involved in the movement.
Static	Under a static stretch the athlete actively moves/stretches the muscles to their maximum flexible state by flexing the agonist muscles while at the same time relaxing the antagonist muscles. This type of stretch is held for between 6–10s and is usually repeated three times.
Isometric	This is a static stretch only this form of stretching is conducted against an immobile force which prevents the limb from moving, but induces a muscle contraction and a high degree of neural recruitment.
Ballistic	This is where a considerable amount of tension is applied to the muscle but at the extremes of ROM and at high movement speeds. Generally associated with jerking or bouncing movements.
Proprioceptive neuromuscular facilitation (PNF)	This can be viewed as an amalgamation of the static or passive methods with the isometric component. With a partner the athlete will move the engaged limb to its maximum ROM at which point they will induce an isometric contraction for between 4–10s. The athlete then relaxes the contraction and the partner moves the limb beyond the pre-existing ROM. This can be repeated a number of times.

Activity 12.2: Modes of flexibility training

For each of the different modes of flexibility training listed in Table 12.4, detail a form of exercise that can be conducted and that would be relevant to your sport. Therefore for each mode listed in Table 12.4 you should list:

- The muscles/muscle groups that would be engaged;
- The type of exercise to be conducted;
- The number of repetitions and sets that would be performed and the amount of recovery between each set;
- The physiological rationale for each exercise listed.

Flexibility within the annual plan

In terms of developing flexibility, this form of training should be introduced in the preparation phase of the annual plan and should be reduced once the athlete progresses into the competition phase of the year. At this stage of the training year the overriding aim is to maintain the flexibility status of the athlete as opposed to developing flexibility in the preparation phase.

However, where most athletes and coaches are inclined to use flexibility is within the pre-training session warm-up, something common to most sports. There is little doubt that the use of flexibility post exercise is beneficial to the athlete in helping to reduce symptoms resulting from training such as delayed onset muscle soreness (DOMS) and general muscle stiffness (Cheung et al, 2003). However the use of flexibility exercises as part of the pre-training session warm-up routine has been questioned. If you wish to know more about the association between flexibility exercise and the pre-session warm-up routine refer to the *Concept box* below.

Concept: 12.1: Flexibility and warm-up

If you observe most athletes during the pre-session routine they will be undertaking or be encouraged by their coach to complete a period of static flexibility work as part of the warm-up. This has historically been part of the warm-up routine for many cited reasons such as reducing muscle tension, increasing ROM and reducing the incidence of injuries (*Sports Medicine*, Australia). Yet there is now a considerable body of evidence which suggests that a pre-training session stretching routine incorporating a period of static stretching is possibly detrimental to performance.

The literature base informs us that following a period of static stretching the engaged muscle groups display reductions in both isometric (Avela et al, 1999; Fowles et al, 2000) and dynamic strength (Nielson et al, 2001; Young et al, 2004). These reductions have been attributed to either a stretching induced change in the length/tension relationship of the muscle, whereby the muscle is actively stretched causing increased muscle length and decrease in the actin-myosin cross bridge attachments, or through an alteration of the neural control of muscle function. This latter point may be attributed to either desensitisation of the neural reflex within the muscle or to neural fatigue associated with static muscular contractions.

Why there should be such profound physiological responses is still being debated, but whichever school of thought you adhere to the overall impression and consensus is that static stretching prior to either training or competing is detrimental to subsequent athletic performance.

Take home message

Throughout this chapter we have come to recognise the role that flexibility plays within the annual plan of all athletes. We need to appreciate the physiological factors which contribute to both acute and chronic stimulation of the muscle and how these responses can be developed through the various modes of flexibility work. Flexibility is often overlooked as a component of fitness, but when considered, it is often misinterpreted within the structure of the annual plan. Therefore I hope that from this chapter you have gained a greater understanding of how to programme flexibility correctly within the annual training plan.

Further study

In order to assist your understanding of the principles of flexibility training the list below has been compiled. The list contains publications related to issues such as proprioceptive neuromuscular facilitation, static stretching and the association between stretching and athletic performance.

Ferber, R, Ostering, L and Granville, D (2002) Effect of PNF stretching techniques on knee flexor muscle EMG activity in older adults. *Journal of Electromyography and Kinesiology*, 12: 391–7

Handel, M, Horstmann, T, Dickhuth, H H and Gulch, R W (1997) Effects of contract-relax stretching on muscle performance in athletes. *European Journal of Applied Physiology and Occupational Health*, 76: 400–8

Hardy, L and Jones, D (1984) Dynamic flexibility and proprioceptive neuromuscular facilitation. *Research Quarterly*, 57: 150–3

Lucas, R C and Koslow, R (1984) Comparative study of static, dynamic and proprioceptive neuromuscular facilitation stretching techniques on flexibility. *Perception and Motor Skills*, 58: 615–8

Rubini, E C, Costa, A L L and Gomes, P S C (2007) The effects of stretching on strength performance. *Sports Medicine*, 37: 213–24

Sharman, M J and Cresswell, A G (2006) Proprioceptive neuromuscular facilitation stretching: Mechanisms and clinical implications. *Sports Medicine*, 36: 929–39

Young, W B (2007) The use of static stretching in warm-up for training and competition. *International Journal of Sports Physiology and Performance*, 2: 212–6

www.bases.org.uk/newsite/home.asp – British Association of Sport and Exercise Sciences: National body for sport and exercise science within the UK. Useful contacts and documents related to physiology, psychology, biomechanics, health and coaching.

www.athleticscoaching.ca/default.aspx?pid=7&spid=34 – Canadian Athletics Coaching Centre: Site containing information relating to coaching and sports science. This link relates to periodisation of training.

www.elitetrack.com/ – Elitetrack: A website which houses both peer reviewed and lay articles. All papers are referenced and are either written by coaches or sports scientists. A very good resource for all disciplines within coaching.

www.everythingtrackandfield.com/catalog/matriarch/OnePiecePage.asp_Q_PageID_E_350_A_PageName_E_ArticlesGeneralCoaching – Everything Track and Field: Articles related to coaching and training.

www.mysport.net – My Sport: An online community for coach education and discussion.

http://www.sport-fitness-advisor.com/flexibilitytraining.html – Sports Fitness Advisor: Website related to the practical application of training techniques and principles. This link is directly related to the use of flexibility training and exercises.

Chapter 13

Speed, agility and quickness

The ability to move rapidly over varying distances is a fundamental aspect of many sports and not solely confined to activities such as sprinting. However, the topic of speed is more intricate than simply a matter of getting from point A to point B as quickly as possible – rather it comprises many factors all contributing to the overall development of speed. This chapter will focus on the forms of speed, physiological adaptations that occur in response to speed training, modes of speed and agility training and how to programme them within the annual training plan. Therefore, upon completion of this chapter you will have:

- addressed the components of speed such as acceleration, reaction, peak speed and speed endurance and how each of these components can be trained;
- examined the concept of agility as a fundamental skill to many sports and how this can be trained and developed;
- addressed the issue of speed as a component of intermittent-based sports and how this component can be trained;
- considered how to programme speed-based training into the annual plan and appreciated the associated physiological and metabolic adaptations that occur.

Speed

As a component of fitness, speed is an integral part of almost all athletic events. Generally, speed is thought of as the ability to get from point A to point B as quickly as possible, as in sprinting. However, speed is an integral part of intermittent sports as well, such as soccer, rugby, hockey, etc., where the athlete is required to either sustain high speed for prolonged periods of time or complete a series of high speed short duration bursts of activity. For more detail on this component, refer to the section on intermittent sports.

Speed is composed of a number of factors which are highlighted in Figure 13.1. From Figure 13.1 we see that there are four factors contributing to the overall development of athletic speed. A summary of each is presented in Table 13.1.

Figure 13.1: Variations in speed, stride length (SL) and stride rate (SR) during an elite 100m race, where point A refers to the reaction to a signal, point B highlights the acceleration phase, point C indicates the top speed of the athlete and point D refers to the ability to sustain speed. Adapted from: Ae, M, Ito, A and Susuki, M (1992) The men's 100 metres. *New Studies in Athletics*, 7: 47–52

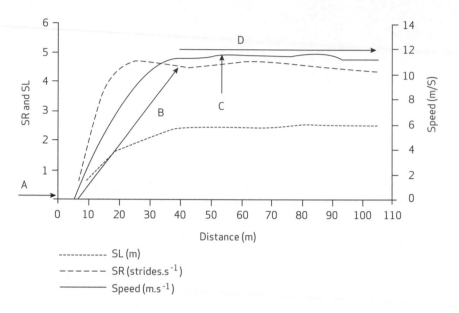

Table 13.1: Classification of the components of speed

Component	Underlying principles
A Reaction	Reacting to a signal or stimulus is an important factor in many sports, whether reacting to a starter's pistol or to a particular style of play within a team game. There are two forms of reaction: reaction to a known stimulus and where the athlete has a choice of reactions due to being presented with a number of stimuli.
B Acceleration	Acceleration is crucial in speed training as athletes cannot attain peak speed instantly but have to increase their speed until this peak is attained. The more quickly an athlete can accelerate the sooner they can reach peak speed.
C Peak speed	Peak speed is the highest speed at which an athlete can move. The ability to sustain this peak is dependent on many factors such as acceleration time, training status and speed endurance capability of the athlete.
D Speed endurance	The ability to maintain peak speed or a high percentage of the peak speed for a period of time is referred to as the speed endurance capability of the athlete. Therefore the athlete who decelerates the least will maintain their speed longest.

Speed foundations

It is perhaps not surprising considering what we have encountered in previous chapters that the development of performance-based speed is dependent upon having established a solid foundation on which the more specific aspects of the 'sporting' speed can be developed. As with strength training (Chapter 11) we should recognise that the foundation which we will classify as 'base' speed has to be established before we attempt to develop the more sports specific speed which we will refer to as 'action' speed.

Training methods for speed development

Before we consider the various approaches to developing speed we should address the notion that speed is closely linked to both strength and power developed in the muscle.

Considerable amounts of speed development are achieved through the use of strength and power work, therefore a speed based athlete must have an annual plan which combines pure speed work (listed below) with the more gym-based work presented in the strength and power training section of Chapter 11. Indeed the suggestion from evidence in the literature and most coaches is that in order to best develop locomotive speed, the muscles engaged in that activity must have been enhanced through either a pre-speed period of strength training or through a simultaneous development of speed and strength (Bompa, 1991).

In order to best address the training methods at the disposal of the coach in relation to speed development, we need to generate a framework that allows us to categorise the components of speed (highlighted in Figure 13.1) into domains of duration; in other words short-term speed and long-term speed. In order to do this we will break down the speed phases into those which are <6s (short-term speed) and those which are >6s but no more than 30s (long-term speed). This means that within the short-term speed training domain we are dealing with the ability to both react to a signal and also the accelerational capabilities of the athlete. The long term speed domain is therefore more associated with the ability to maintain peak speed.

Let us briefly remind ourselves about the energy demands associated with short-term performance. Most of the energy provision under these intense short duration conditions comes from the direct hydrolysis of ATP and the subsequent synthesis of PCr and glycogen. There is also the ability to derive energy from a process termed the adenylate kinase reaction where pairs of ADP molecules combine and through the use of the catalyst adenylate kinase produce ATP. Key points to bear in mind as you read through the following sections are that the ability to achieve peak speed is limited by the ability and capacity to re-synthesise ATP from PCr, while the ability to maintain this speed is dependent on both the ability to both re-synthesise ATP from PCr and also anaerobic glycolysis.

You should further consider that the ability to repeatedly produce speed whether short term or more long term is dependent on the ability to recover from the previous effort and thereby re-synthesise the utilised substrates (Glaister, 2005). To reappraise yourself of more detail of the interplay between the energy pathways and recovery processes, please refer to Chapter 10.

Reaction speed

Reaction speed is related to the exposure to a stimulus (e.g. a starter's pistol; fly half receiving the ball) and the subsequent initiation of muscular movement. If we consider this relationship carefully, we will recognise that reaction speed is associated with the functioning of the CNS and integration of the system with the skeletal musculature.

As a chain of events, the reaction to a stimulus works as follows: there is the exposure and thereby recognition of a stimulus through whichever receptor unit has been engaged (sight, sound, touch, etc.). This signal is then propagated through the CNS and interpreted, resulting in an effector signal being sent back through the CNS to the muscles to be recruited. This process is clearly very fast but there are many ways it can be enhanced through training to quicken the response to the stimulus.

So how is the component of speed trained? This is very much dependent on the specific requirements of the sport in which the athlete is engaged. However, let us begin with the form of reaction training that is most closely associated with Figure 13.1: that of reacting to either an acoustic or visual stimulus at the start of a race. Let us consider an approach taken by track and field coaches working with sprinters, where it is possible for athletes to be held in their starting blocks for anywhere between 1/10 and 5s before the starter's pistol is fired. An athlete not only needs to develop their ability to drive out of the blocks as quickly as possible but also have an ability to remain in a 'coiled' position until the signal is given, something which varies between race conditions. So an obvious form of training would be for the coach to conduct sprint start sessions where they will randomly vary the time that the athlete is held in their blocks, while at the same time instructing the athlete to react as rapidly as possible to the signal.

So far so simple, but the ability to react to the signal is dependent not only on the development of the reactive processes, but also on the development of an appropriate and effective technique. Although technique is discussed in more detail within this chapter we will briefly refer to its significance here. Given that the action is designed to be rapid it becomes more difficult to learn and therefore acquire. An approach that is often adopted by the coach is to break the skill down into smaller components (standing start, raised hand start, no-blocks start) each component being developed before moving onto the next. The key is that the reaction is still trained but the technique is also taken into account.

At this point you will have recognised that the stimulus to which the athlete is reacting is most likely in the form of an audible signal. Many sports, however, do not contain auditory signals but are more visually-based such as reacting to a serve in tennis, reading a deep pass in American football or reacting to the penalty kick in a soccer game. These can be viewed as the fundamentals to each of these sports and therefore the coach must expose the athlete to these processes and scenarios as much as possible. However, we again need to recognise that technique is a critical component to the development of visual reactions and secondly and perhaps critically the athlete has to be able to select the appropriate reaction to the stimulus. This skill is both innate and at the same time trainable but has to be developed and has been associated with the difference between elite and non-elite athletes.

Activity 13.1: Training reaction speed

The examples provided are generic in nature. Use this task to detail TWO types of reaction speed training that you either currently use or could use within your chosen sport. For each session suggest the mode of training to be conducted and the duration of each session/repetition.

Acceleration training

Acceleration is the time taken to reach peak speed and therefore can be viewed as the rate of change for any moving body. The understanding of acceleration is derived from Newton's Second Law of Motion which states that: *when a body is acted upon by a force, a resulting change in momentum takes place in the direction in which the force was applied and this change in momentum is proportional to the force causing it, but inversely proportional to its mass.* Therefore, we can define acceleration through the use of the following formula:

$$a = f/m$$

where a = acceleration, f = force and m = mass.

With reference to this, there are a number of specific speed-based drills that can be used to develop acceleration speed.

Resistive acceleration drills

This could be seen as a form of strength training in that the athlete tows either a weighted sled or a tyre over distance of between 10–40m, trying to pull the object as fast as possible. It results in the athlete moving at much slower speeds but using increased effort to complete the task. As a result there is an element of strength development within this action which can be converted into speed through the use of such techniques as over-speed training.

Over-speed training

This is a form of plyometric training particular for speed work, with common versions on the same theme being down-hill running and bungee cord towing for running-based sports. Both forms of training ensure that the athlete's limbs and body segments are moving at a faster rate than would be normally possible on a flat surface such as a track or pitch. It is used to encourage neuromuscular adaptation and what has been termed 'fast force' development with the optimum aim being transference to the acceleration phase of the specific activity.

These are commonly used methods in any sport where acceleration is a necessity, from rugby through to track and field sprinting. What, however, about in a sport such as track cycling where dragging a weighted sledge or using a bungee cord would be both ineffective and dangerous? An approach used is for the cyclists to follow in the wake of a motorcycle on the track. This allows the cyclist to increase their cadence and achieve speeds that would not generally be possible, with the reason being that being behind the motorcycle reduces the coefficient of drag (resistance through the air) to the cyclist, thus providing an effective and sports specific solution to the problem.

However, some caution should be applied to the use of these approaches for although they develop faster segmental movements, they have been associated with increased risk of injury and when used as the sole acceleration training aid, a decrement in actual athletic performance.

Acceleration sprints

These are used not only to promote the physiological adaptations occurring in response to acceleration training, but also to facilitate the development of correct technique under high speed conditions. The athlete will complete a series of phased sprints over a distance of 20–50m, ranging from paced jogging through to cruising then sprinting. This allows for the technique to be honed at the lower speeds with the aim of transference to the higher speeds.

Activity 13.2: Acceleration training

The examples provided are generic in nature. Use this task to detail TWO types of acceleration training that you either currently use or could use within your chosen sport. For each session suggest the mode of training to be conducted (resistive acceleration drills, over speed training, etc.), and the duration of each session/ repetition and the amount of recovery to be included between sets and repetitions and perhaps even the recovery between each set.

Peak-speed training

Given that peak speed is achieved only once the athlete has accelerated it is not surprising that there is a large overlap between the two phases of speed development. However, we have subdivided the training approaches so as to best exemplify the various approaches that can be adopted.

In order to best understand the approach to peak-speed training we need to re-address the principles of training discussed in Chapters 7 and 8. You will recall that in order to develop both physiological and metabolic adaptations we need to develop fatigue, which if sufficient and associated with recovery will induce a super-compensation.

This should therefore suggest to you that in order to develop peak speed we need to complete a series of repetitions interspersed with recoveries, rather than a single bout of work. As such the majority of training used to develop peak speed is intermittent in nature but the key point to remember is that the recovery needs to be sufficiently long so as to allow each bout of work to be conducted at the required intensity for that session. As such a typical track session may look something like 4x150m with 20min recovery between each repetition or for a track cyclist 4x500m with 30–40min recovery between each repetition.

These highlighted sessions also show us that peak-speed training is only conducted over a limited number of repetitions: too few and we do not create enough fatigue and too many and the athlete becomes fatigued both metabolically and neurologically and so does not attain peak speed in the later repetitions. The aim is for the athlete to exercise as close to their peak speed as possible which may result in them attaining a personal best (PB) for that distance/effort during the training session. While I was competing at an elite level, I came across many coaching styles and approaches, one of which related to peak speed sessions. The philosophy of one particular coach was that if the athlete (elite) attained a personal best during training, irrespective of the repetition number the session would be stopped and the athlete would finish training for that day. The reason offered by the coach was that, 'you can't get better than a PB so anything else that would follow in the session would be less effective'. You may not agree with this approach but it is certainly an interesting one.

As we are trying to achieve peak speed, competition between athletes is seen by coaches as being an effective method of achieving this. This can be achieved either through straight head-to-head competition (where athletes are of a similar standard) or through matched training. In the latter, the more well-trained athlete would complete a greater distance than the less well-trained athlete, thereby generating a hare and hound scenario. The other approach is simply to stagger the start time between athletes, with the slower going off first and the faster athlete having to chase them down.

Speed endurance training

This is often overlooked as a component within speed development primarily because of the overlap into the domain of anaerobic endurance; however despite this overlap it should be considered as a component of speed development. As with peak-speed development, training for this component is usually conducted with repetitions in excess of the race distance, but at near maximal speed with 90–95 per cent of maximal effort. Therefore the primary training method uses interval sessions based around the various methods already mentioned.

The sessions can be manipulated by either altering the duration of the trial or manipulating the recovery period between each trial. Speed endurance within the speed training domain will focus on ATP-PC and anaerobic glycolysis reserves. This is demonstrated in Table 13.2 highlighting the relative contribution of aerobic and anaerobic metabolism to various athletic events.

Agility

Up to this point, we have concerned ourselves with speed in a straight line direction yet as participants in sport and also from supporting data from the literature base we recognise that a vast majority of sports, the so-called 'field and court games' are characterised by changes in direction and the use of specific movement patterns (Gambetta, 1996).

Table 13.2: Estimates of aerobic and anaerobic energy contributions during selected period of maximal exercise

Duration of exhaustive exercise(s)	Anaerobic (%)	Aerobic (%)*
0–10	94	6
0–15	88	12
0–20	82	18
0–30	73	27
0–45	63	37
0–60	55	45
0–75	49	51
0–90	44	56
0–120	37	63
0–180	27	73
0–240	21	79

*Approximately ± 10% at the 95% prediction level. Adapted from: Gastin P B (2001) Energy system interaction and relative contribution during maximal exercise. *Sports Medicine*, 31: 725–44.

Before we address the principles of agility training we need to define what is meant by the term and thereby give us a template from which to establish our understanding. Herein lies the problem, for although it is recognised that agility plays a crucial in field and court games, no current consensus exists within the scientific community as to how to classify agility. This is discussed in great depth by Sheppard and Young (2006) to which you are directed for a further reflection on the complexity of the discussion. For the purposes of our understanding we will classify agility as, 'a rapid whole-body movement with change of velocity or direction in response to a stimulus' (Sheppard and Young, 2006). By adopting this definition we recognise that agility is a combination of what have been termed decision-making components (Abernethy et al, 1999) as well as the more physical components of changes in pace and direction (Sheppard and Young, 2006).

Training approaches

Using the definition of Sheppard and Young (2006) for agility we recognise that the training of this component can be focused on both the physical and cognitive dimensions of the sport. Crucially these two components are linked but for the purposes of training we need to view them initially as separate entities, especially in relation to the development of the athlete.

First, we need to appreciate that the agility training to be completed must be specific to the movement patterns of the sport, so as a coach you need to recognise the directional and pace changes involved in the action, the association between these changes and the decision making requirements of the sport. This involves our understanding of time-motion/notational analysis of the sport and also through the generation of test batteries designed to reflect the demands of the sport. Should you wish to gain a greater understanding of how to assess agility refer to the *Concept box*.

Concept 13.1: Assessing and testing agility

Highlighted below are a series of tests that have been used with selected sports, each showing how the test selected is designed to reflect the relative agility-based demands of that sport.

- *Soccer specific agility* (Balsom et al, 1994): This test was deigned to replicate the 'cutting' actions associated with soccer and the relative changes in pace. As highlighted by Svensson and Drust (2005), this test requires the athlete to complete a series of changes in direction and two turns. The more agile performers are those who complete the course in the quickest time.
- *Cricket wicket agility: 505 test* (Draper and Lancaster, 1985): The test requires the athlete to sprint over an initial distance of 15m whereupon they complete an about turn and sprint back over 5m. The performance of the athlete is assessed as the ability to complete 10m (5m going into the turn, completion of the turn, the following 5m). As such the test focuses on the ability of the athlete to change direction while at the same time maintaining their acceleration speed. Although this test was originally designed for cricket it has been adopted for such sports as netball and hockey.
- *Basketball lateral quickness* (Harley and Doust, 1997): This test was designed to reflect the typical movement pattern implemented during defensive plays. As such, the protocol requires the athlete to complete a series of six lateral movements across the key of the basketball court (6m). The movement pattern requires the athlete to use a side stepping pattern rather than a crossing over routine.
- *Decision-making assessments:* There is some information in the literature which highlights tests for decision-making ability, although many of these are not sports-specific. Recently, sports institutes have started to adopt an approach where images are projected in front of the athlete and they have to react to the image and then make the appropriate decision as to the movement pattern that they would initiate.

Finally, when conducting any test, whether it be for agility or any other fitness component, remember that you must ensure that the environment replicates that used for the sport and that the test being used is specific to the demands of the event. For more detail on tests of agility and other sports specific tests refer to Gore (2000).

When we consider training for agility we should associate the development of this component with the process of skill acquisition (Chapter 3). In so doing, the initial training processes for agility development must focus on the pattern of movement and as this becomes efficient, begin to introduce more of the environmental factors for the sport such as a basketball to dribble, cricket pads and kit to wear and carry and choices of pattern to be offered to the athlete.

Given the close association between agility and speed it is perhaps worth taking a moment to address the transfer of straight-line speed to the performance of an agile movement. The evidence in relation to this is quite compelling, for we are informed that sprinting in a straight line has little or no effect (transference) on the sprinting ability to change direction (Young et al, 2001).

Importance of technique to speed and agility development

Many factors contribute to success in speed and agility development such as genetics, muscle functioning and technique. Technique is crucial to all athletic events but perhaps more importantly when addressing speed. Given that speed relates to the ability to move the body or body segments as rapidly as possible it is not surprising to note that such ability is facilitated and enhanced through the use of a correct technique.

A considerable amount of time in speed development is devoted to honing appropriate mechanical technique which allows for optimal and effective muscular contraction and co-ordination. Many drills will also contain periods of paced speed work to ensure that technique is correct before the athlete progresses onto acceleration or peak speed work.

When training for speed endurance, fatigue begins to set in and there is a loss of technique and form. Because of this, coaches and athletes need to concentrate a considerable amount of time on ensuring that the technique is fully established at lower speeds before transferring to the higher speeds.

The relevance of technique to actions such as sprinting (Vonstein, 1996) and even rowing (Sheppard, 1998) is an important consideration. For example, in track cycling it is interesting to watch young, novice riders attempt to accelerate their machine from a standing start. The initial reaction is to sway the bike laterally under the perception that this will generate a greater degree of transferred force to the pedal. However, when we observe elite athletes such as Chris Hoy (Olympic Gold medallist) we see that the bike remains steady and the technique applied is a direct transfer of force to the pedals.

Quickness

Before we move on, we should briefly concern ourselves with the remaining term that appears in the title for this chapter 'quickness'. A recent trend among strength and conditioning coaches working with field and court games is to use what is termed Speed, Agility and Quickness (SAQ) training. We have identified and classified both speed and agility, but what is the quickness component?

There is little doubt that the term quickness as a component of training and performance is less clear than speed and agility and therefore much harder to define. Indeed, if we look at the limited data from the literature in relation to 'quickness' training we begin to recognise that the terms quickness and agility are used interchangeably, with quickness apparently referring to the ability to react (physically) and generate explosive power. So although the term is bandied around through the use of SAQ training it is currently considered as being an amalgamation of both speed and agility rather than a separate component of fitness.

Intermittent speed

Previously we have alluded to the fact that there are considerable differences between field and court games when compared to those sports which require linear applications of speed. These sports are defined as either intermittent or multiple sprint activities and so can be classified as being composed of a combination of brief but repetitious bouts of high intensity work (speed/agility) interspersed with more low intensity (aerobic) blocks of work. However, our understanding of multiple sprint work is also relevant to coaches working with speed-based athletes, for it underpins the physiological and metabolic principles which help to dictate the way in which speed and agility training sessions are constructed.

Energetics of intermittent speed work

When we consider the metabolic cost of this form of work we need to take into account both the cost of the speed-based action but also that of the intervening recovery between each effort. The consensus from the scientific community is that the mean demand is between 60 and 75 per cent VO_{2max} (Glaister, 2005). However, do not be fooled into thinking that the metabolic cost of intermittent speed work is relatively low, especially in relation to such activities as lactate tolerance training (Chapter 10). Remember that this mean value is an average of both the energy cost of the actual speed work and also the cost of recovery.

Interplay of energy and fatigue during multiple sprint work.

Given our understanding of the physiological and metabolic costs of speed-based work, we can deduce that intermittent speed training will be associated with the use of the high energy phosphates and anaerobic glycolysis, depending on their duration. So when constructing a training session that uses multiple repetitions of high intensity work, we need to address the interplay between the work done and the recovery between each repetition.

The ability to perform well in a multiple sprint activity is dependent on the underlying aerobic capability of the athlete (Chapter 10). What is meant by the term 'perform well'? In this case we are referring to the ability of the athlete to maintain the desired work intensity, without a significant power decline, by which we mean that the power output does not decline significantly and the time taken to complete the repetitions does not increase significantly. This has been highlighted nicely in a study where athletes completed 10 × 6s cycle sprints interspersed by 30s recovery in either normoxic or hypoxic conditions. Under hypoxia the power outputs were lower for the first eight sprints and then significantly lower for sprints 9 and 10 when compared with the normoxic condition (Balsom et al, 1994).

Some examples of intermittent sprint sessions would be 10x20m, with a walk back recovery, a session with minimal recovery which may be adopted in the preparatory phase. A session used for sprint cycling may be 10x10s with 30s recovery or 10x10s with 3min recovery, which given the differences in the recovery interventions, would both produce different physiological responses.

Physiological adaptations to speed training

There are myriad physiological adaptations resulting from speed training which can be broadly classified as metabolic, morphological or neurological in nature as summarised in Table 13.3.

Table 13.3: Physiological and metabolic adaptations to speed/sprint training

Component	Response
Metabolic responses	
Phosphate metabolism	Increases in specific enzymes such as myokinase (MK), creatine phosphate kinase (CPK) have been reported after varying periods of speed/sprint training. An increase in the rate of ATP re-synthesis has also been reported.
Glycolysis	Increases have been shown in phosphofructokinase (PFK) lactate dehydrogenase (LDH) and glycogen phosphorylase (PHOS) following periods of speed/ sprint training.
Aerobic energy system	Studies have reported increases in both succinate dehydrogenase (SDH) and citrate synthase (CS) following longer duration sprint training studies.
Metabolites	Sprint/speed training increases the intramuscular stores of both ATP and PC.
Intramuscular buffering capacity	Sprint/speed training is associated with enhanced buffering capacity as a result of increases in the body's natural buffers such as bicarbonate, haemoglobin, proteins and phosphate.
Morphological responses	
Muscle fibre type	Sprint and speed training results in an increased number of muscle fibres expressing type II characteristics and therefore expressing greater rates of force development and relaxation.
Muscle fibre size	Sprint and speed training are associated with increases in both type I and II muscle fibre area and total muscle volume despite no significant change in absolute muscle fibre size.

Table 13.3: Continued

Component	Response
Neuromuscular responses	
Muscle conduction velocity (MCV)	MCV increases as a result of speed/sprint training.
Nerve conduction velocity (NVC)	NCV increases in response to sprint/speed training with a concurrent decrease in the refractory period of nervous activation.

Adapted from: Ross, A and Leveritt, M (2001) Long-term metabolic and skeletal muscle adaptations to short sprint training: Implications for sprint training and tapering. *Sports Medicine*, 31: 1063–82

If you wish to know more about these specific physiological and metabolic responses to speed/sprint training refer to the *Concept box* below.

Concept 13.2: Clarifying the physiological and metabolic responses to sprint/speed training

Table 13.3 presents us with a number of terms and concepts which require clarification of their physiological significance but also their meaning and description.

- *Myokinase (MK)*: An enzyme which catalyses the re-synthesis of ATP from ADP.
- *Creatine phosphate kinase (CPK)*: An enzyme which catalyses the breakdown of phosphocreatine (PCr).
- *Phosphofructokinase (PFK)*: Key enzyme within the process of glycolysis which catalyses the phosphorylation of the glycolytic intermediate fructose-6-phosphate.
- *Lactate dehydrogenase (LDH)*: Enzyme which catalyses the conversion of pyruvate to lactate.
- *Glycogen phosphorylase (PHOS)*: Enzyme which catalyses the mobilisation of stored muscle glycogen into the glycolytic metabolic pathway.
- *Succinate dehydrogenase (SDH)*: A mitochondrial enzyme involved directly in the tricarboxylic acid cycle (aerobic metabolism).
- *Citrate synthase (CS)*: A mitochondrial enzyme involved directly in the Tricarboxylic Acid cycle (aerobic metabolism).
- *Muscle conduction velocity (MCV)*: A term used to describe the speed of an action potential from the motor end plate (connection of the neuron to the muscle) along the length of a muscle.
- *Nerve conduction velocity (NCV)*: A term used to describe the speed an impulse can be transmitted along a neuron.

Concept 13.2: Continued

- *Refractory period*: The period of complete inexcitability within the nerve cell following a period of stimulation.

What is the primary stimulus for the training response to sprint/speed work?
There is still some debate in relation to this but recent studies suggest that a primary factor in the degree of physiological and metabolic adaptation is the frequency of training undertaken, with training everyday producing no change in either peak or mean sprint power, whereas training every third day significantly increased both. Indeed, this is the approach favoured by coaches working with sprint athletes (Ross and Leveritt, 2001; Francis and Coplon, 1991).

Why do we see different physiological and metabolic responses as a result of sprint/speed training?
This is an interesting consequence of the type of training conducted, with the more short-term responses occurring in relation to acceleration and peak speed training (Jacobs et al, 1987). However, as the duration of effort increases or the recovery interval between each repetition decreases, the physiological adaptations also change with greater reliance on aerobic metabolism, resulting in adaptations associated with glycolytic and aerobic energy provision (Bogdanis et al, 1995).

Take home message

The development of speed is crucial to sports requiring rapid changes of speed such as in sprinting, team sports or racquet sports; however, we must recognise that speed is an integral part of the annual plan for almost all athletic events and disciplines.

When programming this component of fitness we must recognise that speed is a composite of other factors such as acceleration and reaction and that we may only need to train some of these components rather than speed as a whole. We must also consider the difference between general and specific speed and the associated physiological and metabolic adaptations that occur in response to speed training. When programming speed into the annual plan, we must ensure that the speed being developed is being done so at the correct time and is also of the correct type.

Further study

In order to help with your learning and application of the principles of speed training, the following list of literature based resources has been compiled. The list contains information related to the physiological adaptations to sprint and speed training, periodisation of speed training and the different approaches that can be adopted in speed training.

Allemeier, C A, Fry, A C and Johnson, P (1994) Effects of sprint cycle training on human skeletal muscle. *Journal of Applied Physiology*, 77: 2385–90

Bompa, T (1991) A model of an annual training program for a sprinter. *New Studies in Athletics*, 6: 47–51

Dick, F W (1989) Development of maximum sprinting speed. *Track Technique*, 109: 3475–80

Jacobs, I, Esojorrsson, M and Slyven, C (1987) Sprint training effects on muscle myoglobin, enzymes, fibre types and blood lactate. *Medicine and Science in Sports and Exercise*, 19: 368–74

Linossier, M T, Denis, C, Dormois, D, Geyssant, A and Lacour, J R (1993) Ergometric and metabolic adaptation to a 5-s sprint training programme. *European Journal of Applied Physiology*, 67: 408–14

Martin, J C, Davidson, C J and Pardyjak, E J (2007) Understanding sprint-cycling performance. The integration of muscle power, resistance and modelling. *International Journal of Sports Physiology and Performance*, 2: 5–21

McMahon, S and Jenkins, D (2002) Factors affecting the rate of phosphocreatine resynthesis following intense exercise. *Sports Medicine*, 32: 761–82

Nevill, M E, Boobis, L H, Brooks, S and Williams, C (1989) Effect of training on muscle metabolism during treadmill sprinting. *Journal of Applied Physiology*, 67: 2367–82

Simmonaeu, J A, Lortie, G, Boulay, M R, Marcotte, M, Thibault, M C and Bouchard, C (1987) Effects of two high intensity intermittent training programs interspersed by detraining on human skeletal muscle and performance. *European Journal of Applied Physiology*, 56: 516–21

Tabatschnik, B and Sultanov, N A (1981) Differentiated methods of training sprinters. *Soviet Sports Review*, 1: 45–6

Verkoshansky, Y V and Lazarev, V V (1989) Principles of planning speed and strength/speed endurance training in sports. *Journal of National Strength and Conditioning Association*, 2: 58–61

www.bases.org.uk/newsite/home.asp – British Association of Sport and Exercise Sciences: National body for sport and exercise science within the UK. Useful contacts and documents related to physiology, psychology, biomechanics, health and coaching.

www.elitetrack.com/ – Elitetrack: A website which houses both peer reviewed and lay articles. All papers are referenced and are either written by coaches or sports scientists. A very good resource for all disciplines within coaching.

www.everythingtrackandfield.com/catalog/matriarch/OnePiecePage.asp_Q_PageID_E_350_A_PageName_E_ArticlesGeneralCoaching – Everything Track and Field: Articles related to coaching and training.

www.mysport.net – My Sport: An online community for coach education and discussion.

www.sport-fitness-advisor.com/speedtraining.html – Sports Fitness Advisor: Website related to the practical application of training techniques and principles. This link is directly related to the use of speed training and exercises.

www.saqinternational.com – Speed Agility Quickness: Considered the primary internet resource for SAQ information. Contains resources relating to equipment, courses and literature.

www.verkhoshansky.com – Verkhoshansky: Site of Professor Verkhoshansky, which contains articles and data relating to training methods and responses.

PART 4

Athlete monitoring and evaluation

Chapter 14

Talent identification

This chapter is designed to provide an insight into the complexity and rationale behind talent identification programmes. We will address the issues of identification and how talent is quantified in a scientific manner. We will also consider the success and limitations to the approach and what the future holds for talent identification. Upon completion of this chapter, you will have:

- explored the difference between identifying talent and detecting talent;
- examined what is meant by being talented;
- addressed how athletes develop (chronologically) and how development is monitored;
- critically evaluated the stages of talent identification from young child to National/International calibre athlete;
- considered the future directions in athletic identification.

Introduction

A major concern for coaches and National Governing Bodies of sport (NGB) is the ability to identify potential and future talent. The ultimate aim for any NGB is to select and nurture this athletic talent with the desired end result being medal winning performances.

Talent identification has been used as a diagnostic tool within domains as diverse as education, the armed forces and sport (Abbott and Collins, 2004). The approaches taken by each discipline are based around a generic framework, but the intricacies of each approach would be somewhat different. What each of these approaches has in common however, is the need to identify the 'best of the best'; the so-called elite.

In its broadest sense, talent identification is an elitist tool used to positively discriminate between performers within many different fields. Consider the use of entrance examinations for public schools or university; they are open to anyone, but only those candidates producing the best results on the day get offered a place. This positively discriminates in favour of good candidates, but could be viewed by the candidate who fails as a negative measure.

In elite sport, athletic performance represents a significant interaction between both the genetic capabilities of the individual and also environmental factors such demographics, wealth, access to facilities, etc. (Myburgh, 2003). The identification of an elite athlete could be described as the equivalent of searching for a needle in a haystack. We are seeking special individuals from within our population, which means that many factors converge to describe that ideal athlete. An elite athlete will always be found at the extreme of a population distribution, simply because of their differences from the general population.

Despite these large odds on identifying the next Olympic champion, talent identification has become an accepted process by which coaches select and recruit athletes across a wide range of sporting groups, e.g. soccer, rugby, hockey, gymnastics and wrestling. Therefore, this chapter will explore the rationale for talent identification and how the approach can be used to identify athletes from the wider population.

Identification or detection

At this point, we should consider the difference between talent identification and talent detection. *Talent detection* refers to those individuals not currently engaged in any form of sporting pursuit, whereas *Talent identification* refers to the process of recognising individuals currently engaged in sporting pursuits who have the potential to become elite performers. Clearly, there are considerable differences in the approaches, particularly that of the engagement in a sporting pursuit, but there are also common features to both approaches.

Activity 14.1: Talent detection

Talent detection will not be covered in great detail within this chapter but for this task, consider the following factors when establishing a talent detection programme:

- How it would be set-up?
- Who would you target?
- How would age and gender affect the approach taken?
- What limitations can you envisage with talent detection?

The key point is athlete potential. The process of talent identification can only suggest whether an individual has the potential to become an elite athlete. Beyond this stage, the generation of the world class athlete is a combination of structured scientific and artistic support and in some part, luck. So in essence, especially with children, what we are addressing is their potential to excel. We predict from a series of measurements in childhood what they may be able to achieve as a mature athlete.

Athletic development

The time course for elite athletic development lies between 10 and 15 years from the onset of specialised and dedicated training. The research base shows that the highest standards of athletic performance usually occur in the later stages of an individual's competitive career. For a more detailed review, please refer to Chapter 15.

The chronological age associated with an athlete's best performance varies according to the sport, and appears to be associated with the optimal attainment of physiological development. What do we mean by this?

Sporting performance is a combination of skill, technical acquisition and experience (Smith, 2003). Given that different sports place varying demands on the individual it would be fair to suggest that each sport is constructed differently in relation to skill, technical acquisition and expertise. As a result, we have become increasingly aware that certain sports are associated with earlier attainment of peak performance than others.

Athletes generally attain their optimal performance at or around the point of maturation (Armstrong, 2007), in other words in the age bracket of 18–25 years. Therefore, given the amount of time taken to develop that level of performance, the search to identify future talent should begin with children aged 10–15 years.

As already stated, the attainment of peak performance is sport-specific and can be categorised as follows:

Early developers
- Gymnastics
- Figure skating
- Swimming
- Tennis

Late developers
- Soccer
- Rugby
- Volleyball
- Speed skating
- Distance running
- Cross country skiing

Activity 14.2: Early and late development sports

- Consider why the sports listed should be associated with early and late development.
- Make a list of other sports that would fall into these two categories.

The talented child

At some point a coach will have to consider how to identify a child with innate talent that could be harnessed to produce an international athlete? This is a situation that has vexed both coaching and governing bodies for a number of years.

Consider the following scenarios:

- Does the endurance running coach simply get children to run the desired distance and select those with the fastest times?
- Does the shot put coach get children to put the shots as far as possible with those achieving the best distance deemed to be the most talented?

A number of issues need to be considered before embarking on a talent identification programme. First, there are ethical considerations when working with and assessing children (see Chapter 15). Coaches and scientists need to take into account the legal issues surrounding working with children. They should always be fully versed in the law but at the same time, have a strong working knowledge of children's emotional and physical characteristics. Second, and no less crucially, any measurement that is conducted should be reliable, valid and specific to the nature of the sport/exercise to which it pertains. For a more in depth overview of these concepts, refer to Winter et al (2007).

Does simply measuring performance in young athletes meet these criteria and therefore identify elite athletes from within the population? The simple yet rather crude answer to this hypothetical question, is of course, 'No'. Identification is not a simplistic assessment of performance – rather it is a combination of factors which dictate athletic competence. Remember that performance is a combination of physiological, biomechanical, psychological and genetic factors which in varying quantities contribute to the overall athlete profile. Only measuring performance will not be a robust enough approach. Therefore what is required is a more prudent means of athletic assessment, in a form which meets both ethical and practical considerations while at the same time generating the data describing the athletic prowess of the individual.

Talent identification

Criteria for a successful talent identification model

How do we go about establishing a talent identification programme? The success of any screening programme is dependent on its ability to meet a series of criteria that can be both challenged and quantified. This is all about good science. Any theory that is put forward must be strong enough to meet a series of challenges in the form of debate and questions from the scientific and coaching communities. If the questions cannot be answered and the responses quantified, a new approach should be developed. If you wish to know more about developing a model or theory refer to Noakes (1997).

A model of talent identification needs to predict performance from young children, so our framework or base from which we begin must be justifiable. Abbott and Collins (2002) suggest adopting four key criteria which meet the demands of the talent identification model as presented in Table 14.1.

Table 14.1: Criteria for an effective and successful talent identification program

Criteria	Commentary
Positive discrimination	A programme must have the capacity to compare the performance scores of the individuals on the tasks undertaken. Therefore it should have the ability to discriminate between performances.
Appropriate norms	For any data to be of use, it must be compared with normative data from a suitably representative group.
Appropriate weightings	To make predictions based on data directing the candidate towards a selected sporting discipline, the weightings used must be justifiable. The relative importance of the selected test variables to a specific sport must correlate highly with performance in that sport.
Performance stability	In order for the talent identification model to be deemed successful, it must not only meet all the demands identified in the previous criteria, but also be based on assessment variables which remain stable from childhood through to adulthood.

Adapted from: Abbott, A and Collins, C (2002) A theoretical and empirical analysis of a 'State of the Art' Talent Identification model. *High Ability Studies*, 13: 158–78.

Spectrum of talent identification

Given that there is a range of ages associated with the onset of peak athletic performance, it is not surprising that there are phases of talent identification. Each phase highlighted below corresponds to the chronological age of athletic development.

The young athlete

Phase I of the identification process, is in most cases, associated with children from 3–10 years and is not generally coach-led. Rather, it would focus on the health status of the child. Medical-based screenings at this age are more concerned with the determination of pathologies than innate athletic ability.

It is however common practice to undertake functional assessment of key anthropometric variables. The primary anthropometric variables that are assessed in young children are height and mass. In the very young developing child, the ratio between height and mass has been shown to be a powerful indicator of growth and maturation in relation to the general populous (see Chapter 15).

In essence, what are being assessed at this very early stage are raw genetic phenotypes. As a result, we must consider two distinct, but interlinked, questions: why work with children at such a young developmental stage and what potential pitfalls are there?

It is important to ascertain if the young child has any specific physical deficiencies which could prove to be detrimental to long-term athletic development. A crude but apt example would be a child who shows innate physical ability but has a visual impairment. They would be better directed to more physical sports than those having a fine skill element.

Identification of health issues, such as musculoskeletal imbalances, cardio–respiratory complaints or metabolic syndromes early in the child's development will allow clinicians and related groups to either recommend specific treatments or develop an appreciation that the attainment of elite performance in adulthood may be limited unless an alternate pathway is adopted.

We have already identified that different sports are associated with varying developmental rates for performance. Sports such as swimming, gymnastics, tennis and figure skating appear to demand younger performers, so there is an urgent need to identify individuals who show some form of athletic ability at a much earlier age than for the late developer sports like track and field and cycling.

There are some problems and concerns associated with this stage of screening. Thorough clinical screenings do not directly reflect athletic ability; rather they provide evidence in relation to health which can be used to make inferences about future athletic performance. This can be a gamble in that we know that children who are healthy and show elevated growth rates, might be pre-disposed to athletic performance. Generally, at this early stage of screening the child will come from one or two routes.

1. They come from a family with a sporting pedigree (inherited genes);
2. They have shown outstanding talent for a sport in relation to their age matched peers.

The genetic inheritance route should not be overlooked as we know that many innate physical attributes are inheritable (Bouchard et al, 1997). Coming from good athletic stock is an advantage. The child who produces exceptional performances at a tender age may be directed through their family and/or school, or will potentially miss the chance to progress due to socioeconomic status and class, in either case, Stage I of the talent ID process is unlikely to apply.

Another consideration is what to do with the data? This initial screening may well for example, yield information for a child who, when compared to mass and age matched counterparts, is exceptionally tall. Does this mean that we direct that child into sports where height is a pivotal factor, such as basketball?

Consider what this implies: if you are tall at a young age you will be a tall adult. The approach can be applied more readily to the adolescent athlete but not so much to the young child. Also, despite the apparent associations between child height and mass with athletic performance, there are limitations with this approach. It may only yield data indicating early maturation as expressed by a growth spurt. Consequently, although ahead of their peers in terms of apparent physical attributes, there is a reasonable chance that they will not develop further and hence will not progress to the next stage of athletic development (Abbott and Collins, 2002).

This first phase of the ID process could be viewed more as initial health screening than pure talent ID. Notwithstanding, using this approach gives clear benefits for long-term future development, but these should be considered with respect to potential limitations.

The developing athlete

Phase II of the talent identification spectrum is perhaps the most widely recognised and applied component, with established methodologies being used and adopted around the world, e.g. Australia (Hoare, 1996) and Brazil (Matsudo et al, 1987).

At this stage, as with Phase I, the assessment is not sport-specific, but rather makes use of a series of measures that focus on components of the fitness matrix, anthropometrics and motor abilities. Table 14.2 highlights the measures used as part of the Australian Talent Identification Programme (Australian Sports Commission 1998).

Table 14.2 shows that these are not direct measures for any specific sport but that the measures of fitness are used as benchmarks to suggest that a child may have the potential to excel within a particular exercise domain. So how does this work?

In order to understand why such a broad approach is used at this stage, we need to appreciate the 'components of fitness' and how they relate to specific sporting disciplines. We have covered this to an extent in Chapters 7 and 8 in terms of training but we need to address them here in relation to athlete make-up.

COMPONENTS OF FITNESS

These have been used to describe both health and performance and reflect the key physiological and metabolic parameters of human functioning. In their broadest sense, the components reflect body shape/composition, muscular strength, cardio–respiratory functioning, suppleness and co-ordination.

In considering each, we begin to recognise how they describe both general health and athletic capability. So, although Table 14.2 is reflecting different terminology, the approach is the same, with anthropometrics reflecting body shape/composition, endurance showcasing cardio–respiratory function, strength and power reflecting both suppleness and muscular strength and speed relating to coordination and muscular strength.

Now what we have is a picture of overall physical capability but no real reflection of sporting application. This understanding can only be established once we appreciate and reflect upon the demands of an athletic event.

Table 14.2: Assessment variables as used in the initial screening profile of the Australian Talent Identification Programme

Component	Variable	Measure
Anthropometrics	Height	
	Sitting height	
	Body mass	
	Arm span	
Motor ability	Basketball throw	Strength
	Vertical jump	Power
	40m sprint	Speed
	Multi Stage Fitness Test (VO_{2max})	Endurance

Source: Australian Sports Commission (1998).

Physiological and metabolic demands of sport

We need to understand how the broad factors highlighted in Table 14.2 relate to sporting performance; in other words we need to describe the demands in terms of the physiology of different sports. We can then decide if, e.g. cardio–respiratory functioning is more important than muscular strength and so on. For an applied appreciation of training intensities and metabolic load, refer to Chapter 7.

It is also possible to suggest that events which are short in duration or require sudden generation of power (PCr) such as the 100m sprint would be associated with high levels of muscular strength and power.

We also know that a marathon runner would not be suited to the event if they were carrying high levels of excess fat; hence anthropometrics and body shape come into consideration. The two parameters that are less implied from the data are coordination and suppleness.

The suppleness factor can be considered in relation to sports where there must be a considerable amount of limb movement, such as swimming and gymnastics, whereas coordination can be related to sports where hand–eye and limb–eye synchronisation are of utmost importance, such as table tennis and martial arts. Hence, these very simple measures can be used to classify our developing athletes, in terms of both health and classification of sports, i.e. endurance-based, strength-based, etc.

This approach has some considerable advantages. Identifying components of fitness rather than assessing the key physiological parameters of a sport helps to prevent the child from specializing to soon. There is considerable debate surrounding this concept (see Chapter 15) with a number of research groups suggesting that earlier specialisation may lead to premature burnout and demotivation in adulthood (Bloom, 1985). Coaches and parents should consider this as being of paramount importance as we know that young athletes suffering from burnout will struggle to develop into elite performers.

The tests used for this phase of the identification process require the use of non-specialist equipment, which is also not particularly expensive. Furthermore, the administration of the tests does not require specific specialist training. As a result, we have a series of tests that describe exercise sporting capabilities and are user friendly.

There are however limitations to this approach. The initial stage of screening is extremely time-consuming, because in order to provide as many children as possible with an opportunity, a sample size in the thousands is required. We could work with smaller groups, but there is always that nagging doubt over whether someone has 'slipped through the net'.

Based on the assumption that initial screening is intended to assess as many candidates as possible representing the population as a whole, a smaller sample of individuals will eventually be selected. Those selected will have excelled in this initial screening, demonstrating that they display physical characteristics that could predispose them to athletic achievement, but will not yet have had a sporting discipline identified for them.

From this initial screening, a smaller, more select group of children will be identified. They will be assessed using more specific tests which should positively discriminate between performances as suggested in Table 14.1. The tests used by the Australian Sports Commission are detailed in Table 14.3, along with the sport for which they can highlight potential talent.

Table 14.3: Parameters assessed as part of the Australian Talent Identification Programme

Component	Measure	Sports
Counter movement jump	Lower limb explosive power	Athletics, baseball,
Vertical jump	Ability to spring in a vertical plane	basketball,
Cricket ball throw	Arm speed	canoeing, cycling,
Radar speed	Over arm throwing speed	diving, hockey, judo,
Forward shot throw	Upper body explosive power	netball, rowing,
Seated shot throw	Torso related explosive power	rugby, skiing,
Basketball throw	Upper body strength	soccer, softball,
Bench pull	Arm and shoulder strength	swimming, tennis,
Agility run	Agility	triathlon, volleyball,
10 and 40m sprint	Acceleration	water polo,
20m flying speed	Acceleration/maximum speed	weightlifting,
MSFT	Aerobic fitness	wrestling.
Arm/leg ergometer	Aerobic fitness	

MSFT: Multi stage fitness test, a non-invasive field-based measure of VO_{2max}.

From these measures, a weighting is applied to identify the importance and overall contribution of that measure to each sport. So for example, in a sport such as archery, which is predominated by fine motor skills, the weightings would be, e.g.: height 0.00, sitting height 0.00, arm span 0.00, mass 0.00, catch 0.38, basketball throw 0.31, vertical jump 0.31, agility 0.00, 40m sprint 0.00 and MSFT 0.00. For gymnastics the proposed weightings are: height −0.20, sitting height 0.00, arm span 0.00, mass −0.20, catch 0.38, basketball throw 0.19, vertical jump 0.21, agility 0.20, 40m sprint 0.00 and MSFT 0.00. These weightings should be viewed as correlations; in other words they suggest whether a particular component is positively or negatively associated with that sport. So where there is a negative value such as for mass in gymnastics (−0.20) we can recognise that as the mass of the individual increases the effect on performance becomes negative.

Activity 14.3: Tools for talent identification

Using the components identified in Table 14.3 highlight more sports that could be assessed using these methods. You should consider the following:

- The nature of the sport (endurance, skill etc.);
- The measures that could be used;
- The importance of each fitness component to the sport;
- Try ranking the fitness parameters in terms of importance.

This stage of the identification process should be viewed as being fluid, i.e. there is not a single test session that will classify an athlete. There must be an on-going process which assesses current standards and maps the performance criteria in relation to the maturation process. Some athletes at the onset will appear to be future talent but may fall by the wayside as they mature, primarily because they do not develop as was hoped.

The developed athlete

The third phase of the talent identification programme is primarily associated with National/International team selection. In order to meet the criteria for National/ International team selection the methodology used must be much more elaborate and crucially, sport specific. As a result, the tests performed at this point must conform to a series of established guidelines; these are examined further in the *Concept box* below.

Concept 14.1: Guidelines for test selection

Are the tests to be conducted highly correlated with specific requirements of that sport?
Here we must consider the components of fitness and the demands of the event. We know for example that an endurance athlete needs good cardio–respiratory development but not so much anaerobic power, so the tests used must accurately reflect the demands of the event.

Are the tests sophisticated and sensitive enough to highlight any physiological adaptations to training?
There are myriad of tests available to assess athletic performance, however the key is selecting the tools of the trade that are best suited to the task. Here we must consider both validity and reliability of the measures.

Has the ability of the athlete to cope with stress been assessed?
A major facet of elite athletic performance is the ability to cope with pressure and stress. Psychological screenings can be used to assess how well the athlete can cope with these factors. Although athlete psychology plays a major part in elite performance, its contributing factors are far harder to determine and assess.
Despite the limitations psychological screening is a requirement.

The guidelines should then be used to consider two issues in relation to athlete development (and particularly elite athletic development): first, is there still potential for future athletic development, and, second, is the athlete ready to compete?

How successful are such schemes?

Generally, data on the success of such schemes is guarded and not readily available for mass consumption. However, there is some data from the Australian programme which highlights the degree of success. The data presented in the Table 14.4 shows the apparent success of this scheme with athletes involved in the programme between 1994 and 2004.

Table 14.4: Athlete achievements at National and International level for testing conducted between 1994 and 2004

Achievement	Totals
Full Senior open performances	
Olympic Games representation	1
Senior World Championship (medals)	1
Senior World Championship (Top 10 placing)	16
Senior World Championship (representation)	23
Commonwealth Games (representation)	3
Commonwealth Games (medals)	4
Commonwealth Games (Top 10 placing)	5
National Champion	61
National Championships (Placing 1st–3rd)	239
National Championships (Top 10 placing)	577
Team sport performances	
Australian (Senior representation)	4
Australian (Age representation)	17
Stage (Age representation)	79
State (Open representation)	2
Athletes with a disABILITY	
World or Paralympic (representation)	1
National Championships	3
National age Championships (Placing 1st–3rd)	8
National age Championships (Placing Top 10)	9

On initial inspection, the data does not look very impressive with one Olympic games representative and only one Paralympic games representative. However, when viewing the data in the context of the sampling period (1994–2004) the results are more compelling.

The data shown was collected over a ten-year period, during which time the athletes listed would have completed all three phases of the Talent Identification process. By taking this into account we can make some inferences from the data. The initial screening in 1994 would have focused on children aged 7–10 years, therefore it is conceivable that many of these athletes would not have reached their peak athletic state by the end of the sample period. Bearing this in mind, the fact that the system has developed 61 National champions and a further 23 athletes who have competed at World level is testament to both the rationale and depth of screening conducted. Indeed as these athletes start to reach peak athletic status the number of Olympic/World medal winners should increase.

Limitations to such an approach

In order to ascertain whether a talent identification programme is truly successful, the criteria established in Table 14.1 should be examined in the context of the methodologies employed. In other words, do the criteria selected actually do what they suggest?

Positive discrimination

The ability of a structured talent identification program to discriminate positively between performances is comprehensively addressed in a review of the Scottish system (Abbott and Collins, 2002). The methodology used by most traditional programmes is to rank performances against a set of derived normative values for that test (benchmarks).

The data should conform to a normal distribution pattern, i.e. if the sample is large enough it should reflect the spread of the population within its recorded sample. Previous research and studies suggest that a better approach would be to follow the standard percentile ranking, but rather than presenting the data as a distribution curve, use a frequency plot.

Appropriate norms

As was suggested in Table 14.1, an appropriate set of normative values against which the test scores can be compared is of utmost importance. Interestingly, it has been argued that the test data does not need to be distributed normally, as long as the results can be compared with robust normative data. Therefore, what is required is a well-generated set of normative values that are reflective of the population group to which they will be compared.

So a key issue to consider is that the normative data must be representative of the population from which the test data has been generated. For example it would not be wise to collect test data from a group of UK children and use normative data from the USA because there are key sociological differences between the two population samples, and the National attitudes to youth sport would potentially influence the collected data. Therefore within the UK, coaches should be comparing their athletes to normative data from UK children.

Appropriate weightings

As Table 14.1 suggests, the weightings are used to calculate the relative contribution of each measure to the various sports. Think back to the section on components of fitness and the metabolic demands of an event. We can place a level of importance to each component in relation to the sport (weightings). There is logic to such an approach in that vertical jump performance is clearly important to high jumping therefore has a high weighting, while arm span has a low weighting due to the lack of association with high jump performance.

However, the approach has been questioned suggesting that it does not allow for precise discrimination between different sports. Indeed ultra-marathon competition and gymnastics show that physiological and anthropometric measures cannot accurately classify candidates into those selected events.

From this criticism, we have been able to identify two more key concerns to be addressed which are the age and gender of the athlete (Carter and Ackland, 1998). The validity and reliability of physiological and anthropometric measures decline with age, primarily as a result of physical maturity, which has a profound effect on an individual's physiological make-up. So anthropometric variables are less able to distinguish between athletic performance in children who mature late compared to earlier developers.

Furthermore, the data presented in Table 14.4 show no distinction between males and females, contrary to the case with current mass talent identification approaches.

The scores do not take into account the clear somatotype and physiological differences between males and females and the subsequent effects on sporting performances. As a result, there is a lack of positive discrimination between males and females, with females actually being negatively discriminated against.

Performance stability

Table 14.1 identifies that the talent identification process needs to provide recordable measures in children that will predict performance in adulthood, in other words, the measures need to remain stable over time. As a result, a key consideration would clearly be the association between age and performance ability, which as has previously been suggested is not a stable parameter.

The other factor to consider is the change in a child's physique over time. This variable is independent of age and shows large levels of annual variation in the adolescent (Baxter-Jones and Sherar, 2007). The change in physique can have a subsequent effect on performance, leading to either over or underestimation of the affected variables and the identification profile of the athlete. Once again we have a reason to suggest that it may not be possible to positively discriminate between athletes.

Where does this leave us? It would appear that coaches and scientists have adopted an approach which may not be as accurate and reliable as we would hope. As a result, a consensus has arisen suggesting that the factor which should be included and could help to positively discriminate between performances is psychology.

What about athlete psychology?

As previously discussed, there is compelling evidence to suggest that at the elite level of sport, the psychology of the athlete plays a pivotal role in obtaining a podium position. Indeed the concepts of athlete motivation, learning and coping strategies have been found to be key components of an athlete's make-up.

When athlete psychology is studied in greater detail we note that a number of contributing factors are powerful discriminators for assessing the difference between elite and non-elite athletes. Unlike inherited personality traits, factors such as goal-setting, imagery and commitment respond positively to training and have been shown to discriminate between medal winners and non-medal winners (Orlick and Partington, 1988).

This is further supported by the work of Thomas and Thomas (1999) who demonstrated that elite athletes use a wider range of psychological skills such as goal-setting and self-talk during both training and competition when compared with non-elite athletes.

However, the most compelling evidence relating to the psychology of elite athletes is that which highlights the ability of top performers to consistently maintain their level of performance.

The concept of performance maintenance appears to be independent of physical status, with the main discriminating factor being a combination of psychological traits such as the ability to cope with increased demands and pressures. This aptitude has been termed the maintenance of expertise (Kreiner-Philips and Orlick, 1992).

The relevance of an athlete's psychological traits to the talent identification process is apparent. It has been well established that elite athletic performance is a combination of physiological and psychological attributes rather than a single defining factor. Consequently, the use of psychological screening during the talent identification process could help to determine those individuals who have the capacity to cope with stress and emotional demands. Furthermore, psychological screening would help to define those children who are accomplished learners as opposed to those who have a reduced capacity for absorbing instructions and skills.

At present, this approach is not widely assessed within sport, yet there is good evidence from other domains which suggests that the most successful individuals think and learn differently to their less successful counterparts (Simonton, 1994). Therefore we need to consider that the ability to assess motivation for sport would be a key facet in the development and identification of elite athletes.

To date psychological screening is only used once an athlete reaches phase III of the Talent identification process, yet if the traits were assessed earlier the validity of talent identification models may be enhanced.

Activity 14.4: Athlete psychology and talent identification

Why do you think psychological screening is at present undertaken only in Phase III of the talent identification process? When discussing this question, you should consider:

- What is motivation and how can we evaluate it?
- What is stress and how can we evaluate the ability to cope with it?
- Do individuals respond to stress differently?

What does the future hold?

The future for talent identification as it currently stands looks promising. The models presented in this chapter have produced promising results, despite the concerns that have been raised and as with any form of science, it is an iterative process, one that will develop and modify over time mostly as a result of better understanding of the factors contributing to and hence potentially predicting performance. There is little doubt that as sport becomes both a political and economical bargaining chip that there will be a concerted drive to enhance and increase the validity and predictive capability of these models.

This chapter began with a statement suggesting that elite athletic performance was in essence a convergence of both environmental and genetic factors (Myburgh, 2003). To a certain degree current talent identification models take into account environmental conditions, especially if the Phase II screening is on a large scale. The genetic issue is however at present less clear.

An argument often used is that athletes are born and not made; this is what talent identification is trying to show us, however since the recent mapping of the human genome the idea of elite athlete identification may be about to move out of the laboratory and into the field.

A picture is being generated that outlines the level of heritability in the context of sporting and physiological attributes (Bouchard et al, 1997). Data from the HERITAGE study (Health, risk factors, training, genetics and exercise) suggest that heritability ranges from 20 to 75 per cent for selected variables including maximal oxygen uptake (VO_{2max}), sub-maximal oxygen uptake, stroke volume and cardiac output during sub-maximal exercise and exercise heart rate response to training (An et al, 2000).

Further studies have shown significant genetic influences in relation to muscle strength and performance, muscular adaptations to endurance exercise, vertical jump as a measure of explosive strength and the average size of type I slow twitch oxidative muscle fibres in the sedentary state and in response to training.

The current trend within genetic/exercise sciences is to identify specific genetic polymorphisms which can be related directly to specific physiological/performance attributes. Such a step forward could potentially change the face of talent identification and the way performance profiling works. In such a situation, a genetic test would be conducted as part of the traditional talent identification process. Indeed if a specific gene were to be shown to influence performance through a single physiologic pathway then its analysis and determination would be invaluable to the talent identification process.

Unlike traditional tests which assess the multiple interactive effects of genes on performance, a genetic test would identify individual genes, such as those for endurance, power or strength. So far considerable attention has been paid to the angiotensin converting enzyme (ACE) gene and its variants, with results showing significant relationships with elite athletic performance (Montgomery et al, 1998). These studies are the tip of the iceberg and the hunt is now on to find more genetic polymorphisms and their associated links with elite athletic performance.

Activity 14.5: Genetics and athletic potential

Consider and debate the moral and ethical issues surrounding the use of genetic information in the identification and selection of athletes. This is clearly a thorny issue and could be debated from both sides. Perhaps a suitable starting statement would be:

- *Genetic screening for athletic prowess is morally and ethically justified in the context of elite athletic development – Discuss*

Take home message

The ability to identify talent is a process driven by coaches, National governing bodies and scientists and one which aims to positively discriminate between elite and non elite athletes. The methods used have been developed and verified as robust tools as long as the prerequisites identified by Abbott and Collins (2002) are adhered to.

There is little doubt that such an approach has greater success on a large scale although this could be argued as being a measure of statistical power, however the data from Australia is testament to the success of a system. The issues of measurement, the population sample to whom the measures relate and the need for psychological screening are all factors that will need addressing in the ever developing sphere of coach education.

The process of elite athlete identification is advancing at a rapid rate and soon coaches and athletes may be faced with the prospect of genetic screening to assess their athletic potential.

Further study

The following is a list of publications, which will help you in your learning and appreciation of the process of talent identification. The list includes literature related to the association between genetics and performance, the application of talent identification models to specific sports and the relationship between specialisation in sport and the development of talent.

An, P, Rice, T, Gagnon, J, Leon, A S, Skinner, J S, Bouchard, C, Rao, D C and Wilmore, J H (2000) Familial aggregation of stroke volume and cardiac output during submaximal exercise: The HERITAGE family Study. *International Journal of Sports Medicine*, 21: 566–72

Australian Sports Commission. (1998) National talent identification and development program: General testing protocols. www.ausport.gov.au/eTID

Baker, J (2003) Early specialisation in youth sport: A requirement for adult expertise. *High Ability Studies*, 14: 85–96

Dettweiler, A, Daehne, H O and Loots, J M (1991) Physical and physiological aspects of participants in the 1987–1988 Ultraman competition. *South African Journal of Research in Sport Physical Activity and Recreation*, 14: 23–31

Maes, H H, Beunen, G P, Vietinck, R F, Neale, M C, Thomis, M, Vanden Eynde, B, Lysens, R, Simons, J, Derom, C and Derom, R (1996) Inheritance of physical fitness in 10 year old twins and their parents. *Medicine and Science in Sports and Exercise*, 28: 1479–92

Nieuwenhuis, C F, Spamer, E J and Van Rossum, J H A (2002) Prediction function for identifying talent in 14–15 year old female field hockey players. *High Ability Studies*, 13: 20–33

Piennar, A E and Spamer, E J (1998) A longitudinal study of talented young rugby players as regards their rugby skills, physical and motor abilities and anthropometric data. *Journal of Human Movement Studies*, 14: 13–32

Reilly, T, Williams, A M, Nevill, A and Franks, A (2000) A multidisciplinary approach to talent identification in soccer. *Journal of Sports Sciences*, 18: 695–702

Siminton, D, K. (1994) *Greatness: Who makes history and why.* New York, Gilford.

Van Der Walt, T S P (1988) Anthropometrical typecasting amongst competitors in different Olympic events [in Africaans]. *Journal of Sports Sciences*, 18: 183–9

Woods, D R, Hickman, M, Jamshidi, Y, Brull, D, Vassiliou, V, Jones, A, Humphries, S and Montgomery, H (2001) Elite swimmers and the D allele of the ACE I/D polymorphism. *Human Genetics*, 108:230–2

www.ais.org.au/talent/index.asp – Australian Institute of Sport: Massive website devoted to the promotion of elite performance and sport within Australia. This specific link takes you to articles related to Talent Identification programmes within Australia.

www.eis2win.co.uk/gen/wwd_talentid.aspx – English Institute of Sport: National organisation who support and work with elite athletes in England. This link is directly related to Talent Identification processes within the UK.

www.sportdevelopment.org.uk/index.html – Sports Development. A UK-based web resource which acts as a searchable database for articles and research related to sport.

www.uksport.gov.uk – UK Sport. National body supporting elite world class performers. Useful resources related to coach education and drug free sport.

Chapter 15

Long-term athlete development

The purpose of this chapter is to develop your understanding of the stages of athlete development from childhood through adulthood to retirement from sport. This whole approach is centred on the maturation and development status of the athlete rather than their chronological age. On completion of this chapter you will have:

- explored the issues related to the timeframe for development of an elite level champion athlete;
- examined the issues related to early and late specialisation sports and how they can be considered in relation to the developmental plan for an athlete;
- critically reflected upon the difference between chronological age and developmental age and how this is integral to the process of long-term athlete development;
- investigated and appraised the seven stages of athlete development and examined how the athlete's developmental status transcends these stages and the nature of training and competing that they undertake;
- studied the processes of long-term athlete development in an applied manner;
- understood potential limitations with such an approach.

Introduction

A fundamental key in the coach/athlete relationship is the development of the athlete's capabilities over a prolonged period of time, in order to reach the desired athletic goal. The development of 'athletic potential' is a long haul requiring stringent planning and support from the coach.

This concept of the 'long haul' is in stark contrast to many more traditional approaches to coaching and athlete development, where there is a desire for top performances immediately. Sport, like business, is driven by the attainment of results, with short-term gain outweighing the desire for long-term development, where results are not the primary goal.

There is a famous saying which states that, *Rome was not built in a day*, this is the same for the development of athletes. Yes, we can gain short-term results in a young performer by loading on high volumes of training, but at what cost? As previously suggested, there is good evidence that introducing high levels of volume and intensity of training at a young age will lead to athlete burnout and dropout. How often have we watched sport and seen the new young protégé appear, only for them to disappear soon after, due to long-term injury or disillusionment with the sport?

An approach that is being openly advocated and promoted as being appropriate for bringing on athletes in a controlled manner, is through the use of a structured framework encompassing an understanding of the developmental stage of the athlete but also encouraging greater synergy and co-operation between coaches, National Governing Bodies, schools and athletes.

This chapter will explore the concept of long-term athlete development and show how using a structured plan can increase the numbers of fully-developed and peaked athletes.

How long does it take to create a champion?

Empirical data and observations from coaches have demonstrated that the process of athlete development takes around 10–15 years, with many National Governing Bodies of Sport citing the '10-year rule'; in other words, 10 years are needed to develop the athlete.

When considering this value we should do so in the context of the general consensus which suggests that the path to elite athlete development begins at 12.0 years for males and 11.5 years for females.

Further when we examine this path we must consider how much work for the athlete and coach this 10-year plan would entail. Data suggests that this 10-year plan can be equated to 10,000h of training or the equivalent of training and/or competing for just over 3h/day for every day of the 10-year block (Salmela et al, 1998). This is a long, sustained period of continued motivation and commitment to the goal by both the coach and athlete.

However, we need to consider this initial concept with some caution, primarily because a 10-year block of training does not guarantee success; free forms of training in this period will struggle to yield potential, whereas a structured developmental plan should be more successful.

Basics of long-term development

Traditional contemporary approaches to sports participation and coaching focus on the chronological age of the athlete, with children and young adults training and competing in groups of peers of similar age. Think about sports such as soccer, where young players compete at levels of around 10–12 years, 13–15 years, 16–18 years and so on. We see the same approach in track and field, swimming and most of the mainstream sports which aim to encourage sports participation from a young age. It is worth noting however, that recently the FA have adopted a new approach to player progression based on the long-term athlete development (LTAD) model.

As coaches, we are fully aware that there are both early and late developers in all sports, yet conventional approaches to training do not address this. The concept of LTAD is to structure athlete development in response to the developmental level of the athlete (maturation) rather than chronological age. Therefore when we address the structures implemented in LTAD we see that they focus on the physical, psychological and emotional development of both children and adolescents, with progression to each stage being determined by developmental level rather than chronological age.

Although there are a number of LTAD plans in existence, almost all have as a common theme or thread the stages of athlete development.

The general consensus is that there are seven stages to athlete development which must be addressed in order to optimise athlete potential.

Developmental and chronological age

To understand how an athlete or child develops we need to understand the differences between chronological age and developmental age and the interplay between growth and maturation. The terms 'growth' and 'maturation' tend to be used interchangeably when in fact they should be viewed individually and then as a package.

Growth refers to the observable changes in physical characteristics such as height, mass and percentage body fat content. Note that these parameters are easily measurable and can be recorded to observe the growth changes in the child/athlete. When considering maturation we are addressing the progression of the body towards 'maturity', including such developments as the conversion of cartilage to bone. The relationship between maturation and growth gives us what is termed 'development'. Development highlights the relationship between these two parameters in relation to the passage of time.

We should not however become preoccupied with the physical developments of the child and athlete for we should also consider that development encompasses such domains as emotional, sociological, intellectual and motor advancement. Extending this concept further, we see that developmental age represents the level of maturity within the physical, emotional and psychological domains.

Chronological age relates to the number of days and hence time since birth. Although this seems to be quite a simple concept it has fundamental consequences for the coach, in that children of the same chronological age can show differences in biological maturity and development of 3–4 years. It is the difference between chronological age and developmental progression that is crucial to the coaching process and implementation of the LTAD plan.

A consistent message coming from the LTAD plans currently used at international level is the need to identify the stage of maturation, in order to establish training and competition plans that respond to the athlete's development. How do we determine the level of development of the athlete? The common approach is to determine the peak height velocity (PHV), which is an expression of the association between stature (height) and chronological age. This is considered in more detail in the *Concept box*.

Concept 15.1: Peak height velocity: mechanisms and applications

This is perhaps the most widely accepted and recognised method for the determination of maturity and onset of development. The practitioner looks for the association between chronological age and the change in stretch stature (height). The basic premise is to track the age and height of the individual over time, thereby making this a protracted longitudinal study.

By following the child's height–growth charts we can calculate the age at peak height velocity (APHV). Data from a large scale study in the UK demonstrated that girls attain PHV anywhere between 9.3 and 15 years with boys reaching PHV between 12.0 and 15.8 years (Malina et al, 2004). The limitation to this as a diagnostic tool for use by coaches is the requirement of data collection over a prolonged period of time in order to determine APHV.

Another, less demanding, but also less reliable option is to use a developed regression equation to predict the APHV, such as that developed by Mirwald et al (2002).

According to the authors, it can predict the APHV±1.0 years in 95 per cent of cases. The derived formula calculates the interaction factors between various anthropometric variables. The values measured are: age, height (cm), mass (kg), sitting height (cm) and leg length (cm). The regression formula used is as follows:

PHV = maturity offset + chronological age

Maturity offset = (9.236 + (0.0002708 × leg length-sitting height interaction) + ((0.001663 × age-leg length interaction) + (0.007216 × age-sitting height interaction) + (0.02292 × mass to height ratio).

Interactions are calculated by multiplying the two factors.

The advantage to this method is that it does not require a longitudinal study to be conducted and therefore allows us to make a prediction as to the APHV and therefore athlete development.

The main limitation is that it is a prediction equation so the determination is only as good as the regression model that has been produced. An error of ±1.0 years seems to be quite good, but when viewed in the context of the 10-year plan could reduce the time to peak athletic development by 10 per cent.

Stages of athlete development

The seven stages to LTAD are highlighted in Table 15.1 indicating both the outline of the stage and the associated chronological and developmental age.

There are some sports where peak development is associated with younger ages (gymnastics, swimming, etc.) as compared with other sports, where peak development age is somewhat older (endurance sports, power sports, etc.).

This poses an interesting question, i.e. whether the model applies to both early specialisation (gymnastics) and late specialisation (endurance) sports. The answer is: 'No, not fully'! The seven-stage model works for late specialisation sports but needs

Table 15.1: Stages of long-term athlete development

Stage	Chronological and developmental age (years)
Sport for all	
Stage 1: Active start	Males and females 0–6
Stage 2: FUNdamentals	Males 6–9; Females 6–8
Stage 3: Learning to train	Males 9–12; Females 8–11
Excellence	
Stage 4: Training to train	Males 12–6; Females 11–15
Stage 5: Training to compete	Males 16–23; Females 15–21
Stage 6: Training to win	Males -19; Females -18
Lifelong physical activity	
Stage 7: Active for life	Enter at any age

manipulation to incorporate the early specialisation athletes. In order to incorporate these sports, the initial few stages are adjusted by amalgamating current stages 2, 3 and 4 (FUNdamentals, Training to train and Training to compete) into one stage which would be defined as Stage 2. From then on, the model would follow the same developmental pattern as seen for late developers.

When considering the difference between early and late specialisation, we need to address why this should be the case. Evidence suggests that in sports requiring early specialisation, there is a need to master specific motor skills and co-ordinated movement patterns, preferably prior to maturation. As a result, the LTAD plan for these athletes has to incorporate the condensed Stage 2. We should here note some points of caution when considering LTAD and specialisation. As stated by Baker (2003), early specialisation in a late specialisation sport can lead to:

- lack of appropriate motor skill development;
- impaired psychological and sociological development;
- early burnout;
- early retirement from sport;
- overuse injuries.

It is apparent from Table 15.1 that males and females show different rates of response to the training process. This is an important consideration and one that must be appreciated before we embark on developing a LTAD strategy.

Gender-based responses to training

In order to appreciate the levels of response to training in males and females, we need to be conversant in the difference between 'trainability' and adaptations to training. The latter is discussed in Chapter 8, however for the purposes of understanding LTAD, we must make a distinction between the two terms.

Adaptations to training are the body's biological responses to applied stimuli (training), whereas trainability reflects the athlete's response to the applied stimuli (training) at various stages of development. It therefore represents the body's responses to training in relation to growth and maturation. This distinction is important because coaches normally refer to physiological adaptations when working with athletes and studying their responses to a training plan/cycle.

However, when structuring a LTAD plan we need to focus on small 'windows of opportunity' when the young athlete's body is primed to accept an applied stimulus, for in these early stages of athletic development, the greatest gains can be made, but also the greatest mistakes can be made. Table 15.2 highlights the components of fitness and their associated windows of opportunity for trainability.

Table 15.2: Windows of opportunity for trainability within the long-term athlete development plan

Component	Timeframe
Flexibility	In both males and females the ideal age for developing flexibility occurs between the ages of 6 and 10.
Skill	In males the ideal age for skill development is between 9 and 12 and for females it is between 8 and 11 years.
Speed	For both males and females there are TWO windows of opportunity for development of speed. In males these are between 7 and 9, and 13 and 16 years. In females they are between 6 and 8, and 11 and 13 years.
Strength	Strength is best characterised by developmental age rather than chronological age. In males it is around 12–18 months after PHV and in females it is at PHV.
Endurance	For both males and females the optimal time period is at PHV. Caution is recommended in that aerobic power training should not be introduced until after PHV and then only progressively. Prior to this, the focus would be on aerobic capacity training.

A word of wisdom at this point: remember that all components of fitness will respond to training at all times.

Stage 1 – Active start

The aim of this stage is to allow the child to learn and acquire fundamental movements and be able to link them to a playing situation. The overall approach is to encourage the development of motor skills and co-ordination in conjunction with an active and healthy lifestyle.

The emphasis should be on FUN and the play should allow the child to develop basic motor skills such as running, jumping, twisting, hopping, kicking, throwing and catching. There should be a combination of both structured (physical education) and non-structured sessions within the school day and where at all possible, in the home environment. By being FUN, competitive games are avoided and the child learns participation and enjoyment of the activity. It is often suggested that at this stage of development the child should not be inactive for more than 60 min/day except when sleeping.

Stage 2 – FUNdamentals

The aim of this stage is to build on the foundations developed at Stage 1 and encourage the learning of fundamental movement skills and the development of motor skills. By the title of this stage, we can appreciate that development of these key skills must be combined with the sense of fun that was established at Stage 1. Even though there will have been both chronological and developmental advances in the child, there should still not be a direct focus on sport-specific actions, but rather on developing the underlying skills contributing to all sports through sessions that promote the components of fitness through play. The emphasis should be on developing correct bi-motor abilities, such as running, catching, kicking, etc. and in encouraging the child to integrate these into the play sessions. At this stage, we start to see the introduction of more specific components of fitness such as strength training, although this should only be developed through using the child's own mass as resistance.

The games should also encourage bilateral movements (change of direction) but only for very short durations. The child should also be introduced to the concepts of fair play and the rules of participation. The coach or teacher should ensure that any equipment used is specific to the developmental age of the child in order to avoid the development of inappropriate technique and injury. Wider participation should be encouraged in at least 3–4 sports.

Stage 3 – Learning to train

The aim of this stage is to learn the overall skills of the sport. The training adopted by the child will build on that developed in Stages 1 and 2 but with greater emphasis on applying the learnt motor skills to sport-specific situations.

Once again, the training encourages the development of the components of fitness and emphasises trainability rather than structured formulaic training plans. However, as the child develops, the introduction of a single periodised structure is encouraged but only towards the latter part of this stage of development. Exercises such as hopping, leaping and bounding, which help to develop neuromuscular strength and power should be introduced while ensuring that all strength development is through the use of the child's own body mass and not resistive devices. A key facet of this stage is the introduction of competition to the plan.

Competitions should constitute only around 30 per cent of the total work done and can be sub-divided into actual competition and training to compete. The purpose of competition is two-fold. First, it allows young athletes to experience the difference between training and competing, and second because the use of competition allows identification of differences in training and ability. This stage offers unique opportunities to the young athlete in terms of trainability and development, however if not structured correctly through the use of set sessions and unstructured play, the window of opportunity will be lost.

The research base informs us that at this chronological and developmental age, children are highly sensitive to the process of skill acquisition. It should also be noted that children should not specialise too soon, especially in the late specialisation sports, as this can prove detrimental to later and long-term performance.

Stage 4 – Training to train

The primary aim of this stage is to continue the development of skills which have been advanced through the previous stages of the plan, but also to begin building an aerobic base with focus directed towards the enhancement of speed and power near the end of this stage.

The development of the aerobic base is fundamental to all athletic development (see Chapter 10). It is very much like the foundations of a house. A solid, well-constructed foundation is laid, on which we build our solid brick structure, eventually capping this off with the roof, the pinnacle of the build. If we employ a cowboy builder who does not put in a foundation or does not dig it deep enough, the house will probably look great but will be unsafe, as it has been built without a solid base. The house will very soon begin to show signs of damage (cracks in the brickwork) and will eventually collapse.

This analogy can be translated to our developing athlete. The aerobic base is a solid foundation upon which we build all other training; if we neglect or ignore its development, on the surface the athlete will look fine but their ability to produce sustained athletic performances will be diminished with an increased chance of developing under-performance syndrome (UPS) (see Chapter 9).

The optimal point for the introduction of aerobic base work is when PHV is achieved. However, we should not focus on aerobic development at the expense of other athletic adaptations. In Stage 3, we introduced the athlete to training, which develops the core components of fitness (speed, strength, flexibility and skill), these should not be ignored and so the coach's role is to introduce the aerobic base work without overloading the athlete in terms of total work done (see Chapter 9). It would be very easy for the coach to just give the athlete more training on top of that previously introduced at Stage 3, but that would be a potential route to UPS and athlete burnout. Instead, the coach should develop a balanced plan which may involve reducing some of the emphasis on the other fitness components but overall not bombarding the athlete.

The coach should know how much work to give the athlete and also when to give this work to them. They should recognise the maturation status of the athlete; either early, average or late and through this recognition emphasise particular areas for development in relation to that stage. This is important when programming aerobic base work and strength training at this age.

By understanding the developmental age of the athlete, sessions can be programmed that meet their needs rather than focusing on more generalised training. This scenario is exemplified by our recognition of the timing of strength training which is not only maturation stage dependent but also gender specific. Male athletes have one optimal window of opportunity occurring at around 12–18 months after the onset of PHV, whereas in females there are two optimal windows. The first is immediately after the onset of PHV with the second occurring at the onset of menarche.

An important facet of this stage of athletic development is the considerable degree of morphological adaptation which occurs, meaning that at this chronological age the young athlete will experience changes in their tendons, bones and muscles. Therefore flexibility training should be actively encouraged so as to minimise the tightening effect of training on these structures during a period when relative elasticity within these structures is needed to allow them to grow and develop.

We should aim to use a structured training plan (periodised) using either a mono- or bi-cycle approach (see Chapter 9). In this way, the training is programmed to meet the developmental stage of the athlete and phased to optimise their actual response to training through specific training units and more crucially, in recovery.

In Chapter 10, we discussed the role of recovery being the primary stimulus for physiological adaptation and athletic development. The use of a periodised plan also helps the athlete to focus on specific competitions, something which is important at this stage of their development. During Stage 3 (Learning to train) we discussed the use of training to competition weightings of 70 per cent to 30 per cent, respectively. As the athlete is now starting to develop and becoming more accustomed to competing the weighting changes to around 60 per cent training and 40 per cent competition.

Again we must consider balance. If the athlete is introduced to too much competition during this stage it inhibits their overall development as they are losing valuable training time. However, we should accept that failure to introduce them to sufficient competition hinders their competitive development by not exposing them to decision-making, tactical and emotional conditions, all of which are associated with competition.

There is no doubt that Stages 3 and 4 of the LTAD plan are crucial to the overall development of the athlete, but why? They key to success lies in that there are sound physiological reasons for the correct timing of aerobic and strength training especially during stage 4.

In considering the development of aerobic base and endurance capability, we need to address the issue of the 'Trigger hypothesis'. This theory suggests that changes in hormone levels associated with the onset of adolescence and the increased growth rate of the cardio–respiratory and muscular systems makes the young athlete susceptible to aerobic development (Katch, 1983). The development and timing of strength training is somewhat more complex and less well understood, due to conflicting evidence from the literature base. However, what we can interpret is that at this developmental age, a number of factors contribute to the promotion of strength.

In both young males and females at and around PHV, there are increases in levels of hormones associated with growth, including growth hormone, adrenaline and testosterone (in males), all contributing to and rendering the athlete highly sensitive to the adaptation of muscle (hypertrophy) to strength training.

In females, there is also the second window of opportunity associated with the onset of menarche, at which point the young female athlete will experience profound increases in the hormones oestrogen and progesterone, both of which contribute to the morphological development of the body.

However, it should be noted that sensitivity to strength training at this developmental stage is not due to hormonal responses but rather to changes in neuromuscular recruitment, in particular to greater co-ordination of the musculoskeletal system through developmental adaptations of the central nervous system (CNS).

Therefore, sensitivity to strength training could be the result of enhanced co-ordination and the ability to use muscles during any action more effectively. Either way, the timing is still crucial to the overall developmental of the athlete.

Stage 5 – Training to compete

The overall aim of the training to compete stage is continued development of the physical capabilities of the athlete, with greater emphasis being placed on the role of competition and learning how to be an effective competitor. Before addressing this stage of the plan we should consider how progression is achieved from the 'training to train' stage.

The coach should have a checklist of objectives for each stage (but especially for Stage 4) which emphasises the key components of that stage (aerobic base, strength work, etc.). Only when the athlete has met and obtained each objective of Stage 4 should entry to Stage 5 be considered.

Up to this point, the athlete will have learnt and applied basic skills and competencies within their specific sport, however there is a significant difference between training to train and actually applying these skills in a competition-based environment. Hence, the focus of training at this stage, wherever possible, is to simulate competition conditions to allow the athlete the opportunity to apply their fundamental skills base to more specific scenarios.

The competition focus should be emphasised as much as possible throughout this stage of development. Some of the sessions will focus on specific scenarios with some also focusing on high intensity competition training. Remember that the focus is training to compete, not training to train.

Whereas in the previous stage we were building the foundations now we are focusing on the actual walls and specifics of the sport. Therefore emphasising the use of training sessions at competition intensity will not only simulate the skills and conditions but also expose the athlete to the physiological sensations associated with competition, which are markedly different to those experienced during 'normal' training. A term often used is training at 'full gas'; giving everything as one would do in competition thereby developing specific physiological and psychological adaptations.

Two terms helping to define this stage of athlete development are 'specialisation' and 'individual'. The training focus should now be specific to the demands of the sport in which the athlete is competing (by this stage they should be concentrating on one sport) and should be tailored to the needs of the athlete.

The athlete's needs can be determined in a number of ways: goal-setting and needs analysis (Chapter 4), performance profiling and physiological/psychological screening. From these analyses, the coach can define their athlete's respective strengths and weaknesses and design a training plan to meet these individual requirements.

As explained in Chapter 9, training programme design achieves the best results when tailored specifically to meet the needs of the athlete. So the focus has to be on mapping primary competitions for the athlete into the annual plan through the use of mono, bi- and even tri-cycle periodised training plans. Unlike in the training to train stage where the coach can use more generic planning, at this stage the plan is individualised to the athlete.

The use of such tailored plans allows the athlete to achieve optimal physiological adaptation in response to training. Bearing this in mind, the coach should consider the programming of technical sessions which work on specific tactical and specialist components of the sport, such as more advanced plays in basketball or pace judgement control in running (Tucker et al, 2006). An appreciation for the athlete's psychology is fundamental to athlete development and so specific training sessions to focus on this should be introduced into the training cycle.

Perhaps the most important aspect of using such individualised and structured plans is the programming of recovery. This is discussed in much greater depth in Chapter 10; however, we should briefly address the rudiments here.

The primary stimulus for physiological adaptation is the training unit or session, however the primary period for gaining physiological adaptation is during the period of recovery. For this reason we must ensure that the devised training programme – although emphasising a high training volume – has sufficient periods of time to allow short-term recovery and longer blocks of time to allow for more enhanced recovery and supercompensation (physiological adaptation).

Recovery can either be programmed in the form of rest days or through the use of reduced training volume following a period of intense training. Crucially though, although there are generic rules of recovery, these periods should be programmed individually as different athletes respond differently to training. How much training and competition should the athlete now be exposed to?

Once again, remember that the emphasis is now on competition, whether in the shape of actual competitions or through the use of competition training. Therefore, our weightings have to be adjusted accordingly, as summarised in Figure 15.1 which shows that by this stage of the athlete's development the weighting should be 40 per cent base training to 60 per cent competition/training.

Stage 6 – Training to win

This is the final stage of the athlete's development and preparation, so the emphasis is quite simply what many of the National Governing Bodies (NGBs) of sport describe as podium performances: winning medals, preferably gold.

Figure 15.1: Weightings of training to competing during the stage of athlete development. The dark blocks represent the amount of training time devoted to training and the pale blocks represent the amount of time devoted to competing

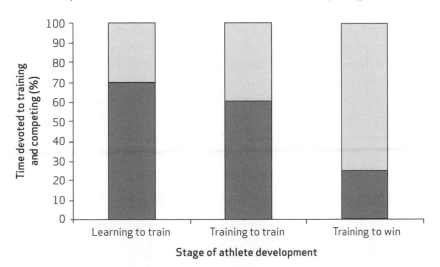

Therefore, the primary aim of winning has to be accomplished through peaking the athlete for competition. The attainment of a peaked athlete is through a combination of appropriate training, planning and tapering to maximise the capabilities of the athlete (Chapter 9).

As with the Training to compete stage, the training programme will emphasise key athletic components of the sport and will be tailored to meet the athlete's needs in terms of strengths and weaknesses. If we refer back to our analogy of constructing an athlete being like building a house, then this stage is the equivalent of putting the roof on and completing the finishing touches. The training therefore has to focus on maximising performance and delivering optimal results in competition.

To achieve this, the training will predominantly be of high intensity and reasonably high volume, however as with the training to compete stage, there should be prescribed blocks of recovery both to achieve supercompensation but also to prevent UPS and over-reaching by the athlete. At this stage of athletic development, there is a fine balance between being optimally trained and prepared and being overtrained and on the path to burnout. Therefore, throughout the training plan the coach should encourage the athlete to take recuperative breaks allowing for physical and mental recovery.

A further aspect of this stage that is often overlooked is ensuring that the athlete and coach have strategies in place to deal with lifestyle management.

Lifestyle management

Lifestyle management encompasses any factor which can affect the performance of the athlete but which lies outside the training and competing domains of sport. The coach and athlete should work together to ensure that the athlete has a controlled and appropriate diet to meet the demands of their sport, that there are no undue influences from work or home and that everything existing outside their sport is compart-mentalised and controlled so as to minimise their influence on performance.

Athletic peaking

Although we discuss the nature of athletic peaking in detail in Chapter 9 we should address it here as a concept related to the stage of athletic development. Peaking is the convergence of all of the components of fitness in order to derive performance, with each being fine tuned to its optimal level. There is also peaking of mental processing and toughness. In essence, we want to achieve peak athletic condition on the day of competition; it is no good being at the peak a week later for by then it will be too late and the opportunity to win will be lost.

Peaking is accomplished through the use of correct training strategies and also by ensuring that the athlete has tapered correctly prior to the competition.

Referring back to Figure 15.1, we can see that once again the weighting of base training to competition and/or competition training has shifted. Now the primary focus is very much on optimal performance under conditions of competition, reflected in the weightings as 25 per cent of the total volume devoted to base training and the remaining 75 per cent focusing on competing and competition based training.

Stage 7 – Active for life

The overriding aim of this stage is to optimise the athlete's transition from a competition-based career in sport to a prolonged period of being active and parti-cipating in sport either in age bracketed events or for recreation. This is the one area of athletic development that is often overlooked and neglected, because quite simply, once the athlete is 'over the hill' athletically, they are no longer podium performers and so no longer of primary concern or focus to the coach and NGB.

This however has changed in recent times, especially in the UK with schemes such as Performance Lifestyle, which is hosted and administered by the British Olympic Association (BOA) and the British Paralympic Association (BPA). This scheme aims to provide the athlete with the resources to progress from a competitive athletic career to a more routine lifestyle, achieved by helping the athlete with skills such as CV production, putting them in contact with companies and organisations looking for suitable employees or helping them get into education.

An avenue often pursued by retiring athletes is one which keeps them in contact with their chosen sport such as coaching, sports administration and sports development.

We see this quite often in sports such as soccer where the best players at a club get appointed as a coach or manager of the team. This approach is also occurring in Olympic sports where it is recognised that many athletes have a wealth of experience and knowledge that they can pass on to new and developing athletes.

We should also recognise that many athletes attempting such transference of skills do not succeed, for they may have been a great athlete but turn out to be a poor coach. This is why schemes such as Performance Lifestyle are important in directing athletes to careers suiting their abilities, very much as a school leaver would seek career advice from the appropriate service.

As it should be, attention is now paid to the sporting transition of the athlete. Athletes are competitive by nature, which is one reason they succeed. This natural desire to compete needs to be channelled and one way is through encouraging the older, retiring athlete to compete in age matched sporting events such as at Master's level.

Here, although competition is intense, it is not as concentrated as that seen during the training to win stage. Athletes compete against age-matched peers, but without the pressures associated with high level podium performance competition.

It should also be recognised that many athletes no longer wish to compete and so could be channelled into recreational based pursuits; in all cases, the aim is to keep them active both physically and mentally.

Many athletes reach their podium potential in one sport but may have the requisite skills to prosper in another at podium level. Most notably, this has been seen in sports such as bobsledding, where many brakemen come from careers in track and field having been world class sprinters; although they can no longer medal on the track, they provide the necessary power to the sled over a short distance.

Great examples are Lenny Paul who went from being a GB sprinter (100m) to being the brakeman in the four-man bob at the Winter Olympics and Rebecca Romero who transferred from GB rowing to GB track cycling.

An area where this transfer from sport to sport has been quite prolific is that in disABILITY Paralympic level sport. It is quite common to find athletes who competed internationally in one sport, achieved all they wanted to achieve or thought they could achieve and transferred to another sport. We have seen considerable movement in recent years from GB swimming to GB cycling with, e.g. Sarah Storey (formerly Bailey) and Jody Cundy – both multi-Paralympic medallists in the pool – successfully transferring their abilities to the velodrome. Paralympic sport also provides another opportunity for able-bodied athletes who are no longer podium potential in their chosen sport. Runners can become guide runners and cyclists can become tandem pilots for blind and visually impaired athletes.

There is another, very unique scenario highlighting the transference of talent between Olympic and Paralympic domains. A considerable number of Paralympic athletes started their athletic careers as able-bodied, but either due to illness or injury have had to retire from able-bodied sport. Consequently, they have transferred their skills to disABLED sport. A phenomenal example of this unique transference is the Spanish cyclist Javier Ochoa who rode such events as the Tour de France, who was rendered physically disABLED after a horrendous road accident in which he was knocked off his bike. This left him with acquired cerebral palsy but he has continued to ride as an athlete with a disABILITY competing at the Paralympic games and continuing to win within his own physical disABILITY category. What we see from these athletes, Ochoa, Storey, Paul and Cundy is a desire to maximise athletic potential and utilise their skills and expertise as an athlete to their fullest.

In essence, this final stage of the LTAD is about maximising the potential of the athlete and channelling this in a direction that is both rewarding and fulfilling in the long term.

Take home message

Long-term athlete development is a plan designed to integrate recognised coaching processes with sport and physical education in schools. This integration allows for children to develop basic and fundamental skills before progressing to more dedicated coaching and support. This approach requires the coach to be fully aware of both the chronological and developmental age of the athlete and to recognise the difference between adapting to training and trainability. Furthermore, this approach to coaching should generate increased numbers of elite athletes with podium positions, while at the same time reducing incidences of athlete burnout and dropout in the early stages of their athletic careers.

The coach must adopt a systematic and structured approach to coaching and support and recognise the needs/strengths and weaknesses of their athlete. Clearly, this approach is not without its limitations, e.g. the integration between the education system and coaches and the continued requirement to assess peak height velocity in the early stages of an athlete's development. These notwithstanding, LTAD is the way forward to achieve podium-driven athletes.

Further study

The following list details key publications which relate to the concepts attributed to LTAD. Within the list are topics related to child development, physiological responses to training in the child and the initialisation and implementation of LTAD plans across the globe.

Balyi, I (2001) *Sport system building and long-term athlete development in British Columbia*. BC, Canada: Sports Medicine

Balyi, I and Hamilton, A (2003) *Long term athlete development: Trainability in childhood and adolescence. Windows of opportunity, optimal trainability*. Largs, Scotland: Strength and Conditioning Seminar

Baranowski, T and Jago, R (2005) Understanding the mechanisms of change in children's physical activity programs. *Exercise Sports Science Review*, 33: 163–8

Boucher, J and Mutimer, B (1994) The relative age phenomena in sport: A replication and extension in ice hockey. *Research Quarterly Exercise and Sport*, 65: 377–81

Danis, A, Kyriazis, Y and Klissouras, V (2003) The effect of training in male prepubertal monozygotic twins. *European Journal of Applied Physiology*, 98: 309–18

Ericsson, K A and Charness, N (1994) Expert performance: It's structure and acquisition. *American Psychologist*, 8: 725–47

Ericsson, K A, Krampe, R T and Tesch-Romer, C (1993) The role of deliberate practice in the acquisition of expert performance. *Psychological Review*, 363–406

Falk, B and Tenenbaum, G (1996) The effectiveness of resistance training in children a meta-analysis. *Sports Medicine*, 22: 176–86

Helsen, W F, Starkes, J L and Van Winckel, J (1998) The influence of relative age on success and dropout in male soccer players. *American Journal of Human Biology*, 10: 791–8

Hoyle, R H and Leff, S S (1997) The role of parental involvement in youth sport participation and performance. *Adolescence*, 32: 233–43

Katch, V L (1983) Physical conditioning of children. *Journal of Adolescent Health Care*, 3: 241–6

Maffulli, N, King, J B and Helms, P (1994) Training in elite young athletes (the training young athletes (TOYA) study): Injuries, flexibility and isometric strength. *British Journal of Sports Medicine*, 28: 123–36

Ottis, C L, Crespo, M, Flygore, C T, Johnston, P R, Keber, A, Lloyd-Kalkin, D, et al (2006) The Sony Ericsson WTA Tour 10 age eligibility and professional development rule. *British Journal of Sports Medicine*, 40: 464–8

Rommich, J N, Richmond, E L and Rogol, A D (2001) Consequences of sport training during puberty. *Journal of Endocrinal Investigation*, 24: 708–15

Rommich, J N and Rogol, A D (1995) Physiology of growth and development: It's relationship to performance in the young athlete. *Clinical Sports Medicine*, 14: 483–502

Rowland, T W and Boyajian, A (1995) Aerobic response to endurance exercise training in children. *Pediatrics*, 96: 654–8

Thumm, H P (1987) The importance of basic training for the development of performance. *New Studies in Athletics*, 1: 47–64

Tolfrey, K, Campbell, I G and Batterham, A M (1998) Aerobic trainability of prepubertal boys and girls. *Pediatric Exercise Science*, 10: 248–63

Vrijens, J (1978) Muscle strength and development in pre and post pubertal age. *Medicine and Sport*, 11: 152–8

Weber, G, Kartodihardjo, W and Klissouras, V (1976) Growth and physical training with reference to heredity. *Journal of Applied Physiology*, 40: 211–4

www.eis2win.co.uk/gen – English Institute of Sport: National organisation who support and work with Elite athletes in England.

www.sportscoachuk.org – Sports Coach UK. National body responsible for regulating and overseeing coach education within the UK. Site contains information relating to coaching courses and contacts through to coaching resources and support.

www.sportdevelopment.org.uk/index.html – Sports Development. A UK based web resource which acts as a searchable database for articles and research related to sport.

www.sportengland.org/national-framework-for-sport.pdf – Sport England: National body that promotes and funds sport and active lifestyles within England. This specific link takes you to the strategic document which sets out the National Policy for sport in England.

www.uksport.gov.uk – UK Sport. National body supporting elite world class performers. Useful resources related to coach education and drug free sport.

References

Abbott, A and Collins, C (2002) A theoretical and empirical analysis of a 'State of the Art' Talent Identification model. *High Ability Studies*, 13: 158–78

Abbott, A and Collins, C (2004) Eliminating the dichotomy between theory and practice in talent identification and development: Considering the role of psychology. *Journal of Sports Sciences*, 22: 395–404

Abernethy, B, Wood, M J and Parks, S (1999) Can the anticipatory skills of experts be learned by novices? *Research Quarterly for Exercise and Sport*, 70: 313–8

Adams, J A (1971) A closed loop theory of motor learning. *Journal of Motor Behaviour*, 3: 111–50

Allen, J B and Howe, B L (1998) Player ability, coach feedback and female adolescent athletes' perceived competence and satisfaction. *Journal of Sport and Exercise Psychology*, 20: 280–99

Ames, C (1992) Achievement goals, motivational climate, motivational processes, in Roberts, G C (ed) *Motivation in sport and exercise*. Champaign IL: Human Kinetics, pp 161–6

An, P, Rice, T, Gagnon, J, Leon, A S, Skinner, J S, Bouchard, C, Rao, D C and Wilmore, J H (2000) Familial aggregation of stroke volume and cardiac output during submaximal exercise: The HERITAGE family Study. *International Journal of Sports Medicine*, 21: 566–72

Annesi, J H (1997) Three-dimensional state anxiety recall: Implications for individual zone of optimal functioning research and application. *The Sport Psychologist*, 11: 43–52

Anderson, A G, Knowles, Z and Gilbourne, D (2004) Reflective practice for sports psychologists: Concepts, models, practical implications and thoughts on dissemination. *The Sports Psychologist*, 18: 188–203

Anderson, J R (1983) *The architecture of cognition*. Cambridge, MA: Harvard University Press

Apter, M J (1982) *The experience of motivation: The theory of psychological reversal*. London: Academic Press

Armstrong, N and Welsman, J (1997) Children in Sport and Exercise. *British Journal of Physical Education*, 28: 4–6

Armstrong, N (2007) *Paediatric exercise physiology*. Edinburgh: Churchill Livingstone/ Elsevier

⊔, J, Kyrolainen H and Komi, P V (1999) Altered reflex sensitivity after repeated and prolonged passive muscle stretching. *Journal of Applied Physiology*, 86: 1283–91

Baechle, T R and Earle, R W (2000) *Essential strength training and conditioning.* Champaign IL: Human Kinetics

Bahr, R (1992) Excess post exercise oxygen consumption: Magnitude, mechanisms and practical implications. *Acta Physiologica Scandinavia*, 605: 1–70

Baker, J (2003) Early specialisation in youth sport: A requirement for adult expertise? *High Ability Studies*, 14: 85–94

Balsom, P D, Gaitanos, G C, Ekblom, B and Sjodin, B (1994) Reduced oxygen availability during high intensity intermittent exercise impairs performance. *Acta Physiologica Scandinavia*, 152: 279–85

Balsom, P D (1994) Evaluation of physical performance, in Ekblom, B (ed) *Football (soccer).* London: Blackwell, pp 102–23

Bandura, A (1977) Self efficacy: Toward a unifying theory of behavioural change. *Psychological Review*, 84: 191–215

Bandura, A (1982) Self-efficacy mechanism in human agency. *American Psychologist*, 37: 122–47

Bar-Eli, M, Dreshman, R, Blumenstein, B and Weinstein, Y, (2001) The effect of mental training with bio-feedback on the performance of young swimmers. *Applied Psychology*, 51: 567–81

Basler, M L, Fischer, A C and Mumford, N L (1976) Arousal and anxiety correlates of gymnastic performance. Research Quarterly, 47: 586–9

Baxter-Jones, A D G and Sherar, L (2007) Growth and maturation, in Armstrong, N (eds) *Paediatric exercise physiology.* Elsevier: Churchill Livingstone/Elsevier, pp 1–26

Bean, J W, Serwatka, T S and Wilson, J W (2004) Preferred leadership of NCAA Division I and II intercollegiate student athletes. *Journal of Sport Behaviour*, 27: 3–16

Bejek, K and Hagtvet, K A (1996) The content of pre-competitive state anxiety in top and lower level of female gymnasts. *Anxiety, Stress and Coping*, 9: 19–31.

Belcastro, A B and Bonen, A (1975) Lactic acid removal rates during controlled and uncontrolled recovery exercise. *Journal of Applied Physiology*, 39: 932–6

Berg, K E and Latin, R W (2004) *Essentials of Research Methods in Health, Physical Education, Exercise Science and Recreation.* 2nd edition. London: Lippincott Williams and Wilkins

Best, D (1978) *Philosophy and human movement.* Sydney: Unwin Education Books

Billat, V L, Demarle, A, Slawinski, J, Paiva, M and Koralsztein, J P (2000) Physical and training characteristics of top-class marathon runners. *Medicine and Science in Sports and Exercise*, 33: 2089–97

Billat, V L (2001) Interval training for performance: a scientific and empirical practice. *Sports Medicine*, 31: 13–31

Blomstrand, E (2001) Amino acids and central fatigue. *Amino Acids*, 20: 25–34

Bloom, B S (1985) *Developing talent in young people.* New York: Baltimore

Bloomfield, J (1998) Flexibility in sport, in Elliot, B and Mester, J (eds) *Training in sport: Applying sport science.* Chichester: Wiley

Bogdanis, G C, Nevill, M E, Boobis, L H, Lakomy, H K A and Nevill, A M (1995) Recovery of power output and muscle metabolites following 30s of maximal sprint cycling in man. *Journal of Physiology*, 482: 467–80

Bompa, T O (1991) A model of an annual training program for a sprinter. *New Studies in Athletics*, 6: 47–51

Bompa, T O (1999) *Periodization: Theory and methodology of training*. 4th edition. Champaign, IL: Human Kinetics

Bonifazi, M, Sardella, F and Luppo, C (2000) Preparatory versus main competitions: Differences in performances, lactate responses and pre-competition plasma cortisol concentrations in elite male swimmers. *European Journal of Applied Physiology*, 82: 368–73

Bouchard, C, Malina, R M and Perusse, L (1997) *Genetics of fitness and physical performance*. Champaign, IL: Human Kinetics

Budgett, R (1990) The overtraining syndrome. *British Journal of Sports Medicine*, 14: 231–6

Cady, E B, Jones, D A, Lynn, J and Newham, D J (1989) Changes in force and intracellular metabolites during fatigue of human skeletal muscle. *Journal Physiology*, 418: 311–25

Carr, W ed. (1989) Introduction: Understanding quality in teaching. *Quality in teaching*. Lewes: Falmer Press

Carter, J E L and Ackland, T R (1998) Sexual dimorphism in the physiques of world championship divers. *Journal of Sport Sciences*, 16: 317–29

Cassidy, T, Jones, R and Potrac, P (2000) *Understanding sports coaching: The social, cultural and pedagogical foundations of coaching practice*. London: Routledge

Chelladurai, P and Saleh, S D (1978) Preferred leadership in sport. *Candian Journal of Applied Sports Sciences*, 3: 85–97

Cheung, K, Hume, P A and Maxwell, L (2003) Delayed onset muscle soreness: Treatment strategies and performance factors. *Sports Medicine*, 33: 145–64

Chilibeck, P D, Syrotuik, D G and Bell, G J (1999) The effect of strength training on estimates of mitochondrial density and distribution throughout muscle fibres. *European Journal of Applied Physiology*, 80: 604–9

Chu, D (1998) *Jumping into plyometrics*. Champaign, IL: Human Kinetics

Corbin, C B (1967) Effects of mental practice on skill development after controlled practice. *Research Quarterly*, 38: 534–8

Costill, D L, Flynn, M G and Kirway, J P (1988) Effects of repeated days of intensified training on muscle glycogen and swimming performance. *Medicine and Science in Sports and Exercise*, 20: 249–54

Côté, J, Salmela, J, Trudel, P, Baria, A and Russell, S (1995) The coaching model: A grounded assessment of expert gymnastics coaches' knowledge. *Journal of Sport and Exercise Psychology*, 17: 1–17

Cotterman, M L, Darby, L A and Skelly, W A (2005) Comparison of muscle force production using the Smiths machine and free weights for bench press and squat exercises. *Journal of Strength and Conditioning Research*, 19: 169–76

Covassin, T and Pero, S (2004) The relationship between self-confidence, mood state and anxiety amongst collegiate tennis players. *Journal of Sport Behaviour*, 72: 230–243

Cox, R H (2002) *Sport psychology: Concepts and applications*. 5th edition. New York: McGraw Hill

Coyle, E F, Martin, W H, Sinacore, D R, Joyner, M J, Hagberg, J M and Hollszy, J O (1984) Time course of loss of adaptations after stopping prolonged intense endurance training. *Journal of Applied Physiology*, 57: 1857–63

Coyle, E F, Hemmert, M K and Coggan A, R (1986) Effects of detraining on cardiovascular responses to exercise: Role of blood volume. *Journal of Applied Physiology*, 60: 95–9

Coyle, E F (2005) Improved muscular efficiency displayed as Tour de France Champion matures. *Journal of Applied Physiology*, 98: 2191–8

Craik, F I M and Lockhart, R S (1972) Levels of processing: A framework for memory research. *Journal of Verbal Learning and Verbal Behaviour*, 11: 671–84

Cregan, K, Bloom, G A, and Reid, G (2007) Career evolution and knowledge of elite coaches of swimmers with a physical disability. *Research Quarterly* 78: 339–50.

Cronin, J, McNair, P J and Marshall, R N (2001) Velocity specificity, combination training and sport specific tasks. *Journal of Science and Medicine in Sport*, 4: 168–8

Cureton, K J, Collins, M A and Hill, D W (1988) Muscle hypertrophy in men and women. *Medicine and Science in Sports and Exercise*, 20: 338–44

Dalleau, G, Belli, A, Bourdin, M and Lacour, J R (1998) The spring-model and the energy cost of treadmill running. *European Journal of Physiology*, 77: 257–63

Daniels, J (2005). *Running Formula*. 2nd edition. Champaign IL: Human Kinetics

Davis, M H and Harvey, J C (1992) Declines in major leaguer batting performance as a function of game pressure: A drive theory analysis. *Journal of Applied Social Psychology*, 22: 714–35

de Vries, H (1986) *Physiology of exercise: For physical education and athletics*. Dubuque: Wm C Brown

di Prampero, P E, Capelli, C and Pagliaro, P (1993). Eneregtics of best performance in middle distance running. *Journal of Applied Physiology*, 74: 2318–24

Draper, J A and Lancaster, M G (1985) The 505 test: A test for agility in the horizontal plane. *Australian Journal for Science and Medicine in Sport*, 17: 15–18

Drewe, S B (2000) An examination of the relationship between coaching and teaching. *Quest*, 52: 79–99

Easterbrook, J A (1959) The effect of emotions on cue utilisation and the organisation of behaviour. *Psychological Review*, 66: 183–201

Edwards, R S (1981) Human muscle function and fatigue. *Ciba Foundation Symposium*, 82: 1–18

Edwards, T and Hardy, L (1996) The interactive effects of intensity and direction of cognitive and somatic anxiety and self-confidence upon performance. *Journal of Sport and Exercise Psychology*, 18: 296–312

Epstein, J (1988) Effective schools or effective students? Dealing with diversity, in Haskins, R and MacRae, B (eds) *Policies for America's public schools*. Norwood, New Jersey: Ablex, pp 89–126

Epstein, J (1989) Family structures and student motivation: A developmental perspective, in Ames, C and Ames, R (eds) *Research on motivation in education*. 3rd edition. New York: Academic Press, pp 259–95

Fiedler, F E (1967) *A theory of leadership effectiveness*. New York: McGraw Hill

Fischman, M and Oxendine, J (1993) Motor skill learning for effective coaching and guidance, in Williams, J (ed) *Applied Sport Psychology*. Mountain View, CA: Mayfield

Fitts, P M and Posner, M I (1967) *Human performance*. Belmont, CA: Brooks/Cole

Fowles, J R, Sale, D G and MacDougall, J D (2000) Reduced strength after passive stretch of the human plantorflexors. *Journal of Applied Physiology*, 89: 1179–88

Francis, C and Coplon, J (1991) *Speed trap: Inside the biggest scandal in Olympic history*. London: Grafton Books/Collins

Gambetta, V (1996) How to develop sport specific speed. *Sports Coach*, 19: 22–4

Gastin, P B and Lawson, D L (1994) Influence of training status on maximal accumulated oxygen deficit during all-out cycle exercise. *European Journal of Applied Physiology*, 69: 321–30

Gastin P, B (2001) Energy system interaction and relative contribution during maximal exercise. *Sports Medicine*, 31: 725–44

Gibbs, G (1988) *Learning by doing: A guide to teaching and learning methods*. Oxford: Oxford Brookes University Further Education Unit

Gibbons, T, McConnell, A, Forster, T, Riewald, S T and Peterson, K (2003) *Reflections on success: U.S. Olympians describe the success factors and obstacles that most influenced their Olympic development*. United States Olympic Committee Publication.

Glaister, M (2005) Multiple sprint work: Physiological responses, mechanisms of fatigue and the influence of aerobic fitness. *Sports Medicine*, 35: 757–77

Gleeson, M (2003) Biochemical and immunological markers of overtraining. *Journal of Sports Science and Medicine*, 1: 31–41

Goldspink, G (1974) Work induced hypertrophy in exercised muscle of different ages and the reversibility of hypertrophy after cessation of exercise. *Journal of Applied Physiology*, 239: 179–93

Gore, C J (2000) *Physiological tests for elite athletes*. Australian Sports Commission: Human Kinetics

Green S. (1994) A definition and systems view of anaerobic capacity. *European Journal of Applied Physiology*, 69: 168–73

Greenleaf, C, Gould, D and Diffenbach, K (2001) Factors influencing Olympic performance: Interviews with Atlanta and Nagano U.S. Olympians. *Journal of Applied Sports Psychology*, 13: 154–84

Hakkinen, K, Komi, P and Tesch, P A (1981) Effect of combined concentric and eccentric strength training and detraining on force-time, muscle fiber and metabolic characteristics of leg extensor muscles. *Scandinavian Journal of Sports Science*, 3: 50–8

Hakkinen, K, Komi, P V and Alen, M (1985) Effects of explosive type strength training on isometric force and relaxation time, electromyographic and muscle fibre characteristics of leg extensor muscles. *Acta Physiologica Scandinavia*, 125: 587–600

Hakkinen, K, Kallinen, M and Izquierdo, M (1998) Changes in agonist-antagonist EMG, muscle CSA and force during strength training in middle-aged and older people. *Journal of Applied Physiology*, 84: 1341–9

Hall, H K, Weinberg, R S and Jackson, A (1987) Effects of goal specificity, goal difficulty and information feedback on endurance performance. Journal of Sport Psychology, 9: 43–54

Hanin, Y L (1986) State trait anxiety research on sports in the USSR, in Spielberger, C D and Diaz, R (eds) *Cross cultural anxiety*. 3rd edition. Washington DC: Hemisphere, pp 45–64

Hardy, L, Parfitt, G and Pates, J (1994) Performance catastrophes in sport: A test of the hysteresis hypothesis. *Journal of Sport Sciences*, 12: 327–34

Hardy, J P L and Fazey, J A (1987) *The inverted-U hypothesis a catastrophe for sports psychology and a statement of a new hypothesis*. Vancouver: North American Society for the Psychology of Sport and Physical Activity

Harley, R A and Doust, J H (1997) *Strength and fitness training for basketball: A sports science manual.* Leeds: National Coaching Foundation

Harter, S (1978) Effectance motivation reconsidered: Towards a developmental model. *Human Development,* 21: 34–64

Hebb, D O (1955) Drives and the CNS (Conceptual Nervous System). *Psychological Review,* 62: 243–54

Helgerud, J, Hoydal, K, Wang, E, Karlsen, T, Berg, P, Bierkaas, M, Simonsen, T, Helgesen, C, Hjorth, N, Bach, R and Hoff, J (2007) Aerobic high intensity intervals improve VO_{2max} more than moderate training. *Medicine and Science in Sports and Exercise,* 39: 665–71

Hickson, R C, Foster, C, Pollock, M L, Galassi, T M and Rice, S (1985) Reduced training intensities and loss of aerobic power, endurance and cardiac growth. *Journal of Applied Physiology,* 58: 492–9

Hill, D W (1993) The critical power concept: A review. *Sports Medicine,* 16: 237–54

Hill, D W (1999) Energy system contribution in middle-distance running events. *Journal of Sports Sciences,* 17: 477–83

Hirvonen, J, Numemela, A, Rusko, H, Rehunen, S and Harkonen, M (1992) Fatigue and changes of ATP, creatine phosphate and lactate during the 400-m sprint. *Canadian Journal of Sports Science,* 17: 141–4

Hoare, D (1996) The Australian national talent search programme. *Coaching Focus,* 31: 3–4

Holmyard, D J, Cheetham, M E, Lakomy, H K A, Williams, C. (1988) Effect of recovery duration on performance during multiple treadmill sprints, in Reilly, T, Lees, A, Davids, K (eds) *Science and Football.* London: F & N Spon, pp 134–42

Hopkins, S R and McKenzie, D C (1994) The laboratory assessment of endurance performance in cyclists. *Canadian Journal of Applied Physiology,* 19: 266–74

Houmard, J A, Hortobágyi, T, Johns, R A, Burns, N J, Nute, C C, Shinebarger, M H and Welbourn, J W (1992) Effect of short term training cessation on performance measures in distance runners. *International Journal of Sports Medicine,* 13: 572–6

Houmard, J A and Johns, R A (1994) Effects of taper on swim performance: Practical implications. *Sports Medicine,* 17: 224–32

Hutton R, S (1992) Neuromuscular basis of stretching exercises, in Komi, P V (eds) *Strength and power in sport.* Oxford: Blackwell Science, pp 29–38

Jacobs, I, Esojorrsson, M and Slyven, C (1987) Sprint training effects on muscle myoglobin, enzymes, fibre types and blood lactate. *Medicine and Science in Sports and Exercise,* 19: 368–74

Jones, A M and Carter, H (2000) The effects of endurance training on parameters of aerobic fitness. *Sports Medicine,* 29: 373–86

Jones, A M, and Poole, D C (2005) *Oxygen uptake kinetics in sport, exercise and medicine.* Abingdon: Routledge

Jones, D A, Newham, D J, Round, J M and Tolfree, S E J (1986) Experimental human muscle damage, morphological changes in relation to other indices of damage. *Journal of Physiology,* 375: 435–48

Jones, D A, Rutherford, O M and Parker, D F (1989) Physiological changes in skeletal muscle as a result of strength training. *Quarterly Journal of Experimental Physiology Cognitive Medicine and Science,* 74: 233–56

Jones, D, Round, J and de Haan, A (2005) *Skeletal muscle from molecules to movement.* Edinburgh: Churchill Livingstone

Katch, V L (1983) Physical conditioning of children. *Journal of Adolescent Health Care*, 3: 241–6

Kent-Braun, J A (1999) Central and peripheral contributions to muscle fatigue in humans during sustained maximal exercise. *European Journal of Applied Physiology*, 80: 57–63

Knapp, B (1963) *Skills in sport*. London: Routledge/Kegan & Paul

Krane, V, Joyce, D and Rafeld, J (1994) Competitive anxiety, situation criticality and softball performance. *The Sport Psychologist*, 8: 58–72

Kreiner-Philips, K and Orlick, T (1992) Winning after winning: The psychology of ongoing excellence. *The Sport Psychologist*, 7: 31–48

Kubo, K, Kanehisa, H and Fukanaga, T (2001) Effects of different duration isometric contractions on tendon elasticity in human quadriceps muscles. *Journal of Physiology*, 536: 649–55

Labuschagne, P (1994) The road to Barcelona 1992. *British Miler's Club News* 2: 6–9

Lambert, E V, Hawley, J A, Goedecke, J, Noakes, T D and Dennis, S C (1997) Nutritional strategies for promoting fat utilisation and delaying the onset of fatigue during prolonged exercise. *Journal of Sports Sciences*, 15: 315–24

Lehmann, M J, Lormes, W and Optiz-Gres, A (1997) Training and overtraining: An overview and experimental results in endurance sports. *Journal of Sports Medicine and Physical Fitness*, 37: 7–17

Lei, D, Slocum, J W and Pitts, R A (1999) Designing organisations for competitive advantage: The power of unlearning and learning. *Organisational Dynamics*, 27: 24–38

Lindsay, F H, Hawley, J A, Myburgh, K H, Schomer, H H, Noakes, T D, and Dennis, S C (1996) Improved athletic performance in highly trained cyclists after interval training. *Medicine and Science in Sports and Exercise*, 28: 1427–34

Loche, E A and Latham, G P (1985) The application of goal setting to sports. *Journal of Sports Psychology*, 7: 205–22

Lydiard, A. and Gilmore, G (1962) *Run to the top*. London: Herbert Jenkins

Lyle, J (2002) *Sports Coaching Concepts: A framework for coaches' behaviour*. London: Routledge

MacDougall, J D, Elder, G C B and Sale, D G (1980) Effects of strength training and immobilisation on human muscle fibres. *European Journal of Applied Physiology and Occupational Physiology*, 43: 25–34

Malina, R M, Bouchard, C, Bar-Or, O (2004) Growth maturation and physical activity. 2nd edition. Champaign, IL: Human Kinetics

Martens, R (1971) Anxiety and motor behaviour. *Journal of Motor Behaviour*, 3: 151–79

Martens, R (1987) Science, knowledge and sports psychology. *The Sports Psychologist*, 1: 29–55

Martens, R, Burton, D, Vealey, R S, Bump, L A and Smith, D E (1990) Development and validation of the competitive state anxiety inventory-2, in Martens, R, Vealey, R S, Burton, D (eds) *Competitive anxiety in sport*. Champaign, IL: Human Kinetics, pp 117–90

Martin, D E, Vroon, D H and May, D F (1986) Physiological changes in elite male distance runners training for the Olympic Games. *Physician and Sports Medicine*, 14: 152–69

Maslow, A H (1954) The instinctoid nature of basic needs. *Journal of Personality*, 22: 326–47

Mathews, P B (1991) The human stretch reflex and the motor cortex. *Trends in Neurosciences*, 14: 87–91

Matsudo, V K R, Rivet, R E and Pereira, M H N (1987) Standard score assessment on physique and performance of Brazilian athletes in a six tiered competitive sports model. Journal of Sports Sciences, 5: 49–53

Matsudo, V K R (1996) Prediction of future excellence, in Bar-Or, O (ed) *The child and adolescent athlete.* Berlin: Blackwell Science, pp 92–108

McArdle, W D, Margel, J R, Delio, D J, Toner, M and Chase, J M (1978) Specificity of run training pm VO_{2max} and heart rate changes during running and swimming. *Medicine and Science in Sports and Exercise*, 10: 16–20

McArdle, W D, Katch, F I and Katch, V L (2007) *Exercise Physiology: Energy nutrition and human performance.* 6th edition. Washington DC: Lippincott Williams and Wilkins

McNair, D M, Lorr, M and Droppleman, L F (1992) *Manual for the profile of mood states (POMS).* San Diego, CA: Educational and Industrial Testing Service

van Mechelen, W, Hlobil, H, Kemper, H C G, Voorn, W J and de Jongh, H R (1983) Prevention of running injuries by warm-up, cool-down and stretching exercises. *American Journal of Sports Medicine*, 21: 711–9

Mento, A J, Steel, R P and Karren, R J (1987) A meta-analytic study of the effects of goal setting on task performance 1966–84. *Organisational Behaviour and Human Decision Processes*, 39: 52–83

Metzler, M (2000) *Instructional models for physical education.* Needham Heights, Allyn and Bacon

Midgley, A W, MacNaughton, L R and Jones, A M (2007) Training to enhance the physiological determinants of long distance running performance: can valid recommendations be given to runners and coaches on the basis of current scientific knowledge? *Sports Medicine*, 37: 867–80.

Mikesall, K A and Dudley, G A (1984) Influence of intense endurance training on aerobic power of competitive distance runners. *Medicine and Science in Sports and Exercise*, 16: 371–5

Miller, B W, Roberts, G C and Ommundsen, Y (2005) Effect of perceived motivational climate on moral functioning, team moral atmosphere perceptions and the legitimacy of intentionally injurious acts amongst competitive youth football players. *Psychology of Sport and Exercise*, 6: 461–77

Millet, G P, Candau, R B, Barbier, B, Vusso, T, Rouillon, J D and Chatard, J C (2002) Modelling the transfers of training effects on performance in elite triathletes. *International Journal of Sports Medicine*, 23: 55–63

Mirwald, R L, Baxter-Jones, A D, Bailey, D A and Beunan, C P (2002) An assessment of maturity from anthropometric variables. *Medicine and Science in Sports and Exercise*, 34: 689–94

Monod, H and Scherrer, J (1965) The work capacity of a synergic muscular group. *Ergonomics*, 8: 329–38

Montgomery, H E, Marshall, R, Hemingway, H, Myerson, S, Clarkson, P, Dudley, C, Hayward, M, et al (1998) Human gene for physical performance. *Nature*, 393: 221–2

Mujika, I and Padilla, S (2000) Detraining: Loss of training-induced physiological and performance adaptations. Part I. *Sports Medicine*, 30: 79–87

Mujika, I, Goya, A, Padilla, S, Grijalba, A, Gorostaga, E and Ibanez, J (2000) Physiological responses to a 6-day taper in middle distance runners: Influence of training intensity and volume. *Medicine and Science in Sports and Exercise*, 32: 511–7

Mujika, I and Padilla, S (2003) Scientific basis for pre-competition tapering strategies. *Medicine and Science in Sports and Exercise*, 35: 1192–87

Myburgh, K H (2003) What makes an endurance athlete world class? Not simply a physiological conundrum. *Comparative Biochemistry and Physiology*, 136: 171–90

Nicholls, J G (1984) Achievement motivation: Conceptions of ability subjective experience, task choice and performance. *Psychological Review*, 91: 328–46

Nielson, A G, Guillory, U K, Cornwell, A and Kokkonen, J (2001) Inhibition of maximal voluntary isokinetic torque production following stretching is velocity specific. *Journal of Strength and conditioning Research*, 15: 241–6

Nieman, D C (1994) Exercise: Upper respiratory tract infection and the immune system. *Medicine and Science in Sports and Exercise*, 26: 128–39

Noakes, T D (1997) Challenging beliefs: Ex Africa Semper aliquid novi. *Medicine and Science in Sports and Exercise*, 29: 571–90

Ntoumanis, N and Biddle, S J H (1999) A review of motivational climate in physical activity. *Journal of Sports Sciences*, 17: 643–65

Nybo, L and Nielson, B (2001) Perceived exertion is associated with an altered brain activity during exercise with progressive hyperthermia. *Journal of Applied Physiology*, 91: 2017–23

O'reilly, K P, Warhol, M J and Fielding, R A (1987) Eccentric exercise induced muscle damage impairs muscle glycogen repletion. *Journal of Applied Physiology*, 63: 252–6

Orlick, T and Partington, J (1988) Mental links to excellence. *The Sport Psychologist*, 2: 115–30

Ozolin, N G (1971) *Athletes training system for competition.* Phyzkultura, Moscow: I Sports

Paavolainen, L, Hakkinen, K, Nummela, A and Rusko, H (1994) Neuromuscular characteristics and fatigue in endurance and sprint athletes during a new anaerobic power test. *European Journal of Applied Physiology and Occupational Physiology* 69: 119–26

Parry, J (2004) Must scientists think philosophically about science?, in McNamee, M (ed) *Philosophy and the sciences of exercise, health and sport. Critical perspectives on research methods.* London: Routledge, pp 21–33

Peters, E M (1996) Exercise and upper respiratory tract infections: A review. *South African Journal of Sports Medicine*, 11: 9–14

Pyne D. (1996) *Designing an endurance training program.* Brisbane, Australia: Proceedings of the National Coaching and Officiating Conference

Raglin, J S (1992) Anxiety and sport performance. *Exercise and Sports Sciences Reviews*, 243–74

Raglin, J S (1993) Overtraining and staleness: Psychometric monitoring of endurance athletes, in Singer, R B, Murphy, B, Tennant L, K (eds) *Handbook of research on sports psychology.* New York: MacMillan

Raglin, J S and Morgan, W P (1994) Development of a scale for use in monitoring training induced distress in athletes. *International Journal of Sports Medicine*, 12: 84–8

Randle, S and Weinberg, R (1997) Multidimensional anxiety and performance: An explanatory examination of the zone of optimal functioning hypothesis. *Sport Psychologist*, 11: 160–74

Roberts, G C, ed. (1992) *Motivation in Sport and Exercise*. Human Kinetics, Champaign IL: Human Kinetics, pp 161–76

Robinson, J M, Stone, M H, Johnson, R L, Fenland, C M, Warren, B J and Lewis, D R (1995) Effects of different weight training exercise/rest intervals on strength, power and high intensity exercise endurance. *Journal of Strength and Conditioning Research*, 9: 216–21

Ross, W D and Marfell-Jones, M J (1991) Kinanthropometry, in MacDougall, J D, Wenger, H A and Green, H J (eds) *Physiological testing in the elite athlete*. Champaign, IL: Human Kinetics

Ross, A and Leveritt, M (2001) Long-term metabolic and skeletal muscle adaptations to short sprint training: Implications for sprint training and tapering. *Sports Medicine*, 31: 1063–82

Rubini, E C, Costa, A L L and Gomes, P S C (2007) The effects of stretching on strength performance. *Sports Medicine*, 57: 313–24

Salmela, J H, Young, B W and Kallio, J (1998) Within career transitions of the athlete-coach-parent triad, in Wylleman, P, Lavallee, D (eds) *Career transitions in sport: A source book for practitioners and researchers*. Morgantown VA: FIT Publications

Schmidt, R A and Wrisberg, C A (2000) *Motor learning and performance*. Champaign, IL: Human Kinetics

Schmidt, R A (1975) A schema theory of discrete motor skill learning. *Psychological Review*, 82: 225–60

Schmolinsky, G (1983) *Track and field*. Berlin: Sportverlag

Schön, D (1987) *Educating the reflective practitioner*. San Francisco: Jossey Bass

Shepley, B, MacDougal, J D, Cipriano, N, Sutton, J R, Tarnopolsky, M A and Coates, G (1992) Physiological effects of tapering in highly trained athletes. *Journal of Applied Physiology*, 72: 705–11

Sheppard, R J (1998) Science and medicine of rowing: A review. *Journal of Sports Sciences*, 16: 603–20

Sheppard, J M and Young, W B (2006) Agility literature review: Classifications, training and testing. *Journal of Sports Sciences*, 24: 919–32

Shields, D L L, Gardner, D E, Bredemeier, B L L and Bostro, A (1997) The relationship between leadership behaviours and group cohesion in team sports. *Journal of Psychology*, 131: 196–210

Shulman, L (1986) Those who understand: Knowledge growth in teaching. *Educational Researcher*, 15: 4–14

Simon, J A and Martens, R (1977) S.C.A.T as a predicator of A-states in varying competitive situations, in Landers, D M and Christina, R W (eds) *Psychology of motor behaviour and sport*. 2nd edition. Champaign, IL: Human Kinetics, pp 146–56

Smith, D J (2003) A framework for understanding the training process leading to elite performance. *Sports Medicine*, 33: 1003–26

Smoll, F L and Smith, R E (1989) Leadership behaviors in sport: A theoretical model and research paradigm. *Journal of Applied Social Psychology*, 19: 1522–51

Spencer, M R (2001) Energy system contribution in 200- to 1500-m running in highly trained athletes. *Medicine and Science in Sports and Exercise* 33: 157–62

Sports Medicine Australia – Victoria Branch. Warm-up: Stretching. Available at: *www.sma.org.au/pdfdocuments/warm_up.pdf*

Spurrs, R W, Murphy, A J and Watsford, M L (2003) The effect of plyometric training on distance running performance. *European Journal of Applied Physiology*, 89: 1–7

St Clair Gibson, A, Lambert M, I and Noakes, T D (2001) Neural control of force output during maximal and submaximal exercise. *Sports Medicine*, 31: 637–50

Stephenson, D G, Lamb, G D and Stephenson, G M M (1998) Events of the excitation-contraction-relaxation (E-C-R) cycle in fast and slow twitch mammalian muscle fibres relevant to muscle fatigue, *Acta Physiologica Scandinavia*, 162: 229–45

Stetter, F and Kupper, S (2002) Autogenic training: A meta-analysis of clinical outcome studies. *Applied Psychophysiology and Biofeedback*, 27: 45–98

Svensson, M and Drust, B (2005) Testing soccer players. *Journal of Sports Sciences*, 23: 601–18

Tanaka, H (1994) Effects of cross-training: Transfer of training effects on VO$_2$max between cycling, running and swimming. *Sports Medicine*, 18: 330–9

Tenenbaum, G, Bar-Eli, M and Yaaron, M (1999) The dynamics of goal setting: Interactive effects of goal difficulty, goal specificity and duration of practice time intervals. *International Journal of Sports Psychology*, 30: 325–38

Terry, P C and Howe, B L (1984) Coaching preferences of athletes. *Canadian Journal; of Applied Sports Science*, 9: 188–93

Terry, P C (1995) The efficacy of mood state profiling among elite competitors: A review and synthesis. *The Sport Psychologist*, 9: 309–24

Tesch, P A and Wright, J E (1983) Recovery from short term intense exercise: Its relationship to capillary supply in blood lactate concentration. *European Journal of Applied Physiology and Occupational Physiology*, 52: 98–103

Thomas, J R and Nelson, J K (2001) *Research methods in physical activity.* 4th edition. Champaign, IL: Human Kinetics

Thomas, K T and Thomas, J R (1999) What squirrels in the trees predict about expert athletes. *International Journal of Sport Psychology*, 30: 221–34

Tracy, B, Ivey, F and Hurlbut, D (1999) Muscle quality: Effects of strength training in 65–75 yr old men and women. *Journal of Applied Physiology*, 86: 195–201

Tucker, R, Lambert, M I and Noakes, T D (2006) An analysis of pacing strategies during men's world-record performances in track athletics. *International Journal of Sports Physiology and Performance*, 1: 233–45

Turner, P E and Raglin, J S (1991) Anxiety and performance in track and field athletes: A comparison of ZOFR and inverted-U hypothesis. *Medicine and Science in Sport and Exercise*, 23: s119

Vealey, R S, Armstrong, L, Comar, L and Greenleaf, C A (1998) Influence of perceived coaching behaviours on burnout and competitive anxiety in female collegiate athletes. *Journal of Applied Sport Psychology*, 10: 297–310

Viru, A (1995) *Adaptation in sports training.* Boca Raton, FL: CRC Press

Vonstein, W (1996) Some reflections on maximum speed sprinting technique. *New Studies in Athletics*, 11: 161–5

Verkoshansky (2007a) Topical problems of the modern training theory and methodology of sports. Available at: *www.verkhoshansky.com*

Verkoshansky (2007b) The training system in middle distance running. Available at: *www.verkhoshansky.com*

Viru, A (1995) *Adaptation in sports training.* Boca Raton, FL: CRC Press

Weigand, D A and Burton, S (2002) Manipulating achievement motivation in physical education by manipulating the motivational climate. *European Journal of Sports Science*, 2: 1–14

Weinberg, R S and Gould, D (2007) *Foundations of sport and exercise psychology*. 4th edition. Champaign, IL: Human Kinetics

Weinberg, R S, Burton, D, Yukelson, D and Weingand, D (1993) Goal setting in competitive sport: An exploratory investigation of practices of collegiate athletes. *The Sports Psychologist*, 7: 275–89

Weinberg, R S, D, Yukelson, D and Weingand, D (2000) Perceived goal setting practices of Olympic athletes: An exploratory investigation. *The Sports Psychologist*, 14: 279–95

Welford, A T (1968) *Foundations of skill*. London: Methuen

Weston, A R, Myburgh, K H, Lindsay, F H, Dennis, S C, Noakes, T D and Hawley, J A (1997) Skeletal muscle buffering capacity and endurance performance after high-intensity interval training by well trained cyclists. *European Journal of Applied Physiology and Occupational Physiology*, 75: 1–13

Williamson, D L, Gallagher, P M and Carroll, C C (2001) Reduction in hybrid single muscle fiber proportions with resistance training in man. *Journal of Applied Physiology*, 91: 1955–61

Winter, E M, Bromley, P D, Davison, R R C, Jones, A M and Mercer, T H (2007) Rationale, in Winter, E M, Bromley, P D, Davison, R R C, Jones, A M, Mercer, T H (eds) *Sport and exercise physiology testing guidelines*. London: British Association of Sport and Exercise Sciences/Routledge

Witvrouw, E, Mahieu, N, Danneels, L and McNair, P (2004) Stretching and injury prevention and obscure relationship. *Sports Medicine*, 34: 443–9

Witvrouw, E, Mahieu, N, Roosen, P and McNair, P (2007) The role of stretching in tendon injuries. *British Journal of Sports Medicine*, 41: 224–6

Wood, D M (1999) Physiological demands of middle-distance running, in Fallowfield, J L, and Wilkinson, D M (eds) *Improving sports performance in middle and long distance running: a scientific approach to race preparation*. Chichester: Wiley

Yerkes, R M and Dodson, J D (1908) The relationship of strength and stimulus to rapidity of habit formation. *Journal of Comparative Neurology and Psychology*, 18: 450–82

Young, W B, McDowell, M H and Scarlett, B J (2001) Specificity of sprint and agility of training methods. *Journal of Strength and Conditioning Research*, 15: 315–9

Young, W B, Clothier, P, Otago, L, Bruce, L and Liddell, D (2004) Acute effects of static stretching on hip flexor and quadriceps flexibility, range of motion and foot speed in kicking a football. *Journal of Science and Medicine in Sport*, 7: 23–31

Zarkadas, P C, Carter, J B and Banister, E W (1995) Modelling the effect of taper on performance, maximal oxygen uptake and the anaerobic threshold in endurance triathletes. *Advanced Experimental and Medical Biology*, 313: 179–66

Zatsiorsky, V M and Raitsin, L M (1974) Transfer of cumulative training effects in strength exercises. *Theory and Practice of Physical Culture*, 6: 8–14

Zatsiorsky, V M (1995) *Science and Practice of Strength Training*. Champaign, IL: Human Kinetics

Index